Citizen Brown

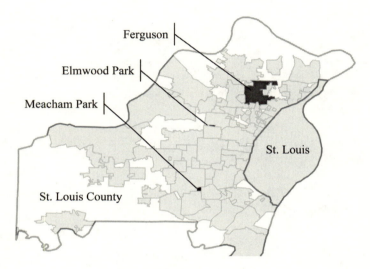

St. Louis County
Source: St. Louis County Department of Planning GIS
dataset (2012); US Census TIGER Line files.

Citizen Brown

Race, Democracy, and Inequality
in the St. Louis Suburbs

COLIN GORDON

University of Chicago Press
Chicago and London

The University of Chicago Press, Chicago 60637

The University of Chicago Press, Ltd., London

© 2019 by The University of Chicago

All rights reserved. No part of this book may be used or reproduced in any manner whatsoever without written permission, except in the case of brief quotations in critical articles and reviews. For more information, contact the University of Chicago Press, 1427 E. 60th St., Chicago, IL 60637.

Published 2019

Printed in the United States of America

28 27 26 25 24 23 22 21 20 19   1 2 3 4 5

ISBN-13: 978-0-226-64748-7 (cloth)

ISBN-13: 978-0-226-64751-7 (e-book)

DOI: https://doi.org/10.7208/chicago/9780226647517.001.0001

Library of Congress Cataloging-in-Publication Data

Names: Gordon, Colin, 1962– author.

Title: Citizen Brown : race, democracy, and inequality in the St. Louis suburbs / Colin Gordon.

Description: Chicago : University of Chicago Press, 2019. | Includes bibliographical references and index.

Identifiers: LCCN 2019005345 | ISBN 9780226647487 (cloth : alk. paper) | ISBN 9780226647517 (ebook)

Subjects: LCSH: African American neighborhoods—Missouri—Saint Louis. | Segregation—Missouri—Saint Louis County. | Equality—Missouri— Saint Louis County. | Urban renewal—Missouri—Saint Louis County.

Classification: LCC E185.93.M7 G67 2019 | DDC 305.8009778/65—dc23

LC record available at https://lccn.loc.gov/2019005345

♾ This paper meets the requirements of ANSI/NISO Z39.48–1992 (Permanence of Paper).

CONTENTS

MAPS AND FIGURES

Introduction

The Hurst Children, 1965

Lottie Mae and Willie Hurst and their seven children lived at 209 Handy Street in Meacham Park, a small, unincorporated African American neighborhood bounded by the St. Louis suburbs of Kirkwood, Crestwood, and Sunset Hills. On the evening of January 16, 1965, the two oldest children, Gladys (age seventeen) and Alice (fifteen), left the house to attend a dance. By eight o'clock, the rest of the family was in bed: the two youngest, Patricia Ann (eleven months) and Arthur Lee (two years), were in the front bedroom with their parents; the others—Willie Jr. (twelve), Helen (ten), Thomas (eight), and Perleen (five)—were in a small bedroom down the hall. Sometime after 10:00 p.m., a fire started near a coal stove in the hallway between the bedrooms. Lottie Mae awoke to screaming, smashed the nearest window, and crawled out with young Arthur. Her husband, his left arm paralyzed by a work accident, escaped through the kitchen—suffering severe burns. Both parents attempted to reenter the house, tearing at the tarpaper walls until their arms and hands bled, but were driven back by the flames.

By this time, a neighbor had called the Meacham Park Fire Department. Only five of the department's twelve volunteers answered the alarm. The department's only fire truck would not start. One of the volunteers retrieved his own car, pulled up alongside the truck, and managed to jump-start it. As the fire raged through this delay, neighbors called the Kirkwood and Crestwood Fire Departments as well. By the time firefighters were on the scene, the fire was out of control. Almost forty minutes after the first alarm, and twenty minutes after the first units were on the scene, firefighters were finally able to get into the house. They found Helen near the back door and the bodies of the other four children where they had been sleeping.[1]

Esther Brooks, 1967

Esther Brooks was born in 1897 and lived at 10008 Roberts Avenue in Elmwood Park, an unincorporated African American enclave of about one hundred families a few miles west of the St. Louis city line. She had been com-
muting (since 1944) to a $32 per week job as a domestic worker in the
tony central-county suburb of Ladue. Her modest Elmwood Park home had
electrical and water hookups and included a living room, a dining room, a
kitchenette, a bath, and two bedrooms. To help make ends meet, she took
on a boarder, who paid $20 per month for the second bedroom.[2] In 1957,
as Brooks approached her sixtieth birthday, St. Louis County officials began
discussing the prospect of "renewing" Elmwood Park.

As renewal plans progressed, Brooks and others dug in against the county
and its efforts to relocate the residents of Elmwood Park. In its first draft,
the renewal plan called for relocation to a public-housing complex planned
for Jefferson Barracks (a decommissioned military base in the southern end
of the county), but this idea was dropped when county voters spurned the
housing development. A revised plan called for staging redevelopment so
that new homes on Elmwood Park's east side would be available before
residents on the west side were faced with relocation.[3] But none of this happened. County officials used the idea of staged development to placate federal officials but privately—and in their communications with Elmwood
Park residents—pressed public housing in St. Louis as the best option. For
Esther Brooks, who had owned her own home in Elmwood Park for over
thirty years, the option of taking an apartment in the city's notorious Pruitt-
Igoe complex (far removed from family, friends, and her place of employment) was "entirely obnoxious to her."[4]

Relocation efforts became little more, as a county grand jury concluded
in 1966, than "an evasion of responsibility and intent [that] . . . practi-
cally wiped out an enclave of Negro property holdings of nearly a century's
duration; a community where there was never any question of the right
of Negroes to buy, own, and rent property." For displaced residents, urban
renewal meant the construction of "dwellings beyond their means, and . . .
commercial and industrial improvements completely irrelevant to their
well-being." This was not an urban renewal program; it was a "race clearance
program."[5] For her part, Brooks received a letter from relocation officials in
early 1962 but no further contact as the redevelopment plans progressed.[6]

As residents—some of whom had deep, multigenerational roots in Elmwood Park—saw their homes and their community being confiscated, they
turned to the courts. In March 1967, Brooks and her neighbors asked the

Missouri Supreme Court for a declaratory judgment, arguing that the state's highest court should intervene because grave constitutional questions were at stake. The court held that the interpretation of Missouri's urban renewal laws might be at stake but not their constitutionality and passed the case on to the Missouri Court of Appeals. When the lower court issued its opinion, Elmwood Park had been blighted for over a decade, the land had been cleared, and rebuilding was well underway. These facts alone were sufficient to guide the court's opinion. Since the redevelopment authority was "now in possession and the owner of the lands in Elmwood Park previously owned by the plaintiffs," the court reasoned, "it is obvious the latter have no legally protectable interest at stake."[7]

Cookie Thornton, 2008

Charles "Cookie" Thornton lived at 351 Attucks Street in Meacham Park. Thornton, who owned a small paving and demolition business, had serious financial problems and a long history of bitter disputes with Kirkwood City officials. As Kirkwood began toying with the annexation and redevelopment of Meacham Park in the 1990s, Thornton expanded his business, signing a five-year commercial lease on an old service-station property on Kirkwood Road that he brashly advertised as the "world headquarters of Cookco Construction." Within six months, Thornton was bankrupt, listing debts for rent, back taxes, unpaid child support, and business expenses of nearly half a million dollars. He went back to parking his equipment at job sites in Kirkwood or in front of his parents' house in Meacham Park. The city of Kirkwood, which had annexed Meacham Park in 1991, began to ticket Thornton for parking violations, improper disposal of trash and debris, and improper storage of building materials.[8]

Over the next few years, Thornton was prosecuted for 114 municipal ordinance violations, including nineteen counts in May 2001 (totaling $12,500 in fines) and another thirty-four counts in October 2001 ($27,808 in fines). In Thornton's view, Kirkwood officials were not only singling him out for code violations; they were also complicit in his failure to win contracts in the area's ongoing commercial development. In June 2001, he assaulted Ken Yost, Kirkwood's director of public works. In May 2002, he was convicted of the assault on Yost and another twenty-six ordinance violations.[9] Thornton began to file frivolous and rambling lawsuits, first for malicious prosecution, then (after being thrown out of two Kirkwood City Council meetings in the spring of 2006) for violation of his right to free speech. Kirkwood, for whom Thornton had become a "chronic antagonist," offered to wipe the slate clean on all outstanding fines and violations if Thornton would promise to stop harassing city officials and disrupting city-council meetings. "I'm never going to let this go," replied Thornton, whose last hope—for redemption and relief from crushing debt—was the federal lawsuit. This was thrown out in late January 2008.[10]

On February 7, 2008, Thornton arrived at Kirkwood City Hall for a regularly scheduled council meeting. He parked his van on Madison Avenue, crossed the street, and walked south into the parking lot across from the city hall and the police station. He shot and killed police sergeant William Biggs, took his gun, and crossed back over Madison to the city hall. Thornton entered the council chambers, holding a poster in front of him to conceal his weapons, and yelled, "Everybody stop what you are doing!" Police officer Tom Ballman, who had twice arrested Thornton for disorderly conduct at meetings, rolled his eyes in exasperation. Thornton dropped the poster and began firing, shooting and killing Ballman, Public Works Director Yost (seated in the front row), and council members Connie Karr and Michael Lynch (who faced the floor from the curved dais), and fatally wounding Mayor Mike Swoboda. Those in the audience rushed to the exits or ducked under desks and chairs. City Attorney John Hessel threw his chair at Thornton, shouted, "Cookie, don't do this, don't kill me. I'm not going to let you do this," and sprinted for the back of the room, throwing more chairs to slow Thornton's pursuit. His path initially blocked by Thornton, Hessel doubled back to the front of the room and made it back down the center aisle and out of the chambers. Police, alerted by Biggs (who managed to sound a distress alarm after he was shot) and the sound of gunfire, arrived at the council chambers and killed Thornton.[11]

Michael Brown, 2014

Michael Brown was born in 1996, in the St. Louis suburb of Florissant. Brown's life was not easy. His parents, teenagers when he was born, divorced when he was young. The inner suburbs of north St. Louis County were marked by economic decline, an aging housing stock, and rapid racial transition. His high school, in the Normandy School District, was one of a handful in the state that had been stripped of accreditation for poor performance. Like many teenagers, Brown dabbled with drugs and alcohol. And he had had a few minor brushes with the authorities: a scuffle with a neighbor, an accusation of a stolen iPod. Yet, against these odds, he was a good kid. He used his size and stature to avoid trouble. He was, by many accounts, "a reserved young man around people he did not know, but joking and outgoing with those close to him." He and his parents were intensely proud of his recent graduation from high school and his plans to enroll in a local technical college. School officials considered him "quiet, shy and a little awkward, hardly one of the 'trouble kids,' of which there were plenty." By the estimate of the school's athletic director, "Mike was probably the person that was the most serious in that class about getting out of Normandy, about graduating."[12]

On Saturday August 9, Brown and his friend Dorian Johnson were walking down West Florissant Avenue in Ferguson. They entered Ferguson Market and Liquor a little before noon, where, in an altercation captured by surveillance video, Brown scooped a handful of Swisher Sweets (a small flavored cigar) off the counter, pushed away the clerk, and left the store. Brown and Johnson walked north, then turned east onto Canfield Drive, where the commercial frontages of West Florissant give way to houses and apartments. There, they were stopped by Officer Darren Wilson. Wilson (who had been on a 911 call nearby) was not responding to the robbery at Ferguson Market; he stopped because Brown and Johnson were walking down the center of the street—in violation of an obscure municipal code proscribing this "Manner of Walking in Roadway." The stop, in turn, was undoubtedly animated by the pressure that Wilson and his fellow officers were under to generate revenue by aggressively enforcing the municipal code, and by a systemic racial bias in local policing. The Ferguson Police Department, as the US Department of Justice would conclude seven months later, was "more concerned with issuing citations and generating charges than with addressing community needs," and much of its activity bore "little relation to public safety and a questionable basis in law."[13]

Officer Wilson instructed Brown and Johnson to "get the fuck on the sidewalk" and then pulled up next to them when they didn't immediately comply. Wilson initially tried to get out of his car, then reached through the car window and grabbed Brown by the throat. The two struggled awkwardly through the open window, and then Wilson fired, breaking the car window and striking Brown. Officer Wilson and Johnson both remember a moment of shock, a hesitation, and then both boys ran. Johnson ducked behind a stopped car. Brown kept running, and Wilson fired a second shot that, as Johnson recalled, "did strike my friend Big Mike in his back 'cause that's when he stopped running." Wilson fired ten more shots, hitting Brown six times in all, twice in the head at close range. As Brown lay in the street, his blood "ran in a wide ribbon several feet down the hill." Brown's body lay in the blood and dust on Canfield Drive for almost four hours while the police plodded through their post-incident investigation. Outrage boiled over into protest almost immediately. Before Brown's body was finally removed, there were two dozen police cruisers, six canine units, and a SWAT team on the scene.[14]

These inexplicable episodes of tragedy, dispossession, and violence all unfolded within a few miles of each other in St. Louis County, the first frontier of suburban development west of the city of St. Louis. Bound together by a common location and a common history, the stories of Michael Brown, Cookie Thornton, Esther Brooks, and the Hurst children underscore pervasive patterns of racial division or exclusion or neglect, and pervasive questions about the status or standing of African Americans in their own communities. Gazing at the aftermath of the 1965 fire, Robert Reim, the mayor of neighboring Kirkwood, conceded that his city was "equally guilty with surrounding cities and St. Louis County in creating a ghetto-like effect in Meacham Park through neglect [and] discrimination."[15] At the unhappy conclusion of Esther Brooks's lawsuit, none of the justices paused to comment on the savage irony of the decision: Brooks and her neighbors filed suit because they felt that their property—and with it their right to citizenship in St. Louis County—had been unjustly confiscated. The fact that this confiscation was complete and successful erased their standing as citizens of Elmwood Park.

In the wake of the Kirkwood shootings, observers immediately underscored—as a precondition or as a mitigating factor—local patterns of racial division. Noting the poisonous racial climate, the Justice Department's Community Relations Service offered to "assist in resolving perceived racial issues in the community." Kirkwood initially rebuffed the offer, but the Meacham Park Neighborhood Improvement Association (MPNIA) pressed the issue, inviting the Justice Department to community meetings in March and April of 2008.[16] In September, MPNIA Chair Harriet Patton abruptly resigned, concluding that "the process has little or no possibility of forging a consensus" and that "we couldn't discuss the racial issues that plagued the community."[17] The final mediation agreement, released in January 2010, called for an array of local reforms, but the response was tepid. Meacham Park activists felt the agreement lacked teeth, and the MPNIA announced its intention to oppose the agreement and its implementation. One Kirkwood councilor voted to reject the agreement because "it's going to cause more of a racial problem, if one exists." The *St. Louis Beacon* concluded glumly that "persistent myths and poor communications continue to haunt the relationship between City Hall and the community."[18]

At the core of both Cookie Thornton's rage and the community response was the unevenness of local citizenship. Thornton wanted to share in the benefits of local politics (the lucrative redevelopment), but once Meacham Park was annexed he experienced only punitive and predatory state action. "He opened a business. He went to court," as Ben Gordon of Webster Groves told a community meeting the day after the shootings, "but the system failed him. . . . We are sorry, we grieve, but [Kirkwood officials] share in this responsibility."[19] "While the acts are unimaginable," as one reporter concluded, "many Kirkwood residents say the frustrations that consumed [Thornton] are very real"—that he was "driven to violence from frustrations that many black residents in Meacham Park describe: Being disrespected by city officials. Being hassled by the police. Being treated like second-class citizens."[20]

The confrontation between Michael Brown and Darren Wilson, in turn, was most elementally a confrontation between citizen and state. This was evident of course in terms of policing and punishment—a state function with the capacity to discipline, disenfranchise, or destroy citizens. But it was also evident in schooling (Brown had just graduated from Normandy High School, a school recently stripped of its accreditation by the state[21]); in the most prosaic patterns of local regulation (the county's inner suburbs are notorious for aggressive code enforcement[22]); in basic democratic representation (the Ferguson-Florissant School District has only rarely and sporadically claimed an African American member[23]); and in the patchwork of municipal incorporation, annexation, and zoning that sorts the local population by class and race.

The aftermath—the protests that roiled through the next year, the Department of Justice investigation, and the ongoing political and legal battles—underscored how tenuous that citizenship was (and is) for many African Americans in Ferguson and in the rest of St. Louis County. Heavy-handed response to the first wave of protests threw fuel on the fire, the images of militarized police confronting local citizens echoing those of Bull Connor in Birmingham a half century earlier. The streets filled again in November 2014, when the grand jury in charge of the court case declined to indict Officer Wilson; in December, when the same happened in the case of Eric Garner in New York; in March 2015, when Ferguson police chief Thomas Jackson resigned; and in April, in response to the death of Freddie Gray in Baltimore. By this point, Ferguson was both a struggling inner suburb of St. Louis and a shorthand for economic, political, and carceral injustice.

Suburban Subjects: Race and Citizenship in St. Louis County

This book is about the place of African Americans in the history of St. Louis County. Spatially and historically, this is a stark setting in which to assess the inclusion and exclusion of citizens from public services, public goods, and public protection. In the United States' central cities, the terms of modern citizenship were forged in a crucible of demographic and democratic change in the quarter century following the end of the Civil War. As the fleeting promise of Reconstruction faded into the horrors of "Jim Crow"[24] and the labor demands of northern industry outpaced those of the agricultural south, African American migrants pushed north (the African American population of the city of St. Louis grew from about twenty-two thousand in 1880 to almost seventy thousand in 1920). In the urban north, the challenge of accommodating and incorporating freed blacks (and the first generation of those born free) was overlaid with the challenge of accommodating and incorporating a generation of new immigrants. In cities like St. Louis, postbellum race relations were hardened and recast and reinvented in a context of intense competition over housing and jobs and urban space. Where African Americans settled, the reach of Jim Crow followed, etching racial lines across the key elements of citizenship: housing, policing, schooling, and economic opportunity.[25]

In suburban settings like St. Louis County, these racial lines were just as indelible—even if the threat they imagined was largely absent (the African American population of the county was just 3,500 in 1890 and 4,700 in 1920). That absence itself, of course, was important. It was, at the onset of the twentieth century and in the ensuing decades, a reflection of larger patterns and policies of segregation that not only confined African Americans to certain neighborhoods in the city but also excluded them entirely from whole towns and counties beyond the city's edge. In turn, that absence encouraged and nurtured a sense of refuge: a conviction that county homes and neighborhoods were (and were meant to be) a haven from the racial threat represented by the city. It sustained a powerful investment in the advantages and opportunities that flowed not just from segregation but also from local and federal policies that boosted the prospects of white families at the expense of others.[26] And it meant that confrontations with African Americans—either those scattered throughout the county before 1970 or those who settled there in increasing numbers after 1970—would be stark and bitter.

Within the county, I look closely at how all of this played out in two kinds of settings: older pockets of African American residency (such as Meacham Park and Elmwood Park), and inner suburbs (such as Ferguson) that experienced successive waves of white flight and black flight. Elmwood Park and Meacham Park were part of a broader pattern of early African American suburban settlement, often in unincorporated enclaves established before both systematic residential segregation and the land-use policies that sustained that segregation.[27] These pockets of black residence preceded even the earliest "streetcar suburbs" that began pushing metropolitan housing out from the central city. Developers ceded (and bypassed) these enclaves as a way of sustaining local segregation, which was reinforced not just by law and practice but also by hard physical boundaries (railbeds, creeks) between black and white residential areas. Homeownership rates in these enclaves were high, but so too were unconventional forms of home finance such as private mortgages and contract sales. The populations of these "little ghettos" swelled with the Great Migration, and by 1940, they housed nearly a fifth of the metropolitan African American population outside the South.[28]

Inner suburbs such as Ferguson, by contrast, were developed and settled in the middle years of the last century as bastions of working-class white flight. Such settings employed the same tactics as their neighbors—including legal restrictions, systematic discrimination in private realty, and exclusionary zoning—but, over time, those tactics failed. Both disinvestment in north St. Louis (and with it the failure of local public goods like schools) and the dislocation caused by urban renewal (shouldered overwhelmingly by African Americans) in the city and in St. Louis County created immense pressures on the older, relatively affordable housing stock of the inner suburbs. The racial premises of both development and redevelopment created and sustained a pattern of population movement in Greater St. Louis, marked by "white flight" into St. Louis County (and beyond) beginning in the 1940s, and by black flight into North County a generation later. The patterns and mechanisms of segregation established on the city's north side drifted into North County and were reinvented there. In the bargain, the consequences of segregation—including concentrated poverty, limited economic opportunity, a paucity of public services (except heavy-handed policing), and political disenfranchisement—moved to these "secondhand suburbs" as well.[29]

The local calculus of race and property—in established and transitional settings alike—was especially stark in Greater St. Louis, a setting irretrievably southern in its race relations and northern in its organization of property. In Missouri (as in much of the Midwest) the prairie beyond the last streetcar stop invited sprawl, while the policies shaping private development, municipal incorporation and annexation, and local land use were remarkably lax. This exaggerated both the incentive and the opportunity to engage in local segregation and discrimination.[30] It deepened the contrast between older African American enclaves (whose development, lacking modern sewers or water lines, was essentially rural) and the cul-de-sacs that surrounded them, and it heightened the economic and political pressure to erase them entirely under the pretext of fighting blight.[31] And it raised the stakes—for white and black alike—in the inner suburbs, where racial transition brought with it deep anxieties about property values and public goods in the wake of a "black invasion" or "ghetto spillover."[32]

Much of the county's suburban development was motivated by the desire to segregate. Development patterns and local zoning segregated land use, separating, or creating buffers between, homes, commerce, and industry. Private development and zoning, whose core logic was the uniform-lot, single-family subdivision, also segregated citizens by income. And both of these strategies were essentially and explicitly racial. The first stabs at zoning (including St. Louis in 1916) were efforts to circumscribe black and white neighborhoods, and the assumption that African American occupancy posed a "noxious" use akin to a junkyard or a glue factory lived on in the language and intent of race-restrictive deed covenants.[33] And the economic sorting accomplished by exclusive single-family zoning was so riven with unequal opportunity and naked discrimination that it quickly and accurately earned the moniker "white flight."[34]

In such settings, the notion that African Americans—either persisting in older pockets or moving into inner suburbs—were "in the wrong place" proved powerful and persistent. Urban renewal of the county's black enclaves included relocation programs crafted to move black residents "back" to the city. The demolition of the city's largest public-housing project in the early 1970s prompted near hysteria that displaced tenants would find their way across the county line. New arrivals in transitional neighborhoods routinely noted the withering of local services and the bolstering of local policing. "I can't recall the streets being cleaned the last year. We now have the most inadequate lighting in the city," an African American resident of Kirkwood told the US Commission on Civil Rights in 1970. "[But] I think we've got more police protection than we required when I first moved here. I don't know if they were protecting me more or protecting someone from me."[35] A half century later, the Justice Department's scathing dissection of policing in Ferguson made essentially the same point: the police see "residents, especially those who live in Ferguson's predominantly African-American neighborhoods, less as constituents to be protected than as potential offenders and sources of revenue."[36]

At its best, this is a lesser form of citizenship, a political margin at which rights and protections and obligations are thinner or less substantial, a diminished or devalued civil status.[37] In pointed and tangible terms, African Americans in St. Louis County were (and are) targets of public policy rather than its beneficiaries, a problem to be solved rather than a population to be served, subjects rather than citizens.

Citizenship and Community

Citizenship, a topic of renewed scholarly and political interest in our global and neoliberal age, offers a keen focus on these historical and enduring patterns of racial segregation and discrimination. At its most basic, citizenship is composed of "rights and mutual obligations binding state agents and a category of persons defined exclusively by their legal attachment to the same state."[38] Those rights, in T. H. Marshall's classic dissection, can be understood as a sequential development of civil rights (by which Marshall meant baseline economic rights—rights to work, to own property, to enter into contracts), political rights (the extension of suffrage), and social rights. The latter was the promise of the modern welfare state, whose redress of market inequalities, as Marshall wrote hopefully in 1950, was "no longer content to raise the floor-level in the basement of the social edifice, leaving the superstructure as it was. It has begun to remodel the whole building, and it might even end by converting a sky-scraper into a bungalow."[39]

Such rights, in turn, should be understood as more than just legal or political formalities. In the classic liberal view, citizenship rests on an equitable "starting gate" distribution of social goods, sustained by the protection of individual rights within (and from) the state.[40] But the enjoyment of those rights also depends on political agency and capacity and on social inclusion or membership in a political community. "Recognition by others as a moral equal treated by the same standards and values and due the same level of respect and dignity as all other members," as Margaret Somers argues, is the prerequisite that gives all other rights substance and meaning.[41] State action and public policy, in this respect, should reflect democratic values and processes; they should "draw citizens into public life" rather than simply regulating, disciplining, or punishing them.[42]

And, just as citizens shape policy, so policies shape citizens—a point Marshall underscores when he observes that "the Poor Law treated the claims of the poor, not as an integral part of the rights of the citizen, but as an alternative to them—as claims which could be met only if the claimants ceased to be citizens in any true sense of the word."[43] In their confrontations or interactions with the state—at a social-service agency, at a traffic stop, at a school—citizens "learn about government, participation, and their own place in the political order."[44] This lived citizenship is especially fraught when categorical or means-tested policies target specific populations. The ways in which such populations are treated or portrayed sends powerful messages "about what government is supposed to do, which citizens are deserving (and which are not), and what kinds of attitudes and participatory patterns are appropriate in a democratic society." Those singled out as especially worthy or deserving (say, homeowners or veterans) find their citizenship enhanced; their claims on state attention are seen as both noble and expansive. Those singled out as dependent or undeserving are treated (and come to see themselves) as objects of state attention rather than democratic citizens. The policies targeting them are coercive and punitive; the government they experience is oppressive and capricious.[45]

As scholarship across a wide array of policy has demonstrated, this reciprocity, or "policy feedback," defines the boundaries of the political community, places conditions on state assistance, shapes civic capacity and agency, and frames future policies. Experience with social-welfare policies can blunt or encourage civic engagement—an outcome shaped both by the hard distinction between social insurance and means-tested programs and by the subtler distinctions in the ways the client-citizens are treated on either track.[46] Racial discrepancies in policing are a form of both discrimination and disenfranchisement; such "pervasive ongoing, suspicious inquiry," as Charles Epp and colleagues conclude, "sends the unmistakable message that the targets of this inquiry look like criminals: they are second-class citizens."[47] These punitive and supervisory policies shape not just formal political rights (to vote, to serve on juries, to hold certain jobs); they also, as Vesla Weaver argues, "transform how people understand their government, their status in the democratic community, and their civic habits—in a word, their citizenship."[48]

The Mixed Promise of American Citizenship

In the American context, citizenship is notoriously uneven in promise and practice. On one hand, the United States boasts strong de jure commitments to individual rights, a relatively early expansion of male suffrage, and similarly strong and early commitments to public education. On the other hand, of course, all of this was conceived in a slave-holding republic and matured in a setting marked by fierce social and political commitments to racial segregation, systematic disenfranchisement, and agricultural labor markets—in the South and the Southwest—that sustained slavery in all but name.[49] "Enduring anti-liberal dispositions," as Judith Shklar notes, "regularly asserted themselves, often very successfully, against the promise of equal political rights."[50] Citizenship for some has always rested heavily and harshly on the exclusion of others.

Such exclusion, embedded in public policies ranging from immigration to labor standards, is most starkly evident in the history of American social citizenship. The foundational social policies of the 1930s and 1940s were premised on near-systematic exclusion of African Americans, the maintenance of a bright line between contributory social insurance and means-tested programs, deference—in program design and generosity—to private job-based benefits, and an increasingly elaborate taxonomy (widows, kids, veterans, parents) of deservedness.[51] "The architecture of protection for white men," as Jennifer Mittelstadt concludes, "was built in part on the backs of those who were denied full economic and social citizenship."[52] And even for those who benefited from all of this, the reciprocal obligations were weak. Social insurance was promoted and defended as a private accomplishment, an entitlement in which the state facilitated protection but did not provide it.[53]

American citizenship conformed not only to the contours of race and region but also to the primacy of the market in ordering social relations and economic rewards. In this sense, American social and labor policies have always offered a weak commitment to either dampening market inequality (through high labor standards or support of collective bargaining) or addressing market failures (through redistribution). Judged by "the ability of civil society, the public sphere, and the social state to exert countervailing power against the corrosive effects of market driven governance," as Somers concludes, the United States has always been a liberal outlier.[54] In the American context, full citizenship has always rested on independence and gainful employment, a fact reflected in the terms and conditions of labor-market policies, social policies, social insurance, and private benefits.[55] For those who do not meet the standard of the upright citizen—worker, taxpayer, consumer, homeowner—the state is a very different beast. It does not just discipline or regulate them; it punishes and preys on them.[56]

In turn, the close equation of market outcomes with civic virtue erodes commitments to public goods and public services. Such goods and services are not—in most instances—considered a benefit of citizenship but are earned, bought, and consumed as if they were private goods. Recipients of social insurance programs defend their "earned" benefits—even admonishing reformers to "keep the government's hands off *my* social security or Medicare."[57] Parents of means choose a good neighborhood in order to choose a good school, fiercely defending their right to "shop" for opportunity with their local taxes.[58] In the bargain, all are left with the presumption that American citizenship must be earned or achieved; that it flows not from birth or nationality but from some combination of market success, good behavior, and exceptional contribution.[59]

The neoliberal turn of the last generation amplifies all of this, but it did not invent it. In some respects, "market fundamentalism" has simply moved the line between public goods and private responsibility: less state, more market, a "risk shift" that has left ordinary Americans less secure.[60] But more fundamentally, it has blurred that line, marking less a retreat of the state than a redirection of its energies. Mass incarceration, in this sense, is but the harshest and clearest example of a much broader set of punitive and paternal policies that harness state power to market demands. Ordinary citizens are not just more exposed to market forces, they are also increasingly governed by them.[61] Any pretense that the welfare state might offer relief from the market, for example, has now been largely displaced by policies and programs for which low-wage employment is the core eligibility threshold.[62] Economic inequalities, in turn, nurture political inequalities. In a setting marked by few restraints on lobbying or campaign financing, the gap between the political capacity (and clout) of the haves and that of the have-nots grows ever wider.[63]

All of this—in its origins, in its history, and in its neoliberal variations—is inextricably entangled with race. Again, the carceral state—for its alarming scale, its starkly disproportionate burden on African Americans, and its direct and indirect constraints on citizenship—offers the bluntest example.[64] As a policy or instrument of social control, however, mass incarceration is the tip of the policy iceberg; it is merely the most visible and glaring fragment of a larger whole.[65] The assault on social programs in modern American history has always been in large part an assault on the legitimacy—or citizenship—of their recipients. Direct and indirect racial arguments underwrote both the exclusionary terms of the original Social Security titles and the backlash against them that began in the 1970s.[66] Whatever the label—the "underclass," "handout nation," the "takers," Mitt Romney's infamous "47 percent"—the underlying message is that reliance on the state makes one less of a citizen. This means that not only is one less deserving of the state's protection, one is more deserving of its scrutiny.[67]

Local Citizenship

While we often think of citizenship in national terms,[68] its promise and its challenges are both replicated and complicated at subnational levels of government: states, counties, cities, school districts. Most interactions between state and citizen occur at the local level—riding the bus, attending a school-board meeting, swimming in the municipal pool, enduring a traffic stop, wheeling the recycling to the curb, applying for a building permit. Citizenship and community are powerful and palpable locally, at a scale where natural solidarities are easier to forge and sustain. Here citizenship rests not on birth or lineage but simply on one's presence in a specific place. Local citizenship—sometimes described as "the right to the city"—involves not just political access and representation but also access to local public goods and services, and to equal opportunity and mobility in local housing and labor markets. But local citizenship is also fragile, its promise easily and routinely compromised by unequal treatment, uneven access to public goods and services, and stark patterns of local segregation or inequality.[69] This changes the equation in a number of interesting ways.

In local settings, citizens have some control—through land-use zoning, incorporation and annexation, and the gerrymandering of school districts—over *both* the boundaries of political jurisdictions and the policies within them. While citizens move through older and arbitrary jurisdictions (townships, counties, states), municipal incorporations are often intended to stem or contain such movement.[70] In our patchwork metropolises, local government acts as a means of parceling out or sorting citizens, rather than addressing their diverse demands and needs. Political jurisdictions are created for the express purpose of segregating or excluding populations, avoiding burdens, and hoarding opportunities.[71] Indeed, most incorporated municipalities provide no or few actual services to their residents; they exist primarily to define citizenship through the regulation of land use.[72] The fragmentation of local governance, as a result, ensures a yawning inequality in outcomes and opportunities across neighborhoods and jurisdictions. Class and racial differences become spatial and territorial, not only carved out in the first instance but also fiercely sustained and defended.[73]

The "right to the city" generated by the centrality and density of urban settings begins to unravel when centrality gives way to fragmentation and density succumbs to sprawl. Segregation by class and race, accomplished and sustained by municipal borders, makes it less likely that diverse citizens will engage with each other politically—and hence less likely that they will broach any of these problems.[74] For those who are well-off, after all, municipal fragmentation yields prosperous enclaves where a combination of citizen demand and high fiscal capacity delivers a relatively robust supply of both private and public goods. Small-scale suburbs assemble those of common backgrounds or incomes in space; fragmentation, in turn, creates a "respectable rationale" to maximize revenues and minimize costs.[75] "In an increasing number of American lives," as Susan Bickford notes caustically, "what counts as civic virtue is maintaining property values, and what counts as social responsibility is paying homeowner association dues."[76] For the poor, this means stark and deeply institutionalized obstacles to equal opportunity or social mobility.[77] Housing policy, in this sense, marks an early inroad of neoliberalism—a setting in which the market, shaped by local zoning, became the primary driver of social and political organization.[78]

The organization of residential space, in turn, shapes access to public goods and public services. Local governance (and its uneven fiscal capacity) is responsible for stark inequalities in education, which is not only a core public good but also a foundation for future political engagement.[79] Other local resources—underwritten by the taxation of consumption and property—are richest where spending and homeownership (and home values) are the most robust. The patchwork metropolis becomes less a source of public goods and services than a marketplace in which consumer-citizens "vote with their feet" for local neighborhoods and services that match their tastes and preferences.[80] Local fragmentation, some of which is driven by a beggar-thy-neighbor competition for local business investment and employment, contributes to job sprawl and a spatial mismatch between residential options and employment opportunities—especially for African Americans in central cities and inner suburbs.[81]

While fragmentation generates uneven citizenship *across* jurisdictions, local patterns of development and policy also stratify citizenship *within* jurisdictions. Central cities quite often encompass zones of abandonment, investment, gentrification, or redevelopment in which the implications and experience of citizenship diverge sharply.[82] Historically, economic and racial segregation have sustained vast disparities in policing, schooling, and other local services. Local citizens may have very different levels of access to public goods and services; they may also be treated very differently by local fragments of political authority. And the sheer number of those fragments effectively confines political representation and incorporation to one jurisdiction while exposing local citizens to state actions—policing, zoning, economic development—by neighboring jurisdictions in which they have no voice or vote.[83]

In turn, the reach of local government is both potent and constrained. Unmentioned in our founding documents, local government employs only that authority extended by the uneven "home rule" provisions in state codes. And local political authority, as an extension of the state's police power, has historically been concerned less with individual rights than with local service provision, regulation, discipline, and order.[84] What this has meant, unfortunately, is that local governments have the capacity to do much harm and not much good. State and local policies, as a rule, focus on "setting rules of conduct and backing those rules by sanctions." Indeed, state and local social policies, in their formative years and in their more recent devolution, have invariably been more punitive and paternal than national social policies.[85] Local taxation historically and routinely bears hardest on those of limited means, countering the modest progressivity of federal taxes.[86] Local policing is animated in large part by the defense of local boundaries; investigatory traffic stops, for example, are overwhelmingly aimed at those (often young, black, and male) deemed "out of place."[87]

And all of this is mediated less and less by standards or protections sustained by higher levels of government. Local political innovation has considerable promise when accompanied by robust state or national standards, including fiscal capacity, civil-rights protections, and universal social programs.[88] But when and where such conditions do not hold, local rule is a devolutionary minefield in which both political responsibility and austerity roll downhill—from federal jurisdiction to state to local—and social policies wither.[89] The "risk shift," in which devolution and policy retreat leave families and individuals increasingly responsible for their own economic security, is particularly potent in local contexts marked by wide variation in economic opportunity, housing costs, and labor standards.[90]

Such fragmented localism is also a powerful mechanism for accomplishing and sustaining racial discrimination. Racial segregation has always been intensely local, policed in local public space and public services during the heyday of Jim Crow and sustained in local public policy and institutions (housing, schools) after Jim Crow and beyond the South.[91] Segregation sought not just spatial separation but also a tiered citizenship—constraining the rights of African Americans to access public goods and services, to choose where they live, and to enjoy the benefits (good schools, recreation, safety, employment, commerce) that come with good neighborhoods.[92] Assumptions about racial difference are inscribed in local spaces by public policies and private realty in such a way that they become institutionalized and, however fictive and cynical in their origins, real. Once the patchwork of development and governance is in place, as Clarissa Hayward has suggested, it creates its own incentives and interests—widening the gap between white places and black places, between white citizens and black citizens.[93]

Local governments, in this sense, do much of the work of creating and sustaining what Somers calls "internal borders of exclusion," mapping degrees of citizenship, or starkly different terms of access to public goods, public services, and public protection.[94] The fragmentation of local government provides the opportunity to mobilize biases or hoard opportunities.[95] The high stakes of local citizenship—especially property values and school quality—provide the motive. Because we view local boundaries as natural or arbitrary, rather than as creatures of segregation and exclusion, deference to local authorities on issues like zoning or economic development amounts to little more than an opportunity or invitation to sustain that segregation. As a result, "spatially and racially defined communities," as Richard Thompson Ford notes, "perform the 'work' of segregation silently."[96]

Greater St. Louis, notorious for both its long history of racial segregation and its uniquely fragmented political structure, offers a telling setting for an assessment of these patterns. It is a setting that has been and remains starkly biracial, the ways "in which citizens make sense of race and place in everyday life" unleavened by new arrivals or new immigration.[97] It is a setting that underscores the long and troubled history of these patterns—starker in the shadow of globalization, deindustrialization, wage stagnation, market fundamentalism, and mass incarceration, but hardly new. It is a setting in which African Americans have experienced an uneven, tiered, and stratified citizenship—their opportunities and outcomes, their rights and obligations, sharply constrained by the structure and actions of local government.

In the chapters that follow, I consider the experience of African Americans, as citizens, in St. Louis County across three arenas of policy. In the first two chapters, I look at the sources and implications of local political fragmentation. Chapter 1 considers patterns of municipal incorporation and annexation and zoning, or the way in which political communities (and their citizens) were defined. In much of the county, across much of its history, political jurisdictions were drawn for the express purpose of sorting the population by race—facilitating white flight, stemming black flight, and quarantining existing enclaves of African American occupancy. Suburban development, in this respect, reflected both the demand side and the supply side of "white flight." Racial transition, economic decline, and the erosion of civic services provided the incentive to flee. Local zoning and housing policies, federal mortgage subsidies, and the deeply racialized practice of private realty reserved that opportunity—at least for the first postwar generation—for white families. And, adding insult to injury, private development and new municipal incorporation bypassed scattered enclaves of African American occupancy. New construction and infrastructure flowed around these "little ghettoes" like rocks in a stream; the resulting economic and developmental contrast eventually targeted them for redevelopment or removal.

Chapter 2 turns to the unevenness and fragmentation of basic public goods and services (sewers, schooling, policing). Here again, uneven citizenship is evident from the most mundane (garbage collection) to the most profound (educating kids) of local responsibilities. This unevenness reflects inequalities both across jurisdictions (including not just municipalities but also school districts) and within them. The population sorting accomplished by municipal incorporation and zoning created jurisdictional fragments with vastly different capacities to deliver or pay for basic services. Older African American enclaves were often marked off by streets, sewer mains, and water lines that stopped at their borders. Secondhand suburbs (like Ferguson) undergoing racial transition suffered from both a meager fiscal base and steep service burdens. And, across the county, African Americans suffering lesser schools and services could always count on more attention when it came to policing or code enforcement.

Chapter 3 turns to urban renewal and redevelopment, a policy used sparingly by the county and its municipalities but almost exclusively to erase pockets of African American occupancy. In practice, both the designation of "blight" and the relocation policies that accompanied redevelopment were animated by concerns about the impact or legitimacy of African American citizenry in the suburban landscape. Redevelopment, animated by the desire to find the "highest and best use" of land, invariably ranked African American occupancy near the bottom of that scale. Not only did the presence of African Americans threaten the "neighborhood homogeneity" so prized by realtors and developers but—as midcentury planners routinely argued—it dampened the value of surrounding parcels as well. Following this logic, urban renewal looked to clear the way for "higher use" by erasing the "blight" of black occupancy. Homeownership—so integral to the American ideal of citizenship[98]—was sustained and subsidized for white families not just by denying the same opportunity to black families but also by actively dispossessing and relocating black families. In Meacham Park and Elmwood Park, these larger patterns of urban renewal and displacement played out in dramatic and dramatically uneven ways. Elmwood Park (the home of Esther Brooks) was wiped from the map and rebuilt in the 1960s, a process that—by intent and by neglect—scattered its original citizens across the deeply segregated housing markets of Greater St. Louis. In Meacham Park (the home of Cookie Thornton), redevelopment dragged out over nearly four decades and yet ended up in very nearly the same place, embroiled in controversy over the displacement of its citizens.

Chapter 4 turns our attention to the inner suburb of Ferguson, tracing its development from an early bastion of white flight to a "secondhand" suburb undergoing rapid racial transition. The conditions sketched above—including segregation and political fragmentation—shaped the city and its suburbs, bearing most heavily on older "inner" suburbs like Ferguson that were caught between the sustained decline of the central city and the sustained flight of wealth and resources to the outer suburbs. As black flight followed white flight, municipal fragments like Ferguson suffered both the success of local segregation and its failures. All of this was the backdrop to the death of Michael Brown in August 2014. Uneven development yielded uneven fiscal capacity and a double burden for the county's poorest residents: in areas where services were at their most meager, where public schools were struggling, local tax rates were invariably higher. Facing this combination of escalating demands and declining revenues, local governments drew even sharper distinctions between their citizens—abating commercial taxes in a desperate play for new investment, while using predatory policing and local courts to extract even more from those least able to pay.

The overarching argument, in one respect, is about the different institutional and political mechanisms shaping local citizenship—*fragmenting* and *segregating* citizenship through local incorporation and service provision, *bulldozing* citizenship under the auspices of urban renewal, and *arresting* citizenship through predatory policing. At the same time, the argument has a historical arc, suggesting the ways in which local policies sought to sustain segregation in response to shifting demographic, political, and fiscal challenges.[99] Mid-twentieth-century innovations in municipal incorporation and zoning, in this respect, were quite explicitly and candidly crafted to sort the local population by race and class. Where and when these strategies failed—especially where pockets of African American occupancy predated white-flight suburbanization—local authorities invoked urban renewal to erase the last vestiges of "blight." This tack, however, was soon confounded by the slow collapse of the hard racial boundary between St. Louis City and St. Louis County and by black flight into the inner suburbs of North County. With this, the definition and maintenance of local borders—and the day-to-day distinction between citizen and subject—fell increasingly to the police and the courts.

ONE

Fragmenting Citizenship:
Municipal Incorporation and Annexation

Conventionally, we think of citizenship as a bundle of rights and obligations that vary across jurisdictions or historical settings. But citizenship does
not just set the terms of political engagement or participation; it is also
"a mechanism to distribute people among political entities" and to establish the practical and physical boundaries of inclusion in a political community.[1] The terms of citizenship, in other words, are shaped by both the
norms and rules within a given jurisdiction and by the scope or boundaries
of that jurisdiction. In the political patchwork of American cities, this has
meant that fragmented governance yields fragmented citizenship, but also
that the opportunity to draw and redraw political boundaries makes that
fragmentation an intentional and ongoing project. Local boundaries are
not, as the Supreme Court assumed in *Milliken v. Bradley* (1974), established
by "neutral legislation" in which the resulting distribution of people and
resources are mere accidents.[2] They are—especially in settings like St. Louis
County, and illustrated starkly in the relationship between the county's municipalities and its unincorporated black enclaves—often pointed efforts to
skew the distribution of resources and to hoard opportunities. Like political
gerrymandering, municipal incorporation and annexation can be powerful
mechanisms of segregation or exclusion.

Once in place, this fierce localism can do (and has done) tremendous
damage. "The political splintering along income and racial lines," as the Advisory Commission on Intergovernmental Relations concluded in 1969, "is
akin to giving each rich, middle-class, and poor neighborhood the power to
tax, spend, and zone. Such decentralization of power can and does play hob
with the goal of social justice."[3] When a metropolitan area is governed by a
patchwork of insular corporate units that are uneven in size, capacity, and
composition, the fruits of local growth will accumulate in a small subset of

affluent localities. Patterns of economic and racial segregation will harden over time, as will the cumulative advantages and disadvantages (in schooling, economic opportunity, health) that flow from economic segregation. Civic participation and public goods will suffer. All of this will come at the expense of the greater metropolis, setting local citizens and local jurisdictions against each other in a scramble for resources or investment or tax capacity that leaves everyone worse off. And, once in place, this localism only exaggerates the incentives that created it. "Local politics as currently organized," as Stephen Macedo underscores, "make all of us into stakeholders in undemocratic exclusion and the perpetuation of inequality."[4]

This chapter looks first to the background of "home rule" and municipal authority in Missouri and sketches some of the broader implications of both fragmentation and local control over zoning and land use for urban (and suburban) citizens. It then turns to the fates of Elmwood Park and Meacham Park, two African American enclaves that predated the suburbanization of St. Louis County. In these settings, local citizenship was shaped not by the conventional sequence of subdivision, residential development, incorporation, and zoning but by the ways in which those patterns and policies developed at their borders—effectively isolating and quarantining the county's few African American residents. In this pattern of "municipal underbounding," incorporation and annexation bypassed older low-income and racially segregated enclaves—leaving them mapped out of local democracy and local citizenship.[5] In these "little ghettos," citizens received few municipal services (save for intensive policing) and faced a constant threat of annexation, redevelopment, and removal.

The Development of "Home Rule" in Missouri

At its 1876 constitutional convention, Missouri formalized its rules for local governance—setting local debt limits, proscribing the passage of "special laws" in the statehouse, establishing a classification system for villages, towns, and cities, and giving cities over a certain population threshold (initially set so just St. Louis qualified) the option of adopting a charter of self-government.[6] In response, St. Louis City pushed its boundaries west, to their current location, and opted for formal separation from St. Louis County. At the time, separation from the county made sense for city interests, and details of the 1876 agreement were crafted and implemented largely at the city's behest.[7]

But over the ensuing decades, four things happened to alter the terms of this deal. First, the metropolitan area grew and soon pressed against the western border established in 1876.[8] To sustain the city as a natural unit of government, its reach coterminous with that of its population and its economic base, the logical step was to add new territory by annexation. But this option was blocked by the hard line drawn between St. Louis City and St. Louis County in 1876, and by the state boundary between the city and its industrial suburbs on the Illinois side of the Mississippi. As a result, urban growth continued, but beyond the regulatory reach of the city. Second, the right of self-government that had been extended to St. Louis alone in 1876 was soon made available to almost all comers. By 1945 home rule had become an option for any Missouri city with over five thousand residents and any county with an assessed property value exceeding $4.5 million.[9] Third, the emergence of municipal zoning (an exercise of home rule sanctioned by the courts in 1926) gave suburban enclaves the incentive to incorporate as a means of cementing restrictive and exclusive patterns of land use. And fourth, the African American population of St. Louis grew rapidly, more than doubling from 1890 to 1920 and more than doubling again from 1920 to 1950.[10]

What all of this meant, in effect, was that the temporary advantage afforded to the city of St. Louis in 1876 soon became a grotesque liability. Natural urban growth, changing state law, and changing demographics combined to give surrounding communities, especially those multiplying west of the city limits, both the opportunity and the incentive to poach St. Louis's wealth and resources and to pick and choose among local citizens. Because the city could not expand, new residential developments to the west fell under other jurisdictions or created their own. The central planning goal of these private developments and new municipalities, in turn, was to insulate themselves from local costs or threats or burdens—especially industrial land use, multifamily housing, and African American occupancy.[11] The damage here was done not by the divorce of 1876 but by the offspring of that divorce: the extension of home rule to a hundred-odd municipal fragments that were—in purpose and in practice—predatory, insular, and deeply discriminatory.[12]

State and local law regarding incorporation, annexation, and consolidation varied wildly but in most settings made it easy to incorporate new localities on the city's fringes. "By the early twentieth century suburbanites had begun carving up the metropolis," the urban historian Jon Teaford concludes, "and the states had handed them the knife."[13] Nowhere was this truer than in Greater St. Louis. St. Louis County claimed six incorporated municipalities in 1900 and only twelve more by 1930—but that number had more than doubled by 1940 and doubled again by 1950.[14] During this era, most new housing stock was erected in unincorporated subdivisions. The character of these suburbs was determined by the terms and standards of private construction and realty, including house and lot size and deed restrictions.[15] Residents sought incorporation as a means of sustaining local standards. Professional planners, for their part, routinely discouraged their St. Louis County clients from annexing new territory. Instead, they argued that smaller municipal units were sufficient to provide local services and necessary to avoid the threats posed by mixed density or use. The result, noted as early as the late 1920s, was a "considerable number of small communities," each "separate from the metropolitan city and . . . aloof from its neighbor."[16]

It was not, of course, the mere fact of this fragmentation that caused the damage but what the proliferation of local governments meant for local citizenship. First and foremost, home rule nurtured segregation. The early twentieth-century city was an organic and haphazard cluster of diverse and densely interrelated populations and economic activities, "bustling streets with a mixture of factories, offices, apartments and homes crowded together amidst heavy traffic, noise, dirt, and excitement." By the middle of the twentieth century, these same cities were shaped by lines of incorporation that separated the offices and the factories from the homes and the homes from the apartments. As independently incorporated suburbs segregated residential and commercial development, they increasingly viewed local government not as a means of managing the city but as a protector of "hearth and home" against the threats posed by the city.[17] And local segregation was deepened and subsidized by state and federal policy. During its heyday from the late 1930s through the late 1950s, the Federal Housing Administration (FHA) wedded its mortgage-guarantee programs to an elaborate system of rating prospective borrowers, properties, and neighborhoods. In St. Louis and elsewhere, FHA policies assumed that stable housing values required that neighborhoods "be occupied by the same racial and social classes," and pushed investment away from the "crowded neighborhoods" and "older properties" of the central cities.[18]

These underwriting standards—which the FHA borrowed whole hog from the real-estate industry—also shaped local control over land zoning. Through the late nineteenth century and the early twentieth century, exclusionary zoning was allowed only on the basis of public health, public safety, or public morals. Courts consistently held that zoning could not be used to sustain property values or the qualities of certain neighborhoods. But as home rule encouraged fragmented incorporation, states ceded zoning authority to local governments, and emerging suburbs sought to protect "community standards," exclusionary zoning became a much more potent tool. Such exclusionary practices—including requirements for minimum lot size and minimum dwelling size, and restrictions on (or outright prohibitions of) manufactured or multifamily housing—were pioneered, in many respects, by the FHA's desire to sustain "the character of the community" in early postwar developments.[19]

In the St. Louis suburbs, local planners and elected officials quite candidly viewed zoning as a mechanism for sorting the metropolitan citizenry by race and income and for sustaining the spirit of race-restrictive deed covenants past their expiration. The direct examples here are telling. The city of Berkeley in St. Louis County grew out of a dispute over school-district boundaries with neighboring Kinloch—one of the few black enclaves in the county. When white residents failed to sustain school segregation by dividing the school district, they created a new town in 1937 instead (an episode I return to in chapter 2). The city of Black Jack was hastily incorporated and zoned in 1970 to stave off a mixed-income housing project. The sprawling West County municipality of Wildwood (incorporated in 1995) was driven largely by fears that St. Louis County was not willing to sustain large-lot single-family residential development. Such exclusionary gambits are now quite familiar. A less familiar, and in some respects more striking, case is that of Meacham Park and Elmwood Park—two older African American enclaves that were reluctantly drawn in to this frenzy of suburban development and incorporation.[20]

The Suburban Quarantine

At the onset of the twentieth century, urban development extended little beyond the borders of St. Louis itself (see maps 1.1 through 1.5). The inner suburbs immediately west of the city's central corridor—University City, Maplewood, Clayton, Richmond Heights, Shrewsbury, and Brentwood—were all incorporated between 1906 and 1920, their establishment spurred by the growth of St. Louis and by the World's Fair in 1904. Northwest of the city, only Bridgeton (a ferry landing on the Missouri River, incorporated in 1843), Florissant (an old trading post on the Missouri, incorporated in 1857), and Ferguson (a transportation depot on the North Missouri railway, incorporated in 1894) interrupted the rural landscape. A few towns—including Webster Groves (1896), Kirkwood (1865), and Pacific (1859)—were strung from east to west through southern St. Louis County along the Missouri–Pacific and St. Louis–San Francisco rail lines. And scattered new residential development was encouraged by the opening of new streetcar lines. In 1892, the Page Avenue trolley was extended west through St. Louis County to Creve Coeur Lake. In 1900, a new North–South line connected Ferguson and Kirkwood.

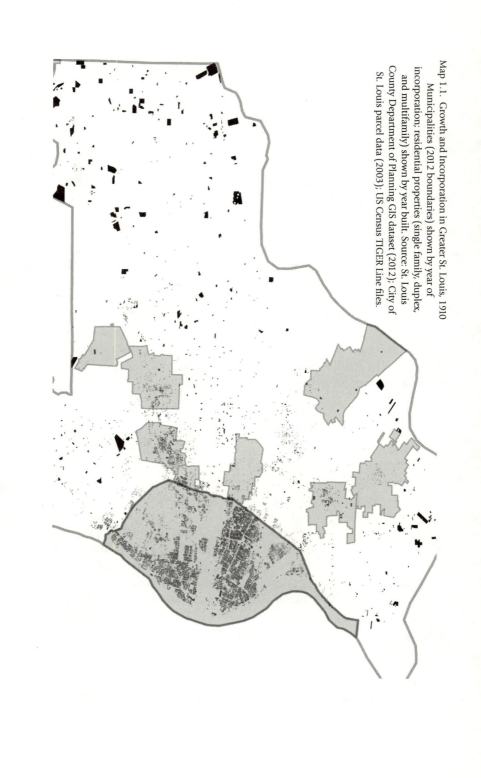

Map 1.1. Growth and Incorporation in Greater St. Louis, 1910 Municipalities (2012 boundaries) shown by year of incorporation; residential properties (single family, duplex, and multifamily) shown by year built. Source: St. Louis County Department of Planning GIS dataset (2012); City of St. Louis parcel data (2003); US Census TIGER Line files.

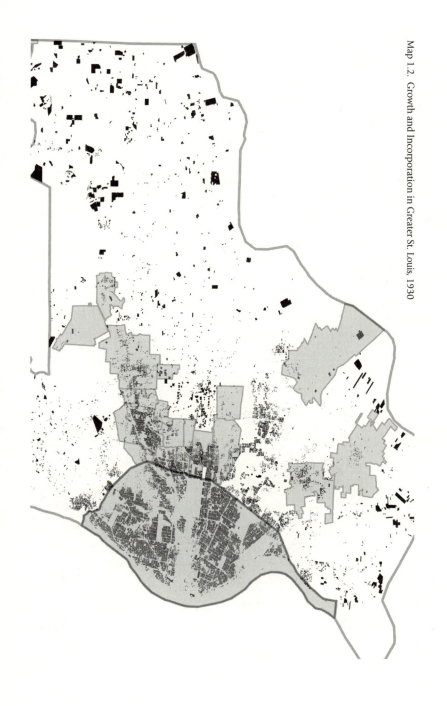

Map 1.2. Growth and Incorporation in Greater St. Louis, 1930

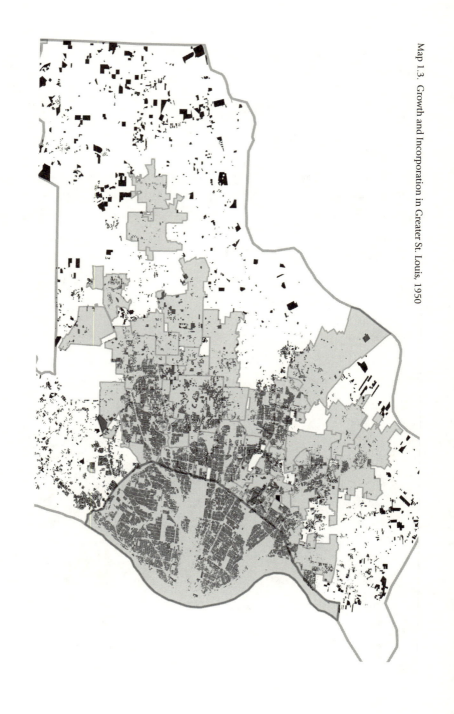

Map 1.3. Growth and Incorporation in Greater St. Louis, 1950

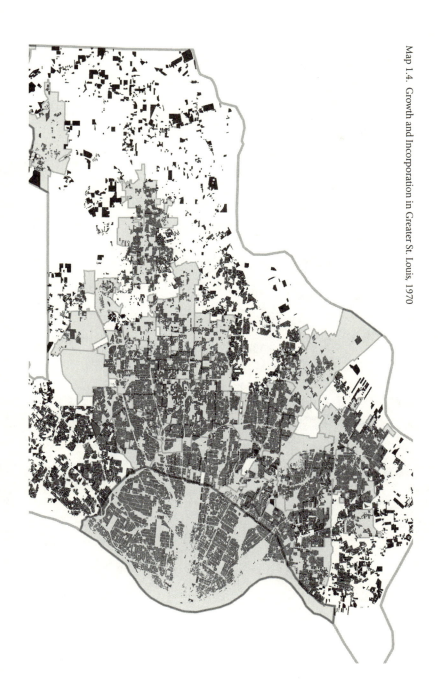

Map 1.4. Growth and Incorporation in Greater St. Louis, 1970

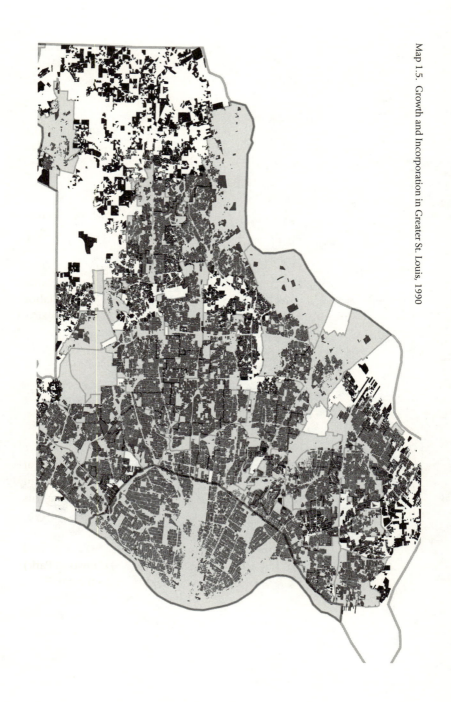

Map 1.5. Growth and Incorporation in Greater St. Louis, 1990

During this era of urban growth, less than a generation removed from the end of the Civil War, patterns and practices of segregation were hardening in settings like St. Louis. Although spared the full brunt of "Jim Crow" that emerged elsewhere in the former Confederacy, the free blacks of St. Louis faced a sustained battle over the terms of their political incorporation, and an increasingly formalized system of residential segregation—the latter sustained by urban planning (including the development of exclusive "private streets"), legal instruments (including race-restrictive deed covenants), and the tactics of private developers and realtors.[21]

Such practices and assumptions took hold outside the city limits as well. Free black settlement in St. Louis County was confined to a few discrete pockets, including Robertson and Kinloch to the north, Elmwood Park and Clayton in the central county, and Meacham Park to the south. Those communities—most of which have long since disappeared—shared many common traits. Most were either developed as black settlements or became so once a few black families moved in. Most were shaped by local labor markets (providing workers to nearby truck farms, brickworks, or quarries, for example), although they also provided homes to middle-class professionals as residential options for African Americans narrowed. And most were starkly segregated from existing or future white settlement by a combination of hard physical boundaries (railways, wetlands, gravel pits) and the purposefully uneven development of public services (schools, fire districts) and basic infrastructure (roads, water and sewer lines).[22]

Elmwood Park (map 1.6) and Meacham Park (map 1.7) were developed by Elzey Meacham in the early 1890s. The subdivision plats were filed with the county in 1892, and both developments pitched their lots (at $25.00 to $50.00, smaller and cheaper than those of most other suburban developments) to African American homesteaders.[23] Many of the first lots went to former slaves or their children, and both communities were soon dominated by extended families.[24] At the 1900 census, the occupational mix included day laborers, farm laborers, clay- and brickyard workers, and servants—some of whom would walk or ride the Colorado (Elmwood Park) or the St. Louis–San Francisco (Meacham Park) rail lines into the city.[25]

Both communities grew along with the metropolitan area. Elmwood Park (map 1.6) consisted of thirty-five black and thirteen white households in 1910, for a total population of just under two hundred (73 percent black). It did not grow over the next decade but did become more segregated: in 1920 there were still thirty-five black households but only seven white households, and the population (now just over 150) was about 85 percent black. Elmwood Park grew over the next twenty years, largely due

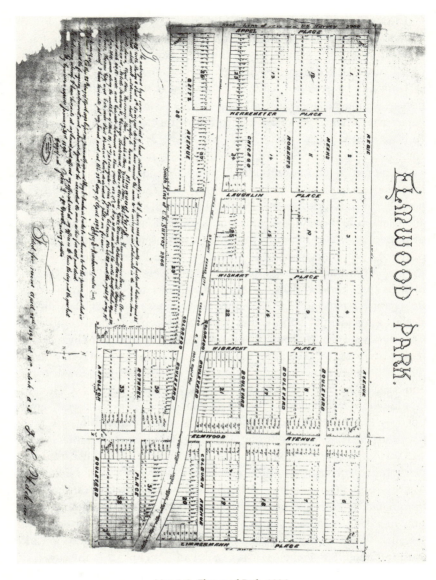

Map 1.6. Elmwood Park, 1896
Source: 1896 Plat Map, Records of the St. Louis County LCRA,
St. Louis County Economic Council, Clayton, MO.

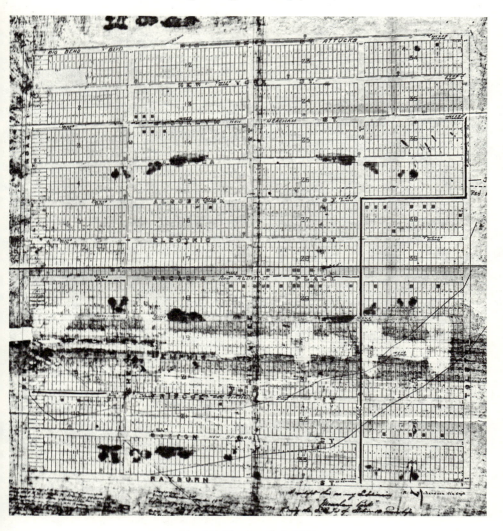

Map 1.7. Meacham Park, 1892
Source: 1892 Plat Map, Kirkwood Historical Society, Kirkwood, MO.
Photo by Taylor Desloge.

to local migration (over three-quarters of 1930 residents were born in Missouri). At the 1930 census, black households had more than doubled (to seventy-two), and the population (318) was now almost 93 percent black. By 1940, there were 109 black households, and the population (now over five hundred) remained about 93 percent black. The demographic trajectory of Meacham Park (map 1.7) was similar, although it was both larger and less segregated. In 1940, Meacham Park's population (266 households, 994 persons) was 75 percent black.[26]

During this era, Meacham Park and Elmwood Park developed as largely self-sufficient enclaves—a reflection (at their origins) of their relative isolation and (as they grew) their segregation from the larger pattern of suburbanization. Meacham subdivided and sold the land, but not much more: purchasers built the first generation of homes, dug wells, and maintained a rudimentary pattern of cinder streets and wooden sidewalks. Despite its close street grid, Meacham Park was essentially rural: "everyone had chickens, some had cows, many people had smokehouses, crime was non-existent, and the well in the southeast corner of 'the Park' was the social center of the community."[27] Local community and commercial services—churches, taverns, food stores, and hairdressers—cropped up to meet local needs. And, even as they were surrounded by new suburban development, residents of Meacham Park and Elmwood Park remained largely responsible for local services—including schooling, water and sewer, and fire protection.[28]

In the middle years of the twentieth century, conventional suburban subdivision and growth engulfed but bypassed Meacham Park and Elmwood Park. Indeed, private development, municipal annexation and incorporation, and municipal zoning were crafted in such a way as to effectively quarantine these older enclaves and their citizens—a process that not only erected new physical and political boundaries but also segregated the basic municipal services provided within those boundaries. New development brought Elmwood Park and Meacham Park physically closer to the center of the metropolis, but the terms of that development left those enclaves' citizens even more politically removed.

In St. Louis County, as in so many other suburban frontiers, municipal growth and municipal services were largely shaped by private developers. Whereas the earlier generation of developers (including Meacham) had simply speculated in the rudimentary platting and sale of lots, the new "community builders" crafted the modern subdivision—selling not only fully finished homes but also basic services (sewers, sidewalks) and the assurance of private regulation and planning. The latter was enforced by subdivision rules and deed covenants, which included both prohibitions (on commercial use, racial occupancy) and basic standards (for lot size, building setbacks).[29] The municipal patchwork spread west through the county as existing cities annexed completed subdivisions or those subdivisions simply incorporated themselves under Missouri's lax incorporation standards.

This process worked smoothly as long as developers were building cul-de-sacs in the cornfields, but it was ill-suited to dealing with already-developed enclaves—especially those featuring small unserviced lots and a population that was expressly prohibited by the deed covenants accompanying most new developments. Both neighboring municipalities and county officials fretted constantly about these underdeveloped and unincorporated pockets and their place in a suburban setting increasingly dominated by large-lot single-family development. Between 1930 and 1940 (by which time residential subdivision of the county surpassed the city's sixty-square-mile footprint), over 92 percent of new lots platted in St. Louis County were over five thousand square feet, and the average lot was over seventeen thousand square feet. As early as 1940, the county considered moving forward with its own zoning ordinance (in the wake of state legislation giving counties this power) in order to protect the "fine residential development" occurring in some unincorporated areas. A few years later, county officials underscored their desire to eliminate uneven land use and small-lot zoning: "such development must be corrected . . . the future welfare of the County depends upon the spacious character of residential development."[30] Such "correction" would come a generation later, under the auspices of urban renewal. Until then, the county and its municipalities worked to isolate and quarantine these "curious communities" through selective annexation.[31]

Under pre-1953 Missouri law, the process and standards for annexation were remarkably lax. Incorporated cities could annex new territory simply by passing an ordinance defining its new boundaries. The passage of the Sawyer Act in 1953 raised the bar, requiring incorporated cities to file annexation proposals with the circuit court—where approval rested on the reasonableness of the proposed annexation, its relationship to the city's development, and the city's ability and willingness to service the annexed area. The 1960 Missouri Supreme Court decision in *City of Olivette v. Graeler* refined the standard of "reasonableness," allowing courts to consider the countywide or regional implications of the sort of competitive, tax-grabbing annexation pursued by many St. Louis County municipalities. In 1963, the Sawyer Act's judicial review was extended to Missouri towns and villages.[32] By this time, much of the damage—the corporate fragmentation of St. Louis County, the starkly uneven provision of services, the pointed neglect of unincorporated areas and their citizens—was already done.

During the twentieth century, new residential development pressed west through the county. These subdivisions were, over time, either incorporated as municipalities or annexed by existing municipalities. Those decisions—made by private developers, homeowners, and city planners—were motivated in large part by the desire to sustain economic and racial segregation: to use the suburban patchwork to sort citizens, public goods, and resources. These patterns are starkly evident in the local history of incorporation and annexation in the municipalities surrounding—and ultimately quarantining—Elmwood Park and Meacham Park.

Elmwood Park

The geography of Elmwood Park was shaped by two neighboring cities, Overland to the north and Olivette to the south (maps 1.8 to 1.11). In Overland, residential subdivision began early in the twentieth century, fanning out from either side of Woodson Road between Lackland Road (to the south) and St. Charles Rock Road. Residents made a push for incorporation in 1937—in part as a pretext for funds from the New Deal's Works Progress Administration—and established the municipality of Overland in 1939. The 1939 boundaries included the subdivisions of East Overland Park, Sycamore Lane, Baldwin, Overland View, and Charlack, as well as a substantial (but lightly developed) commercial area south of Lackland. The postwar residential boom added the subdivisions of Pagewood, Iveland, Midland, Gocke, and Meadowbrook Downs. And each of these was followed or accompanied by an expansion of the municipal footprint, with major annexations east of Woodson Road (1945), west of Burns Avenue (1947), west of Sims (1950), and south of Page (1953).[33]

Olivette developed along similar lines. In the early twentieth century, the central county area south of Page Avenue and the Colorado rail line was composed mostly of small vegetable and fruit farms, punctuated by the unincorporated communities of Olive, Central, Tower Hill, and Strattman. In 1930, these joined together to establish Olivette, bordered to the east by University City, to the west by Warson Road, to the south by a section line about 1,600 feet south of Bonhomme Avenue, and to the north by a section line about a thousand feet north of Olive Boulevard. The city was sparsely developed on the eve of World War II, "far enough removed from the intensively developed portions of St. Louis," as city planners concluded in 1939, "that it should primarily be used as a desirable residential suburb." Most of the early (pre-1950) residential development occurred in small subdivisions running south from Bonhomme (Covington Meadows and Covington Lane, The Orchards, Chevy Chase, Price Lane and Price Court, and Ladue Hills) and on either side of Olive Boulevard near the boundary with University City (Fairlight Downs, Hilltop Woods).[34]

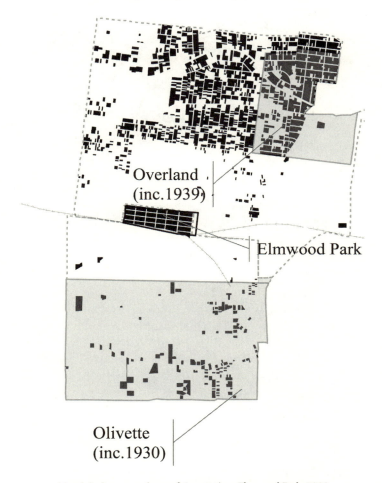

Overland
(inc.1939)

Elmwood Park

Olivette
(inc.1930)

Map 1.8. Incorporation and Annexation, Elmwood Park, 1930
Current boundaries shown by dotted line; incorporations and annexations
marked by date; residential properties (single-family, duplex, and multifamily)
shown by year built. Source: St. Louis County Department of Planning GIS dataset
(2012) and Carolyn Nolan annexation files; US Census TIGER Line files.

In 1949, Olivette annexed a small pocket north of Olive Boulevard, and in 1950 it extended its borders north to the Chicago–Rock Island rail line and the southern boundary of Overland. These additions accompanied and accommodated the housing boom of the early 1950s. Developers held options on much of the farmland north of Bonhomme Road and were poised for subdivision into small (5,000 to 7,500 square feet) lots, but local

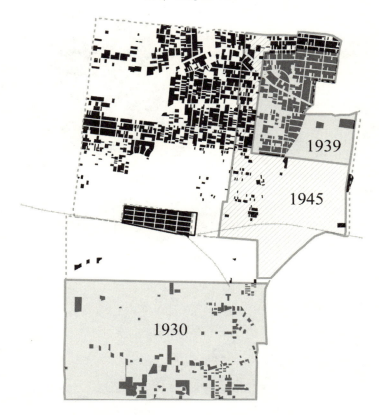

Map 1.9. Incorporation and Annexation, Elmwood Park, 1945

pressure forced a pattern of larger-scale "fine residential development"—
including Indian Meadows (370 homes), Oak Estates (141), and Arrowhead
Park (135). The extension of Olivette north to the rail line was part of a sustained effort to build an industrial tax base.[35] The justification presented to
the St. Louis County Boundary Commission was simply that the annexation
would even out Olivette's irregular northern border.[36]

As annexation followed new development in Overland and Olivette,
the net effect was to surround and isolate Elmwood Park and to exclude
its residents from municipal citizenship. "Olivette did not want to annex
Elmwood Park because we had no tax base or anything and neither did
Overland," as one resident recalled; it was a process "that just left us here
in a little huddle." Overland, most starkly in its 1953 annexation, skirted
Elmwood Park—pushing around the older enclave even as its borders to

the west and east reached the railbed and the new (1950) northern border of Overland. Olivette's 1950 annexation included a small slice of Elmwood Park, about forty homes south of the tracks along Geitz Avenue, and came at the same time that the city first submitted plans for redevelopment ("this section is to become a new modern part of the county when 'redevelopment' is completed," as one observer put it). Olivette officials hoped to both attract industrial development and use such development as a buffer between its own residential neighborhoods and the rest of Elmwood Park. After annexation, there was no extension of city services (most of which were privately contracted by Olivette's constituent subdivisions) to the area, and Geitz Avenue residents were unaware of any change—at least until 1955 when they were notified that their properties were to be auctioned for back

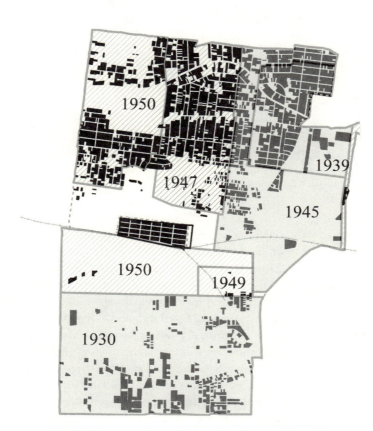

Map 1.10. Incorporation and Annexation, Elmwood Park, 1950

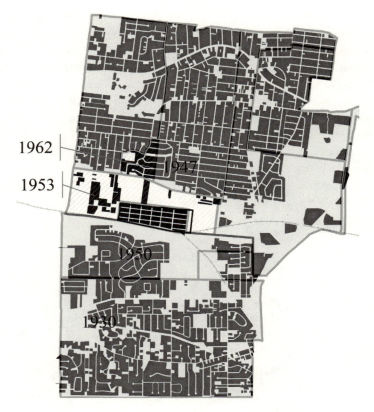

Map 1.11. Incorporation and Annexation, Elmwood Park, 1965

taxes. Assured they were buying "vacant" land, at least one winning bidder tore up his check when he learned of the circumstances.[37]

Land-use zoning added insult to injury (map 1.12). The original (1930 and 1939, respectively) footprints of Olivette and Overland were largely residential, with small commercial strips running along Lackland and Woodson Roads at the southwest corner of Overland, and along Olive Boulevard near the northern border of Olivette. Olivette passed its first zoning ordinance in 1941, acting on the conviction that "the town is predominately a suburban section of single-family homes, and such use should be protected in the future." Overland passed its first zoning ordinance in 1958, a land-use plan that also described, and sought to preserve, a well-established pattern of private residential subdivision. Just as telling, as both cities refined their zoning plans in response to new annexations, was the disposition of land surrounding Elmwood Park. Overland zoned a commercial strip south of Page and designated the rest of its 1953 annexation (surrounding Elmwood Park) as industrial. Olivette's 1958 ordinance both enabled the development of the massive Indian Meadows subdivision (built between 1958 and 1961) and protected it with an industrial zone—the latter running along the northern edge of its 1950 annexation and swallowing the southernmost parcels (along Geitz Avenue, Rothwell Place, and Napoleon Boulevard) of the original Elmwood Park. Olivette's 1969 land-use plan hardened this pattern, designating the old Elmwood parcels as industrial, except for one small strip of single-family housing on an industrial collector street, separated by parkland from a nearby residential area. Taken together,

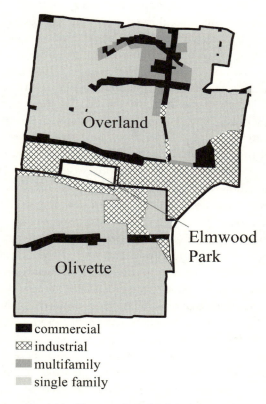

■ commercial

▨ industrial

▩ multifamily

░ single family

Map 1.12. Olivette and Overland Zoning, ca. 1965
Source: St. Louis County Department of Planning GIS dataset (2012) and Carolyn Nolan annexation files; US Census TIGER Line files; St. Louis County Municipalities Collection, Western Historical Manuscripts Collection, University of Missouri–St. Louis (Olivette 1963 in box 19, folder 215; Overland 1965 in box 20, folder 233).

local annexation and zoning ensured that Elmwood Park would remain an "isolated pocket" of unincorporated land "consistently ignored by adjacent communities."[38]

Meacham Park

As in Elmwood Park, the corporate fate of Meacham Park was shaped largely by the desire of neighboring municipalities to harden the boundary between new development and the old African American enclave, and to exclude Meacham Park residents from the benefits of local citizenship. At its creation, Meacham Park sat directly south of Kirkwood, a square mile of development that straddled the Missouri–Pacific at Denny Road (later Lindbergh Boulevard). In 1899, Kirkwood added about a quarter mile to its borders in all directions, pushing its southern border to the St. Louis–San Francisco railbed just north of Meacham Park. Residential development (maps 1.13 to 1.16) proceeded slowly on and near this corporate footprint, with most new residential construction before 1945 coming in residential subdivisions (Woodbine Heights, Louisa Heights, Montauk Hills, Doerr Hill Place, Rose Hill Place) just south of the Missouri–Pacific, and in those further south subdivisions (Windsor Acres, Geyer Court) south of the St. Louis–San Francisco, in areas annexed in 1927 and 1941. The city of Crestwood, to the east of Meacham Park, was incorporated in 1947, its original borders tracing the subdivisions (Crestwood, Elmont Park, Ridgewood, Clover Hill) south of Big Bend. Annexations in 1949 and 1951 expanded Crestwood to Meacham Park on the west and south across an array of new developments on either side of Sappington Road. In 1957, the city of Sunset Hills was incorporated west of Crestwood and south of Kirkwood and Meacham Park.[39]

Local citizens and planners fully understood the pointed exclusion of Meacham Park, and its implications. In 1956, Kirkwood officials and Meacham Park residents discussed the prospect of annexation. As St. Louis County was in the process of drawing up redevelopment plans for the area, Kirkwood held off. Furthermore, the Sawyer Act (passed in 1953) had set a higher threshold for services in newly annexed areas. Kirkwood could not annex Meacham Park without a clear plan for the area—and the fiscal capacity to follow through. A year later, Kirkwood annexed just the east side of Kirkwood Road, essentially pushing its border (south of Big Bend) one hundred feet to the east, poaching Meacham Park's only real commercial properties for its own tax base, and leaving the rest of Meacham Park unincorporated. This gambit left a "feeling of distrust for Kirkwood," according to one resident: "We really didn't have much say in the matter. They came in and

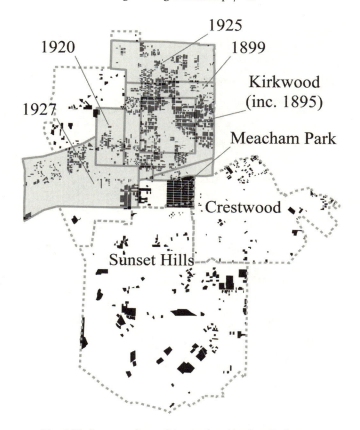

Map 1.13. Incorporation and Annexation, Meacham Park, 1940
Current boundaries shown by dotted line; incorporations and annexations
marked by date; residential properties (single-family, duplex, and multifamily)
shown by year built. Source: St. Louis County Department of Planning GIS dataset
(2012) and Carolyn Nolan annexation files; US Census TIGER Line files.

took what they could use, and they left us with the problem areas." With
the common borders of Kirkwood, Crestwood, and Sunset Hills largely settled, Meacham Park remained "a poor ugly orphan which surrounding cities
carefully avoided as they were expanding."[40]

For the next thirty years, the fate of Meacham Park cropped up repeatedly
in the plans of both Kirkwood and St. Louis County. In 1956, the county's Land Clearance for Redevelopment Authority (LCRA) (the new agency
charged with managing federal urban-renewal programs in unincorporated areas) identified Meacham Park (along with the county's other black

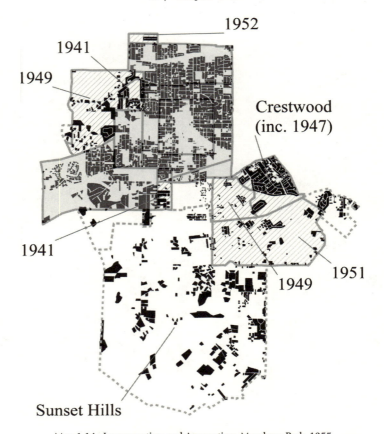

1952

1941

1949

Crestwood
(inc. 1947)

1941

1951

1949

Sunset Hills

Map 1.14. Incorporation and Annexation, Meacham Park, 1955

enclaves) as a target for renewal although—as we shall see in chapter 3—those plans staggered along. In the mid-1960s, Interstate 44 was completed across the central county. Its route cut across the southeast corner of Meacham Park, vacating about seventy parcels on the footprint of the highway and orphaning another forty parcels (about six acres) on the wrong side of the highway (these would be absorbed by Sunset Hills in 1992).[41]

At about the same time, the fire that took the lives of the Hurst children in January 1965 spurred Kirkwood officials to look again at the prospect of annexation. But interest on both sides was muted. Meacham Park residents keenly resented the commercial land grab of 1957 and viewed new annexation talk with skepticism. Kirkwood was reluctant to take on the burden of servicing and policing Meacham Park, but city officials also recognized that the suburban quarantine was an unsustainable solution. "Mosquitoes, bred in the failing septic tanks in Meacham Park[,] or potential criminals, raised in an atmosphere devoid of police protection," as Kirkwood's *Proposed Plan of Action* for Meacham Park observed in 1966, "are not respecters of municipal boundary lines."[42]

This tug-of-war between Meacham Park and Kirkwood, and within each, spilled into the 1970s. Meacham Park residents wanted decent public services. But they were wary of inviting a hostile police presence and cynical (especially in the wake of the 1957 annexation) of Kirkwood's motives. Kirkwood officials didn't know whether the threat of Meacham Park was best addressed by isolation or inclusion—but were willing to pursue the

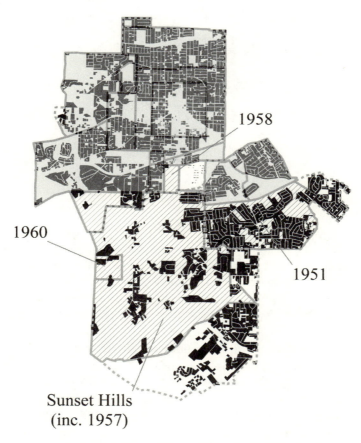

Map 1.15. Incorporation and Annexation, Meacham Park, 1970

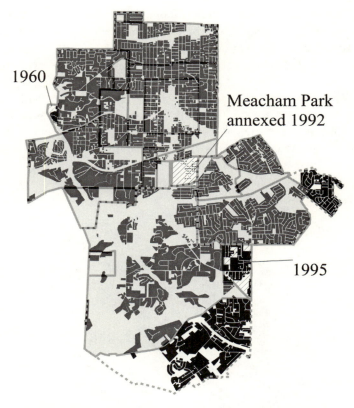

1960

Meacham Park
annexed 1992

1995

Map 1.16. Incorporation and Annexation, Meacham Park, 1995

latter only with substantial county and federal assistance. As long as redevelopment plans stalled, so too did any prospect of annexation. Kirkwood's annexation, zoning, and development policies, as Mayor Reim acknowledged in 1965, had "creat[ed] a ghetto-like effect" because they had "included valuable commercial and industrial areas, but . . . avoided the Meacham Park area."[43]

While services and physical conditions improved somewhat during the 1970s, prospects for annexation languished. The basic dilemma was underscored in 1971, when efforts to develop a new park in Meacham Park fell apart over the conviction that Kirkwood was more interested in segregating recreation (getting the Meacham kids out of Kirkwood parks) than in expanding services. St. Louis County concluded an exhaustive survey of conditions in Meacham Park in 1976, but the report coincided with the evaporation of federal funding for urban renewal. A follow-up annexation study (1977) was quietly filed away after public meetings revealed continued resistance in Kirkwood to taking on "the problems of Meacham Park" and continued concern in Meacham Park that annexation would mean some combination of rezoning for industrial use, higher taxes, and oppressive policing.[44]

The idea of annexation did not emerge again until the late 1980s, by which time the motives and anxieties of the interested parties had changed little. St. Louis County wanted to iron out the provision of basic services to a community that had "slowly and steadily deteriorated into a jumbled heap of dilapidated housing and dirt streets." Kirkwood officials wanted to reign in Meacham Park and fulfill its development potential. Meacham Park residents wanted better services and better representation in local government. But they also wanted to know how Kirkwood ordinances would be enforced and sought some assurance that their residential base would not be lost to commercial redevelopment—specifically requesting that commercial redevelopment go no further east than Shelby Road (which runs north to south through Meacham Park one block east of the pre-annexation border with Kirkwood). Kirkwood and county officials estimated that services to Meacham Park would cost about $300,000 annually and that the area would yield about $185,000 in taxes. In the short term, this gap was to be closed by county grants for streetlights and drug prevention, with the longer-term expectation that commercial redevelopment would eventually bring costs and revenues in line.[45] The annexation measure passed by a wide margin, its strongest support (at 83 percent) in Meacham Park itself, and in 1991 Kirkwood finally annexed Meacham Park.[46]

Again, local zoning and land use reinforced the quarantine (map 1.17). Crestwood (incorporated 1947) and Sunset Hills (1957) pushed single-family housing to their respective western and northern borders, as Interstate 44 and its right-of-way provided a sufficient barrier between Meacham Park and their single-family use zones. Kirkwood used commercial development along Kirkwood Road as a buffer between Meacham Park and its own residential districts. And, over time, it simply pushed this commercial zone further east, crossing Kirkwood Road in 1957 and over the western third of the newly annexed Meacham Park in 1992. Indeed—confirming the pre-annexation fears of Meacham Park residents—planning immediately began for Kirkwood Commons, a retail strip anchored by Target, Walmart, and Lowe's (this redevelopment is detailed in chapter 3). This project took up fifty-five acres (a little more than one-third) of Meacham Park, and revenues from the new tax base helped finance substantial improvements elsewhere. But the project

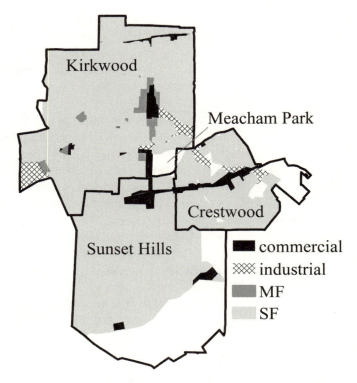

Map 1.17. Kirkwood, Crestwood, and Sunset Hills Zoning, ca. 1970
Source: St. Louis County Department of Planning GIS dataset (2012) and Carolyn
Nolan annexation files; US Census TIGER Line files; St. Louis County Municipalities
Collection, Western Historical Manuscripts Collection, University of Missouri–St. Louis
(Kirkwood 1965 in box 16, folder 163; Sunset Hills 1962 in box 2, folder 34); Harland
Bartholomew Papers, Washington University Archives (Crestwood 1968 in Series 4: Bound
City Planning Reports: Unlabeled Black Binders, 1957–1966, box 15, folder 20).

also widened old wounds. "That was a city ghetto sitting in a suburban community," argued Herb Jones (mayor of Kirkwood from 1984 to 1992), "now
it looks like a normal neighborhood." But response in Meacham Park was
mixed. "In the taking of Meacham Park, Kirkwood has gotten rich off the
backs of blacks," as one resident put it in the wake of the Kirkwood City Hall
shootings in 2008. "Kirkwood adopted us, only for the check."[47]

Mayor Jones's characterization of Meacham Park as a "city ghetto sitting
in a suburban community" captures the logic and motives of midcentury

planners, municipal officials, and white homeowners across St. Louis County. Despite the fact that both Elmwood Park and Meacham Park were well established before the postwar suburban boom, they (and their residents) were seen as obstacles to proper development and as blights on the suburban landscape. Residential development, municipal incorporation, and piecemeal annexation flowed west from the borders of St. Louis only to break around and bypass Meacham Park and Elmwood Park.

The isolation of these enclaves—through incorporation, annexation, and zoning—was both intentional and consequential. It proceeded on the assumption that African American residents were out of place in the suburban hinterlands of St. Louis County; indeed, the effective quarantine of development and zoning was soon followed by plans for redevelopment and renewal. And it fundamentally shaped the terms of local citizenship—determining who was a member of the community and who was not, who received local services and who did not, and who enjoyed local opportunities (jobs, schooling, homeownership) and who did not.

TWO

Segregating Citizenship: Schools, Safety, and Sewers

Municipal boundaries shaped patterns of development and land use and, coupled with local zoning, sorted local housing opportunities by race and class. The municipal patchwork determined not just who could live where but also set the boundaries of local democracy and shaped the scope and quality of local state obligations. Fragmented governance also fragmented the allocation of services integral to the meaning and enjoyment of citizenship: the protection of life (firefighters and police), liberty (courts), property (zoning), health (water and sewers), and equal opportunity (schools).[1]

The segregation and fragmentation of local services follow different logics and different patterns. When public goods or services are provided from general local revenues, they will reflect local fiscal capacity. When they rest on special or discretionary assessments, they may seem more like private goods—less a right of citizenship than an article of consumption.[2] In either case, local political fragmentation will, by intent and design, generate uneven service provision from one jurisdiction to the next. But provision can also be uneven *within* jurisdictions, especially when the discretion of providers opens opportunities for discrimination, disproportionate contact, or neglect (as is the case with policing). In the worst cases, neighborhoods in some jurisdictions may even be subject to near abandonment—to the "targeted withdrawal of hard and soft city systems" as a way of managing decline.[3]

In the geography of metropolitan St. Louis, service segregation occurred within and across jurisdictions.[4] In the first half of the twentieth century, explicit mechanisms of segregation—including the widespread use of race-restrictive deed covenants—created lasting neighborhood boundaries within the city of St. Louis. But, increasingly, municipal boundaries did most of the work of sustaining segregation. Suburban development drew a sharp jurisdictional line between the city of St. Louis and St. Louis County.

On each side of this line, the provision of basic services—schools, policing, fire protection, garbage collection—stopped and started at county or municipal borders. The city of St. Louis (which also had the status of a county) had its own sheriff, police department, fire department, and school district, their jurisdictions all ending at the "Berlin Wall" between city and county. In service provision, only the metropolitan sewer district, a junior college district, and a taxing authority that supported local museums and zoos breached this line.[5]

In turn, the patchwork of suburban development *within* St. Louis County drew equally stark distinctions between its municipalities and between incorporated and unincorporated areas. Across the county, local services closely followed local housing stock and local fiscal capacity. Modern suburban infrastructure ended abruptly where the city of Kirkwood met Meacham Park or where the cities of Olivette and Overland met Elmwood Park. Even as boundaries changed, older presumptions of citizenship persisted. When Olivette annexed a small slice of Elmwood Park in 1949, it provided no notice of this fact to the neighborhood's African American residents, extended no municipal services, and moved to auction off the lots for back taxes a few years later. And service provision eroded with demographic shifts. "Our trash pickups were regular and practiced with dignity. The street lighting was always up to par," as one resident told the United States Commission on Civil Rights in 1970. "But as the neighborhood changed those services have almost completely gone to pot. . . . I can't recall the streets being cleaned last year. We now have the most inadequate lighting in the city. We would be in complete isolation were it not for the complaints."[6]

The effect was twofold. Basic local services—the provision and maintenance of schools, streets, sewers, garbage collection, fire protection, policing—lagged (in timing and quality) in the unincorporated enclaves of Elmwood Park and Meacham Park. The latter was "literally a cesspool," as Kirkwood mayor Robert Reim acknowledged in the mid-1960s: "there were no streets, no sewers, no adequate police or fire protection." In turn, this cemented the conviction that Meacham Park and Elmwood Park—"island[s] of blight and poverty in the midst of new, modern, residential and industrial development"[7]—should be targeted for renewal. Local and county officials only reluctantly and belatedly extended services and then used the paucity of those services to buttress arguments for redevelopment.

When services were extended, the motives were often tangled. Kirkwood officials, for example, were perpetually torn between isolating Meacham Park entirely or annexing (and servicing) it. In this confusion, they often pursued a cynical middle ground, selectively extending services or resources in such a way as to deal with some of the problems posed by Meacham Park without assuming real or lasting responsibility. The first item here, not surprisingly, was policing—viewed by Kirkwood as an unfortunate necessity and by Meacham Park residents as a threat as much as a service. The same ambivalence surrounded a proposed park development (1971), rebuffed by Meacham Park residents as a thinly veiled effort to segregate local recreation.[8]

Under the law, such patterns of discrimination were difficult to identify or address. For most of the last century, local and state courts clung to the assumption that local governments should be given broad discretion to shepherd limited resources and employ the local police power as they saw fit.[9] But, especially as challenges to segregated schooling wound through the courts, legal decisions also underscored the legal and political implications of uneven service provision. Local government, having levied taxes, had a fiduciary responsibility to extend services and a constitutional obligation to do so in congruence with the "equal protection" promised by the Fourteenth Amendment.[10] Courts increasingly held that the provision of police and fire protection, the extension of basic infrastructure, and the availability of potable water were as fundamental as education. "It need only be asked whether dirty, filthy streets, unlit at night, beckoning the criminal, awash during winter storms," as one legal commentator observed, "engender in those who live in such under-serviced areas [quoting *Brown v. Board of Education*:] 'a feeling of inferiority as to their status in the community that may affect their hearts and minds in a way unlikely to be undone.'"[11]

But it was not until 1971, fully seventeen years after *Brown*, that similar arguments for equal protection were extended to local services. In *Hawkins v. Shaw* (1971) a federal appeals court cast aside the usual deference to local governmental discretion and concluded bluntly that no such argument "could possibly justify the gross disparities in services between black and white areas of town that this record reveals."[12] The conditions described in *Shaw* (in which everything from street paving to water pressure followed the local color line) echoed the patterns of deep and lasting discrimination generated in Greater St. Louis by segregation and municipal fragmentation. The municipal patchwork was also a fiscal patchwork, sustaining uneven provision and capacity. Fragmented provision encouraged local residents to think of themselves as consumers exercising their tastes or preferences or choices and not as citizens entitled to public goods. "City borders, once zoned to segregate people by income level," as Gerald Frug argues, "function like the boundaries of private property: a suggestion that one should pay for services for nonresidents is experienced as a demand for the reallocation of wealth."[13] Those left entirely behind by municipal incorporation and annexation (including the residents of Meacham Park and Elmwood Park) relied on a spare single tier of county services.[14] "These families are *citizens* of the community," as the St. Louis Urban League noted bitterly in 1956, eager to "accept the responsibilities expected of them and make their contributions to the city in which they reside."[15] Yet, for many, those contributions yielded little in return.

Schools

The uneven provision of municipal services, as well as its underlying racial logic, is perhaps most profound—and most devastating—in the history of schooling. Education is not just a benefit of citizenship (a local service provided to parents and children) but also a *source* of citizenship—a setting in which students are taught skills and, as John Dewey and others have underscored, socialized to associational and democratic norms. Public schooling represents the "moral requirement that democratic institutions allocate sufficient resources to education," as Amy Guttman argues, "to provide all children with an ability adequate to participate in the democratic process." We view public education, in this respect, as a foundation of civic engagement, as a source of social mobility, and as a "starting gate" leveler of other distributional inequalities.[16]

That this promise—measured by opportunities or outcomes—has gone largely unrealized is most directly a consequence of race relations and their role in organizing, segregating, and distributing local educational resources.[17] This story, pivoting on the *Brown v. Board of Education* decision of 1954, is by now a familiar one: for the first century after Reconstruction, "separate but equal" schooling in the South systematically segregated public education while discriminatory housing practices and policies in the North effectively accomplished the same. The result, implied by the social science behind *Brown* and exhaustively documented by the Coleman Report twelve years later, was a tangle of disadvantages, including uneven commitment and resources in the schools themselves and stark racial and economic segregation in the neighborhoods surrounding them.[18] Desegregation, in turn, was promising but fleeting. *Brown* compelled desegregation *within* school districts but bogged down in metropolitan settings where segregation was abetted or accomplished by district boundaries. Resistance to *Brown* slowed its implementation, and legal setbacks (most importantly the 1974 *Milliken v. Bradley* decision, which reasserted local control and undercut metropolitan cross-district desegregation plans, and the 1991 *Board of Education of*

Oklahoma City v. Dowell decision, which made it easier for districts to satisfy and escape court orders) invited resegregation. Between 1988 and 2016, the share of public schools whose student population was more than 90 percent nonwhite more than tripled, from 5.7 percent to 18.4 percent.[19]

All of this was especially fraught in Greater St. Louis, where municipal fragmentation was mimicked by school-district boundaries and where racial segregation was so deeply embedded in local politics and policy. The state of Missouri prohibited the schooling of black children in 1847 and mandated separate schools for "white and colored children" in 1865—the latter provision was not struck from the state's constitution until 1976. Leaning against these laws and conditions, African American citizens' councils in St. Louis worked diligently—and with some success—to ensure their share of local educational resources.[20] But separate, of course, was not equal: a 1916 survey found that "Negro schoolhouses" in Greater St. Louis were "miserable beyond description."[21]

This misery played out very differently in the city and the county, in a sense following three spatial logics. Within the city of St. Louis, neighborhood segregation (and particularly the "Delmar Divide" between the north and south sides) created a system of segregated schooling within a single district. Fragmented municipal governance in St. Louis County, as well as the white flight that motivated it, was echoed by fragmented school districts for whom local control and maintenance of the boundary between city and county were equally important goals.[22] Finally, the organization and consolidation of school districts within St. Louis County were designed to displace or segregate black students—both in older enclaves such as Meacham Park and Elmwood Park and in transitional inner suburbs like Ferguson. In the county, the broader assumption held that African Americans were lesser citizens or that they were out of place and "belonged" in the city. In 1921, the state of Missouri mandated consolidated (and segregated) black schools in counties with at least one hundred thousand residents and required districts with more than eight black students to either build a "colored" school or cover the costs of their education in another district.[23] St. Louis County districts, for the most part, chose the latter option: in the twenty years before *Brown*, county districts covered the tuition and transportation costs of over 2,600 black students who attended segregated schools in the city.[24]

For its part, the St. Louis City school district was ready for the legal revolution of the 1950s and 1960s: it brought on a desegregation consultant in 1947 and had a plan in place when the Supreme Court struck down "separate but equal" schooling in 1954. The city mapped out a staged response to *Brown*, integrating junior colleges and special schools in September 1954, high schools and adult education in February 1955, and elementary schools in September 1955. The plan centered on neighborhood schools, with transfers or busing as necessary to address overcrowding. While the city's embrace of *Brown* was a national model ("solidly conceived and brilliantly carried off" in the estimate of the US Civil Rights Commission), conditions for African American students across the region changed little. The problem, as observers noted right away and documented across the post-*Brown* era, was that the devotion to neighborhood schools simply traded the de jure segregation at the schoolhouse door for the de facto segregation of the surrounding neighborhood. Underlying (and unchallenged) patterns of housing segregation hardened a pattern of all-black neighborhood schools, and limited busing within the city (mostly of whole classes from overcrowded north-side schools) simply created "separate but equal" enclaves at otherwise all-white school sites. By 1970, over fifteen years into the *Brown* era, fully three-quarters of the city's schools were single-race schools.[25]

Housing segregation was deeply entrenched in the city by 1954 and, in many respects, made worse by the patterns of in-migration and white flight that followed. Housing policies and practices nurtured not just racial segregation but also a cycle of overcrowding, real-estate arbitrage, and disinvestment in African American neighborhoods that spilled over into neighborhood schools. Public policies were little help. The first generation of public housing and urban renewal, by intent and design, sustained and succored segregation. Mortgage-assistance programs aimed at low-income homeowners were, in north St. Louis, simply instruments of segregation and blockbusting. Even after 1968, when federal programs were bound by an unambiguous commitment to housing equity, their local administration often betrayed that promise. "Once again a river of public money washed through parts of the city," as Gary Orfield observes in his summary of the housing issues frustrating school desegregation in St. Louis, "and, once again, left more children attending segregated schools in segregated neighborhoods."[26]

The school system itself could, and did, do little to stem these patterns. Investments in school infrastructure followed housing so that new school construction, which many had hoped would facilitate desegregation, only magnified the challenge. Busing, aimed at overcrowding rather than segregation, was managed in such a way as to deepen the racial divide. Overcrowding in north-side schools, for example, was often addressed with "intact busing," which moved a class of students and their teacher to a predominantly white school during off-hours. However neighborhood patterns and enrollment numbers fell, the St. Louis School Board repeatedly refused to place white students in predominantly black schools or classrooms. And, through all of this, county districts continued to bus most of their African American students into the city.[27]

In turn, the city could do little about the mechanisms of segregation—the patchwork of twenty-seven school districts that sprawled across St. Louis County—that fell beyond its jurisdiction. In the county, school segregation rested less on neighborhood housing patterns than on municipal and school-district boundaries. In some respects, county districts responded calmly to *Brown*, but only because they knew full well that local policies ensured that the Supreme Court's ruling would have little immediate effect. Most county municipalities used zoning to ensure the prevalence of large-lot single-family housing, a strategy explicitly pursued as a means of sustaining other forms of racial restriction.[28] County municipalities (and the county itself) dug in their heels against the construction of public or subsidized housing. State officials, fearing a political backlash if they "forced housing down the throats of people who are against it," largely deferred to local sentiment. Federal housing officials waged a long battle with St. Louis County over its resistance to public housing—even when such housing was a clear condition of federal urban-renewal programs. As a result, virtually all public housing was constructed in the city—"just where it would be of least value for school desegregation," as Orfield observes.[29]

These conditions finally sparked a legal challenge in 1972. Minnie Liddell, a north-side St. Louis parent of a first grader, sued the school district for allowing its "neighborhood schools" policy to abet segregation in city schools. The district offered little dissent but argued that it bore no direct responsibility for the housing policies at the root of the problem. It was not until the early 1980s that the US Justice Department broached the underlying logic of local segregation and ordered the state to craft an interdistrict solution that would "eradicate the remaining vestiges of government-imposed school segregation in the city of St. Louis and St. Louis County." The state of Missouri, whose culpability rested largely on its implicit blessing of "white flight" districts in the suburbs, dug in its heels. Only five inner suburban districts (Kirkwood, Ritenour, Clayton, Pattonville, and University City) in St. Louis County signaled any willingness to cooperate with the voluntary transfer program, while the eighteen[30] other county districts openly resisted. The trial judge threatened to make the plan compulsory by imposing a single metro-wide school district over the city and the county, and the recalcitrant districts grudgingly signed on.[31]

The final settlement in 1983—a notoriously expensive solution crafted in the face of substantial local political opposition—was a voluntary transfer program that required suburban districts to integrate, either by increasing black enrollment by 15 percent or by reaching a threshold student population that was 25 percent black. The program also included magnet schools in the city (designed to attract voluntary in-busing of white students), a "quality of education" commitment to capital improvements in poorer schools, and a state stipend covering the educational and transportation costs of transfer students. The agreement (which also gave cooperating suburban districts a reprieve from legal action) went into effect for the 1983–1984 school year. The results were mixed: funding for magnet schools and capital improvements lagged, and the voluntary transfer program drew too few white students into city schools and too many good black students out of them. Indeed, the litigation over St. Louis integration, which began in the early 1970s, was not fully resolved until 1999.[32]

The tangle of race and exclusion in local education was evident in different ways across the county line. Here, district boundaries were drawn and redrawn alongside the municipal patchwork—and for the same reasons. Here, as in much of white-flight suburban development, realtors and developers made "good schools" a central element of the sales pitch to prospective homeowners.[33] Here, the conviction that African Americans—or, in this context, African American children—were out of place was particularly strident.

Consider the history of schooling in Meacham Park and Elmwood Park. The villages surrounding Elmwood Park established a rudimentary school district in the 1870s. African American residents of Elmwood Park pressed for their own school, and the district rented a house for that purpose in 1880. With the help of the local Baptist church, Elmwood Park established its own elementary school building and struck a deal by which the district would provide a teacher for three months of the year and "two small loads of coal." District enumeration at the end of the nineteenth century counted about 550 students, of which about fifty were black—including the children of Elmwood Park and those of neighboring districts who bused their scattered black enrollees to the Elmwood Park school. The district (Ritenour) established its first black high-school class in 1913, but students were bused to Sumner High School in St. Louis City, and later to Frederick Douglass High School in Webster Groves.[34]

Patterns in Meacham Park, which fell in the Kirkwood School District, were similar. The first Meacham Park school (1908) was for white children only; the neighborhood's black children walked nearly three miles to Booker T. Washington, Kirkwood's all-black elementary school. Black parents from Meacham Park lobbied unsuccessfully for a local school and won a back-handed victory in 1919 when fire damage at Booker T. Washington forced the district to move black elementary students to a two-room portable in Meacham Park. Finally, in 1924, by which time Meacham Park kids made up the bulk of the enrollment at Booker T. Washington, the district opened the Meacham Park School (renamed J. Milton Turner Elementary in 1932). Beginning in 1920, high-school-age black children could attend Sumner High in St. Louis or Douglass High in Webster Groves—although the Kirkwood District was notoriously lax about making the requisite tuition payments. When Kirkwood's Washington School was razed in 1950, Turner School became the area's black elementary and junior-high school.[35]

After 1954, integration of county schools proceeded slowly and fitfully. The Ritenour district surrounding Elmwood Park integrated in 1958, but the Elmwood Park school remained all black, and other county districts continued to bus black elementary students to Elmwood Park into the 1960s. No move was made to integrate the Elmwood Park school until 1974, at which point local parents filed suit against the school district because the remedy (busing Elmwood Park students into Overland) seemed to place much of the weight of desegregation on the shoulders of their children. In the early years of the plan, parents rode the buses alongside their children in order to protect them. The Elmwood Park school building, briefly used for vocational classes, was closed and sold in 1976.[36]

The Kirkwood district dropped formal segregation in 1954 for elementary students and in 1955 for high school students, but the district's schools still reflected the underlying segregation of housing markets. In the 1974–1975 school year, the district had an enrollment of about 6,500, 13 percent of whom were black. Turner Elementary was 99.5 percent black, three others (Rose Hill/Robinson, Pitman, and Nipher Junior) were about 25 percent black, and seven schools (of the thirteen in the district) had black enrollments of under 3 percent. "You would have to consider it a little South of Mississippi," as one observer described the pattern of segregation in Kirkwood schools.[37] Regional administrators for the Office of Civil Rights pressed the district on a more active desegregation plan, which it adopted in early 1975. Under the plan (which the district saw as a chance to cut its budget as well), four elementary schools—including Meacham Park's Turner School—were closed, and expanded busing for those students would accomplish the desegregation of the district's remaining schools. Meacham Park parents opposed the plan and lobbied in vain to reopen Turner. As in Elmwood Park, residential segregation was left untouched, black families lost their neighborhood school, and the burden of school desegregation fell largely on black children.[38]

Local patterns of segregation, in turn, sustained local fiscal inequalities. Patchwork development across and within county municipalities sorted not just citizens but also assessed property values—the primary source, across most of this history, for school funding. In 1956, in the immediate aftermath of the *Brown* decision, the mean assessed value per student, across all districts in Greater St. Louis, was just over $12,000. The wealthy central-county districts, such as Clayton and Ladue, were able to raise twice that amount from local sources while maintaining the lowest tax rates in the county. North County districts, by contrast, suffered both higher tax rates and lower revenues, some (including Kinloch) falling under $6,000 per student. In the late 1970s, a series of equal-protection challenges prompted Missouri (and most other states) to introduce a foundation-funding formula, backfilling local revenues with state aid in order to reach a basic per-student threshold of funding in every district. State aid in Missouri, however, is chronically underfunded, leaving disparities based on local revenues largely intact. These inequities, as one circuit court judge noted in the early 1990s, sustained a school system in which districts still ranged from "the golden to the God-awful."[39]

In the county's inner suburbs, equitable access to education was challenged both by older boundaries of exclusion and by a dramatic racial transition that threatened (and sometimes moved) those boundaries. The spatial logic and racial motives of county schooling are neatly captured by the history of the Kinloch school district in North County. Into the 1930s, the Kinloch district encompassed the African American enclave of Kinloch itself, and most of what is now the city of Berkeley (map 2.1). While the district included white and black kids, its schools did not. In keeping with Missouri law, the district included a high school and an elementary school for white children and an elementary school for black children; the district paid to have black high-school students attend Sumner High in St. Louis. The county turned back two efforts to split the district along racial lines, but in 1937 it allowed white parents another route to sustained segregation. Months after the second failure to split the district, the county approved the incorporation of Berkeley. The footprint of the new municipality formed a ragged horseshoe around Kinloch, its boundaries almost identical to those of the "white" school district proposed a few months earlier. The new municipal boundaries also included a small portion of another adjoining district, so that residents could take advantage of a state law that allowed residents of any incorporated city falling across more than one school district to establish a new district. The first legislative act of Berkeley's newly seated

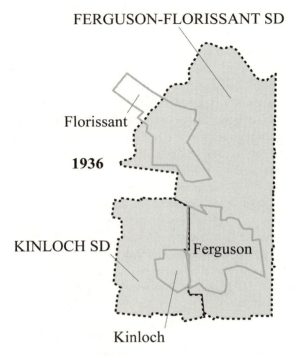

FERGUSON-FLORISSANT SD

Florissant

1936

KINLOCH SD

Ferguson

Kinloch

Map 2.1. Kinloch and Ferguson-Florissant School Districts, 1936
Municipalities shown with gray borders; school districts shown gray with dashed
borders. Source: St. Louis County Department of Planning GIS dataset (2012) and
Carolyn Nolan annexation files; Kinloch History Committee Records, Western Historical
Manuscripts Collection, St. Louis; *United States v. State of Missouri et al.* 515 F.2d 1365
(1975); St. Louis County Superintendent of Schools, *Annual Report* (various years).

board of aldermen was to file a plan to "form a school district coterminous
with the boundaries of the city"[40] (map 2.2).

The consequences were both immediate and long-lasting. The following
September, enrollment across the two districts was fully segregated: a handful
of white students lived in Kinloch (sixteen of 6640), and a few black students
lived in Berkeley (six of 878), but, by law, these students enrolled according
to the color line rather than the district boundaries. All of the teachers and
administrators in Berkeley were white; all of the teachers and administrators in Kinloch were black. For the next thirty-odd years—half of them leading up to the *Brown* decision, half of them coming after—this segregation
went essentially unchallenged. No white student enrolled in Kinloch before
the 1970–1971 school year, and a year later the student population was still

99.3 percent black. Berkeley did not hire its first black teacher until 1960, and Kinloch did not employ any white teachers before 1967.[41]

The split, in turn, left the lion's share of the old district's tax capacity in Berkeley. In 1961, assessed value per pupil in Kinloch ($2,507) was the lowest in the county; fourteen of the county's twenty-one districts had per-pupil valuations that were more than three times as high, and the wealthiest district (Clayton at $23,230) was almost ten times higher.[42] A decade later, Kinloch still had the lowest assessed value per pupil of any school district in the county. The average teacher's salary in Kinloch was barely three-quarters of the average in Berkeley, and the school facilities were so markedly inferior that, as one assessment put it, "no one should go to school there."[43] Indeed, routinely Kinloch ranked dead last in the county on achievement. "Clearly, if the people of St. Louis County are committed to the goal of equalizing to an acceptable level educational opportunity for all children," as a 1962

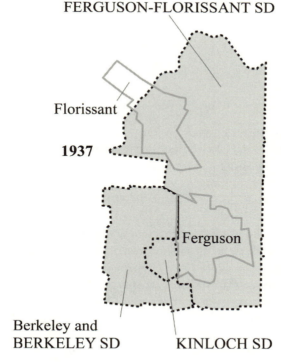

Map 2.2. Berkeley, Kinloch, and Ferguson-Florissant School Districts, 1937

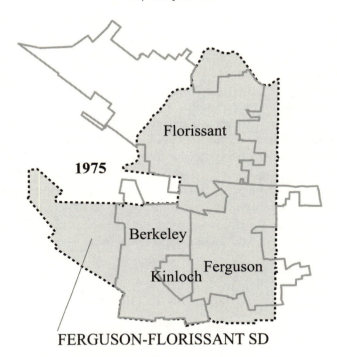

Map 2.3. The Ferguson-Florissant School District, 1975

study of school-district organization, conducted by researchers from the University of Chicago, concludes, "they may begin here."[44]

In 1971, the Justice Department challenged this fragmentation on equal-protection grounds, ultimately winning a reorganization of district boundaries in 1975 (map 2.3). "The cumulative effect of the actions of the state and local defendants," as the plaintiffs argued, "has been the creation, operation, support, and general supervision by the State of Missouri of a small school district which is unconstitutionally segregated and whose students are denied an equal educational opportunity." The isolation of Kinloch's schoolchildren from this elemental source of citizenship was especially striking given a pattern of district consolidation elsewhere in the county. Between 1948 and 1970, the number of school districts in the county fell from eighty-four to twenty-five, with most of the consolidation driven by the fiscal woes of small districts. After 1948, every district in North County saw some adjustment or consolidation, but each plan avoided Kinloch and—as the county grew—further isolated it.

In 1975, the district court finally compelled a settlement, combining the Kinloch, Berkeley, and Ferguson school districts. In these negotiations, Berkeley (now a relatively integrated district) suggested that Kinloch be annexed to Ferguson, while Kinloch and Ferguson thought that Kinloch should be rejoined with Berkeley. None favored the three-district plan, but it was clear that this was the only solution that achieved a new district that would be both substantively integrated and fiscally sound. As the court underscored, there was more than enough blame to go around. While Berkeley bore responsibility for the original split in 1937, Ferguson (and other municipalities) had dug in since then against any reorganization that included Kinloch.[45]

By the 1970s, school districts in the county (and especially in North County) had to contend not just with the integration of older enclaves like Kinloch but also with racial transition as African Americans—fleeing conditions on the city's north side, displaced by urban renewal, and grasping the housing opportunities opened by the civil-rights movement—moved from the city to its inner suburbs. In the half century after *Brown*, the county's African American population increased more than tenfold, from just 19,000 in 1960 to over 193,000 by 2000. In 1940, the city of Ferguson, as the local appraisal by the federal Home Owners Loan Corporation notes, was "restricted so as to prohibit residences of Negroes in its limits."[46] By 2000, over half of Ferguson's population was African American.

The result was not an end to segregation and unequal schooling but an unsettling of its boundaries. The fiscal challenges that had long plagued city schools moved to the inner suburbs as well. As in the city, white children in transitional areas, and some black middle-class children, fled the public school system—leaving the public school population blacker and poorer than the neighborhoods in which it was located. As of 2016, almost all school-age African American children in Ferguson-Florissant, but barely a third of the white children, attend the district schools. The county's inner suburbs simply became the next frontier for "a subtle, ongoing racial injustice," as Nikole Hannah-Jones notes, a "vast disparity in resources and expectations for black children in America's stubbornly segregated educational system."[47]

The persistence of this disparity and its implications for local citizenship were underscored by two legal confrontations, both of which predated the death of Michael Brown but roiled to the surface in its aftermath. The first, *NAACP v. Ferguson-Florissant School District*, concerned the voting rights of local parents. School boards are not just the shepherds of educational resources but also democratic institutions in their own right, providing citizens with direct engagement with local educational policy and priorities.[48] The Ferguson-Florissant district, whose very footprint represented "a long and ugly history of racial discrimination," employed an at-large system of electing members to the board. Local segregation (much of the growing African American population lived in the southeastern corner of the district) disadvantaged African Americans who, despite representing almost half of the voting population and more than three-quarters of the public school population, struggled for representation on the board.[49] In 2016, the trial judge held for the plaintiffs and ordered the implementation of a cumulative voting at-large electoral system that would address both local segregation and changing demographics.[50]

The second legal issue has both offered redress for educational inequalities and cast a harsh light on the assumptions and prejudices behind them. In 1993, the Missouri legislature gave children in school districts that had lost their accreditation the right to transfer to an accredited district nearby. The unaccredited district paid tuition and transportation fees to the receiving district, which had no option but to accept the transfer. Suburban districts, leery of migrants from failing schools, challenged the law, as did parents who had voluntarily open-enrolled in other districts and wanted the failing district they had fled to pay the costs. The St. Louis City school district lost its accreditation in 2007; that, and continued migration to North County, put enormous stress on adjoining districts. In 2009, the state closed down the Wellston district, an all-black, five-hundred-student district that state officials deemed "deplorable and academically abusive," and merged it with the Normandy district. In 2011, the state pulled Normandy's accreditation. As of 2014, almost half of African American students in the county—compared to just 4 percent of white students—were enrolled in unaccredited districts.[51]

The result, as the reporting of Nikole Hannah-Jones has explored, was an illuminating real-time experiment in school integration and community response. For students stuck in the Normandy schools, which ranked dead last among Missouri's 520 districts, disaccreditation offered a glimmer of equal access and opportunity. "Just like that," as Hannah-Jones notes, "the court's decision erased the invisible, impenetrable lines of segregation." Hoping to limit the number of transfers (for which they had to pay tuition and transportation), Normandy school officials designated Francis Howell—a largely white district twenty-six miles away at the western edge of the county—as the transfer district. Nearly three thousand Francis Howell parents voiced their dismay at a community meeting in July 2013, arguing—in candidly racial terms—that the transfer policy threatened the opportunities enjoyed by *their* children. For some in the room, it was a confrontation reminiscent of the desegregation battles—and anxieties—of the 1950s.[52]

The postscript to this story is equally telling. Francis Howell parents and administrators pressed the state to suspend the transfer program. Their unlikely ally in this was the Normandy district, which was slowly going broke covering transportation and tuition payments for transfer students. The solution was a legal sleight of hand: the state reorganized the Normandy district as a "state oversight district," meaning that, while still not an accredited district, it was no longer "unaccredited" as defined by the transfer policy. In August 2014, a circuit court enjoined Normandy and the target districts (Francis Howell, Ritenour, and Pattonville) from ending the transfers. "Sadly, the evidence is crystal clear that the students will suffer if their request is not granted," wrote the judge. "Every day a student attends an unaccredited school (instead of an accredited one) he/she could suffer harm that could not be repaired after the fact. . . . By enacting the transfer statute, the people of Missouri, through their legislature and the Governor, recognized that leaving children in unaccredited school districts with no option to transfer from those districts, is harmful to those children."[53]

Across this long, contested history of local education, the state, the school districts of Greater St. Louis, and the schools within those districts allocated resources and opportunities in sharply unequal patterns. In some respects, schools and districts were constrained or hemmed in by larger patterns of political fragmentation and residential segregation. But in other respects, the choices made by schools and school districts created, embraced, or reinforced those patterns. All of this would be less troubling if these resource and opportunity gaps closed steadily and substantially after *Brown*. Instead they persisted, or they moved with the region's African American population from the city to its inner suburbs. At stake, of course, was not just the right to a public education but also the civic capacity and economic opportunity—the present and future citizenship—of the children of Greater St. Louis.

Safety

Citizenship is calibrated not just by the public services offered or provided to local residents but also by the services, obligations, or expectations that are imposed on them. Policing, in this respect, is not just a public service aimed at securing safety and order. It is a highly discretionary exercise of "coercion, containment, repression, surveillance, regulation, predation, discipline, and violence" that represents for many—and certainly for the most marginal—the single most important point of contact between citizen and state.[54] In policing, in other words, local disparities have rested less on unequal provision than on unequal treatment: on who—in given settings—is policed and who is protected. For African Americans in deeply segregated St. Louis County, this has meant both close surveillance and attention in their own neighborhoods and disproportionate suspicion and contact almost everywhere else.

This experience was shaped by race: by the disproportionate attention given to African Americans generally by the police and courts. And it was shaped by place: by the assumption that, outside a few enclaves of black occupancy, African Americans were threats or interlopers.[55] "I think we got more police protection than we required when I first moved there," as Adel Allen (an African American resident of Kirkwood) told the Commission on Civil Rights in 1970, adding that "I don't know if they were protecting me or protecting someone from me."[56] As the better-off suburbs hoarded opportunities (and the tax base that paid for them), they also sought to protect and police the boundaries they had created. Policing, in this respect, was both an analogue to and an extension of exclusionary zoning; it was a mechanism for sorting and segregating local citizens and for protecting property values.[57]

Policing shapes, and limits, citizenship in a number of ways. First, and perhaps most notoriously, police have considerable discretion as to which citizens they choose to surveil, pursue, or punish. The identification of African Americans as unique threats to public safety and public order accompanied and reinforced both the institution of "Jim Crow" in the South and the articulation of systematic segregation in the urban north.[58] These patterns were both reinvented and reinforced by the expansion of "get tough," "law-and-order," or "broken windows" policing as the war on poverty gave way to the war on welfare.[59] The results, now amply documented, include stark racial inequalities on every metric from school suspensions to executions, pervasive entanglement with the police and courts for young black men in particular, and an era of mass incarceration without historical or comparative precedent.[60] "The meting out of punishment in the American criminal justice system," as Tracey Meares and Ben Justice underscore, ". . . provide[s] Americans with a powerful and coherent set of messages and experiences that define who is a citizen, and who is a problem."[61]

Such sharply uneven experiences diminish, devalue, and discourage citizenship in other ways. A criminal record can short-circuit other avenues of productive and meaningful citizenship—including educational and employment opportunities, access to housing, and the right to vote.[62] Both the rate and the manner of interactions with the police, of which the Justice Department's investigation of the Ferguson Police Department offers but one jarring account, undermine African American citizens' faith in the ability of their government to make fair and objective decisions.[63] Not only are African Americans often not treated like full-fledged citizens, but their mistreatment, as Vesla Weaver and Amy Lerman argue, "weakens attachment to the political process and heightens negative perceptions of government."[64]

All of this was magnified in the politically fragmented and deeply segregated setting of St. Louis County. In one respect, this was an extension of the larger pattern of municipal neglect, in which unincorporated pockets were underserviced and underprotected. Surrounding municipalities, and the county, were reluctant to extend the most basic services into the African American enclaves of Elmwood Park and Meacham Park. Neither community, for example, fell into any of the county's fire districts. Both maintained small volunteer units, affiliated with the countywide Negro Volunteer Fire Department (which also served Robertson and North Webster Groves).[65] The limits of this arrangement were tragically underscored by the 1965 fire—after which Meacham Park contracted for fire protection directly with the county.

Policing and code enforcement, whose extension into these "suburban ghettos" was an important part of the efforts to contain and control them, were an exception to this pattern of neglect. Through the 1960s and 1970s, Olivette, Overland, and St. Louis County police employed concrete road barriers to monitor and constrain access to Elmwood Park. Kirkwood and county officials similarly viewed the policing of Meacham Park as essential to public safety beyond its borders. "Potential criminals," as Kirkwood's 1966 *Proposed Plan of Action for Assistance to the Meacham Park Area* argues, "are not respecters of municipal boundary lines." This view was only hardened when then Kirkwood mayor Robert Reim brought St. Louis County executive Lawrence Roos to Meacham Park where (as Reim recalled) "he was greeted by young fellows loitering in the streets, playing crap games right out in the open." Roos and Reim left the community meeting only to discover that someone had stolen the battery out of the county's limousine.[66]

As part of that 1966 plan, Kirkwood proposed extending police jurisdiction into Meacham Park. For their part, Meacham Park residents resented the proposal—not only because they were leery of the presence of Kirkwood's all-white police force but also because they were understandably bitter that this was the *only* municipal service that Kirkwood seemed ready to extend.[67] Meacham Park contracted with the county instead. Local policing, whether it was the county's nominal presence in Meacham Park or the treatment of Meacham Park residents when they ventured into Kirkwood or beyond, left many "bitter, angry, and frustrated." When annexation was raised again in the mid-1970s, local opposition rested largely on police harassment—"that's what we are going to be paying our taxes for," as one resident argued, "to be discriminated against."[68] Even after annexation, the borders were clear, and rigidly policed: "To those who are not familiar with the area," one resident noted, "it's Kirkwood. But to us, and the police, and everybody that was born and raised in Kirkwood, it's still Meacham Park." Before and after annexation, Kirkwood police closely monitored the entrance to Meacham Park, routinely tailing cars as they left the neighborhood.[69]

Suspicion that neighboring towns were more interested in policing Meacham Park and Elmwood Park than they were in servicing them also played out over the issue of code enforcement—most dramatically in the Cookie Thornton tragedy. As unincorporated pockets of St. Louis County, Meacham Park and Elmwood Park were lightly serviced but also lightly regulated. The county's zoning ordinance was less stringent than those of the county municipalities—and in any case, the small lots and mixed uses in these older enclaves preceded county zoning and persisted as nonconforming exceptions. But when Meacham Park was finally annexed by Kirkwood in the early 1990s, the latter's stricter rules kicked in. For Meacham Park residents—especially those who, like Thornton, saw joining Kirkwood as a precursor to their share of redevelopment business—annexation brought more pain than opportunity. Kirkwood officials began enforcing city codes in Meacham Park, including those prohibiting street parking of heavy equipment, business use of residential property, or the storage of construction materials (or debris) on city lots. Thornton's running feud with Kirkwood was an exceptional case, but it underscored a broader problem. Time and time again, before the 1992 annexation and after, Meacham Park residents felt themselves as targets rather than citizens of local government.[70]

In Meacham Park and Elmwood Park, policing was—like the larger pattern of incorporation and annexation it mimicked—a strategy of containment or quarantine. Across the county, policing was animated both by enforcing borders of exclusion and by identifying and surveilling those deemed "out of place"—especially as racial transition began to accelerate in the inner suburbs of North County.[71] In practice, this pattern of policing was at once systematic and chaotic. Patchwork governance, after all, yields patchwork policing: as of 2017, the county contained ninety-one municipalities, eighty-one municipal courts, and sixty-one police departments. Local testimony—from the 1970 hearings of the United States Commission on Civil Rights to the work of Arch City Defenders and others in the wake of Michael Brown's death—document exposure to serial traffic stops and low-level harassment from one municipal fragment to the next, and a tangle of local warrants and fines that often trap those charged with even minor offenses on a "municipal shuffle" from one court docket to the next.[72] And this "byzantine maze of overlapping jurisdictions" has made it harder to accomplish any meaningful change in policing or in the courts: "whatever you do in St. Louis City," as the activist Kayla Reed observes, "you have to replicate 90 times throughout the County."[73]

In neighborhoods undergoing racial transition—north St. Louis in the 1950s, and north St. Louis County a generation later—the presumption that black residents did not belong and were a threat to those who did was both powerful and persistent. In the county, local efforts to sustain segregation and control black occupancy eventually faltered in the face of continued migration west from St. Louis itself and slow legal progress on equal housing. Downtown urban-renewal programs displaced thousands of families—some of whom were accommodated in new public-housing projects, most of whom simply moved west and north ahead of the bulldozer. In the 1960s, redevelopment in the county uprooted thousands more. The slow collapse of public infrastructure and public services in North St. Louis also encouraged population flight, although the outmigration of African Americans did not really take off until civil-rights law began to open county housing markets. All of this converged on North County's inner suburbs, including Ferguson. Segregation drifted into the inner suburbs, as did its consequences—including concentrated poverty, limited economic opportunity, a paucity of public services (except for heavy-handed policing), and political disenfranchisement.

There was a savage irony here: many black families left the city in the 1970s because they felt vulnerable and unprotected there; in their new neighborhoods in the county, *they* were the threat.[74] In a sense, local policing picked up the slack where other mechanisms of segregation (zoning, discriminatory real-estate practices) had faltered. In their investigation of the Ferguson Police Department, the Department of Justice underscored "the persistent exercise of discretion to the detriment of African Americans; the apparent consideration of race in assessing threat; and the historical opposition to having African Americans live in Ferguson, which lingers among some today," in describing local practices more interested in enforcing segregation than in ensuring public safety. The police "see some residents, especially those who live in Ferguson's predominantly African-American neighborhoods," the Justice Department concluded caustically, "less as constituents to be protected than as potential offenders."[75]

Such assumptions—in Ferguson and across the county—are evident in a long history of disproportionate contact between African American citizens and their local police. This attention has been animated in equal parts by presumptions of criminality that followed African Americans (especially young men) wherever they went in Greater St. Louis and by the added suspicion, in the county and its municipalities, that African Americans were not where they belonged. African Americans, whether they had lived in the county for generations or were joining the "black flight" from the city's north side, were seen as lesser citizens: at least an offense to property values, at worst a threat to public safety. And African Americans experienced a lesser citizenship—they were as likely to be dodging or avoiding state surveillance as they were to be benefiting from state programs. "I don't think there is a black man in South St. Louis County," as Adel Allen testified bitterly in 1970, "who hasn't been stopped at least once if he has been here more than two weeks."[76] Nearly a half century later, the Justice Department underscored the Ferguson Police Department's predilection for "suspicionless, legally unsupportable stops," which yielded arrest and citation rates that fell heavily and almost exclusively on the city's black residents.[77]

One measure of this disparity is the rate of police contact relative to a racial group's share of the population. Since 2000, the state of Missouri has required local police departments to report traffic stops (and their resolutions) by race. Figure 2.1 plots the resulting disparity as a "disparity index" for all police jurisdictions in the nine-county St. Louis region, for blacks and whites, from 2000 to 2016. At a disparity index of "1," the share of traffic stops matches that racial group's share of the population.

For whites, the hundred-odd police jurisdictions (each represented by a dot) in the St. Louis region are clustered at or below 1 in every year surveyed. For African Americans, the median disparity index is closer to 2 and the seventy-fifth percentile is over 3 for all but four of the years surveyed. A quarter of these police jurisdictions, in other words, stopped black motorists at a rate more than three times their share of the population. These disparities were even starker when a traffic stop led to a search or an arrest. In 2013 (the year before Michael Brown was shot), the police departments of Ferguson, Olivette, Overland, and Kirkwood searched the vehicles of black motorists at twice the rate of those of whites and arrested black motorists at almost three times the rate.[78] In Bel-Ridge (just south of Ferguson) that year, more than three-quarters of all traffic stops involved black motorists; of the 775 black motorists stopped, eleven were subject to searches and thirty-two were arrested. Traffic stops of motorists who were *not* black yielded not a single search or arrest.[79]

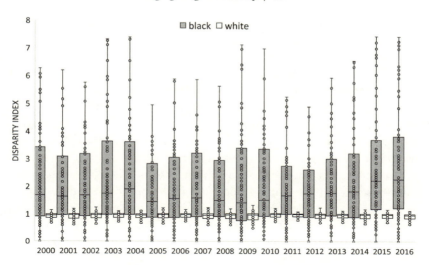

2.1. Traffic Stops by Race, St. Louis County, 2000–2016
Source: Attorney General of Missouri, "Vehicle Stops Report," https://www.ago.mo.gov
/home/vehicle-stops-report. On this graphic, each dot is a police jurisdiction in
St. Louis County, plotting their "disparity index" (the vertical axis) by year from 2000
to 2016. The box shows the 25th to 75th percentiles in a given year, and the middle
line indicates the median disparity index for that year across all jurisdictions.

Such policing practices "arrest citizenship" not just because citizens are unevenly targeted but also because the conduct of the police and the charges themselves violate basic norms of social and legal equity. "African Americans' views of [Ferguson Police Department]," as the Department of Justice observes, "are shaped not just by what FPD officers do, but by how they do it."[80] The problem here is threefold: First, as we have seen, police discretion is clearly shaped by race and place—by assumptions about who belongs where. In deeply segregated St. Louis County, African Americans have always been disproportionately surveilled in their own neighborhoods and disproportionately targeted when they leave them.

Second, local policing in St. Louis County has always leaned heavily on enforcement of the municipal code—a constitutional fog patch of petty offenses and citations. Michael Brown was stopped under the auspices of Ferguson Municipal Code section 44–344, "Manner of Walking along Roadway," an exhortation to use the sidewalk that was, before its repeal in 2016, employed almost exclusively as a pretext for stopping black pedestrians.[81] More broadly, much of the harassment that passed for policing in settings such as Ferguson rested on "contempt of cop" charges such as "Failure to Comply," "Disorderly

Conduct," "Interference with Officer," or "Resisting Arrest"—all of which the police wielded overwhelmingly against black pedestrians and motorists.[82] The result, as the Department of Justice tallies in its Ferguson Report, were systematic violations of the First Amendment and of the "probable cause" and "excessive force" provisions of the Fourth Amendment.[83] And these abrogations of basic citizenship continued when such charges were pursued in the municipal courts, where "ongoing violations of the most fundamental guarantees of the United States constitution" included "denial of counsel, denial of pretrial release, and the de facto operation of debtors prisons."[84]

And third, this pattern of unequal protection was accompanied by the thinnest veneer of procedural justice.[85] Routine stops for petty or manufactured infractions of the law, as Bennett Capers argues, "suggest a public discounting of worth, an asterisk on our protestations of equality, a caveat to our rhetoric about applying strict scrutiny to the state's use of racial distinctions." How African Americans were treated in these interactions with the state sent a clear and powerful message about citizenship to those targeted, and to onlookers. "These stops are a dressing down," as Capers underscores, "a public shaming, the very stigmatic harm that the Court has often, but not often enough, found troubling."[86]

Police interactions with African Americans in St. Louis County have historically been marked by indifference toward and neglect of those seeking the protection of the law (including those who were early arrivals in transitional areas), and disrespect, unequal treatment, and excessive force for those who are the targets of the law. "I've been stopped, searched, and I don't mean searched in the milder sense," as one man testified at the 1970 hearings, "I mean laying across the hood of the car." The Department of Justice emphasized that "police and municipal court practices have sown deep mistrust between parts of the community and the police department, undermining law enforcement legitimacy among African Americans in particular." In their scathing 2015 assessment of the county's municipal courts, Arch City Defenders underscores this point: "For most individuals, the only substantive interaction they have with the Missouri justice system or with their municipal government is through the municipal courts, and the impressions instilled by those courts reflect on the entire municipality."[87]

W. E. B. Du Bois captured this dismal combination of inadequate protection and disproportionate attention when he observed (reflecting on his move to Philadelphia's Seventh Ward in 1895) that "murder sat on our doorsteps, *police were our government*, and philanthropy dropped in with periodic advice" (italics added).[88] More than a century later in suburban St. Louis, the same stark inequality prevailed. For white citizens living adjacent to black enclaves like Meacham Park and Elmwood Park, in zones of racial transition like Ferguson, or on the next exurban frontier of white flight, the police could be relied on to enforce boundaries and punish those who transgressed them. For black residents navigating the same space, the police were instead a threat—routinely suspicious of their presence and dismissive of their rights.[89]

Sewers

In the case of schooling and of public safety, fragmented municipal governance—and the local segregation that motivated it—yielded starkly unequal access or exposure to basic public services. And, in both instances, claims to equal citizenship and equal protection were clear and unambiguous. Both schooling and public safety represent state provision of essential services, putatively available to all and financed out of general revenues. More mundane services—such as street paving, streetlights, trash pickup, or sanitary sewers—are trickier legal and political terrain. Such services are arguably less essential. The initial construction of urban infrastructure is often privately financed in the course of residential development, and local provision or extension of such services, in many settings, is often financed through special assessments rather than general revenues.[90] Even *Hawkins v. Shaw*, the 1971 case that extended the logic of *Brown* to streets and sewers, held that municipalities were under no obligation to provide such services and that equal protection came into play only when such services were financed from general funds.[91]

At the same time, uneven provision of basic municipal services has been a powerful, and powerfully felt, marker of local inequality. Many settings—before and after the early 1970s—echoed the built environment of Shaw (a small Texas town of 2,500): stark racial segregation, in which the streets on the "wrong side of the tracks" were unpaved, undrained, and poorly lit and many of the houses relied on wood stoves, wells, and outdoor privies. The extension of services to new developments often bypassed older enclaves and effectively cemented past patterns of discrimination.[92] What might have been seen as luxuries early in the twentieth century (running water, sewer hookups) were, by the century's end, considered simply adequate to modern urban life.[93] "Inadequate sanitation services are viewed by many ghetto residents not merely as instances of poor public service but as manifestations of racial discrimination," the Kerner Commission concluded bluntly in 1968. "This perception reinforces existing feelings of alienation . . . not only with the administrators of the sanitation department but with all representatives of local government."[94]

These patterns—and their implications for local citizenship—were starkly evident in the contrast between the county's old African American enclaves and its newer suburbs. Elmwood Park and Meacham Park were platted and developed long before the extension of modern waste and water infrastructure, and—like all such rural enclaves—both cobbled together such services locally. As of 1920, for example, most Elmwood Park homes had cisterns that were filled by a local water service; there was also a well on Chicago Avenue for public use. Homes had outdoor pit toilets or septic systems, although the clay-over-limestone subsoil in St. Louis County was a poor base for the latter. Even where rudimentary sewers existed, they did little but remove waste to the nearest stream or ditch. The result was a "hodge-podge, crazy-quilt pattern of sewers, many with no place to go but an open-ditch, of septic tanks, individual and community, and of no sanitary facilities at all"—much of it draining untreated into the Mississippi.[95] Public health officials identified these heavily polluted local watersheds, "offensive to sight and smell," as the probable cause for outbreaks of mosquito-borne encephalitis in 1933 and 1937 that killed over three hundred county residents.[96]

As subdivision-based development began to spread west of the city, property developers assumed the task of extending sewer and water lines, the costs of which were rolled into new home prices. This meant that both sewer and water service branched out intermittently, following the path of new construction but skirting the footprint of older communities.[97] Connection to sewer or water mains was a private obligation and expense, so even when new lines were extended, many residents of older homes could not afford to establish service.[98] Along with new suburban development and its street grid, basic sanitary infrastructure surrounded and bypassed Meacham Park and Elmwood Park. This underscored and cemented local inequalities, sharpened the distinction between "standard" and "substandard" housing stock, and made the underserviced enclaves targets for redevelopment.

In the early postwar era, new residential development tapped into an existing patchwork of small private and municipal sewer systems. While new homes were fully serviced, the system itself was woefully underdeveloped. Many of the county's small waterways had been "turned into stinking, open sewers," running "almost to the brim with raw human waste, garbage, trash and gray sludge from septic tanks." This prompted the creation of the Metropolitan Sewer District (MSD) in 1954, a rare creature of cooperation between St. Louis City and St. Louis County. The MSD was organized into three subdistricts, the bulk (most of the inner county and the city) draining to the Mississippi, the Coldwater Creek subdistrict draining to the Missouri in North County, and the Sugar Creek subdistrict (Kirkwood and South) draining to the Meramec. The MSD was financed by a new levy (a flat annual charge, since city water supply was unmetered), and a mix of general obligation and revenue bonds were used to finance new construction and major renovation. In its first decade, the MSD built nearly nine hundred miles of new sewers, seven major trunk lines, and a new treatment plant for the Coldwater Creek subdistrict.[99]

As of the early 1960s, Elmwood Park was serviced by an uneven web of water mains and two sanitary sewer trunks, but few of the homes were connected to either. The Olivette health commissioner noted that "the portion of Elmwood Park which lies in the City of Olivette is in deplorable condition, having no sanitary facilities whatsoever." Residents of the unincorporated portion of Elmwood Park largely agreed, complaining to the county in 1960 that a local outbreak of polio was unsurprising given the neighborhood's ramshackle infrastructure: "just open sewage, you know, ditches and all." The Elmwood Park redevelopment project, launched in 1962 (a little later on the Olivette side) and completed about a decade later, modernized this infrastructure, running new water lines and sanitary sewer lines alongside the new street grid and establishing a new storm-sewer system. As this project wound to its conclusion, MSD officials boasted that "almost all of the homes within the boundaries of the Metropolitan Sewer District, with rare exceptions, are presently served with adequate sewer facilities."[100]

Meacham Park—quarantined from new development, bypassed by the MSD, and excluded from the county's renewal plans—remained one of these "rare exceptions." A 1970 survey of Meacham Park's 216 residential properties found more than two-thirds suffering some degree of "septic failure," and fully half of which still relied on outdoor privies. One quarter of Meacham Park homes lacked adequate water supply. And poor stormwater drainage had been exacerbated by the recent construction of I-44, which cut across Meacham Park's southeast corner. Most of Meacham Park drained to a sorry tributary of Gravois Creek—"a littered, polluted, and abused channel" that also collected runoff from I-44 and much of Sunset Hills.[101]

In the absence of sweeping redevelopment, extension of sewer service to Meacham Park residents (maps 2.4 to 2.7) faced an array of obstacles. The first of these was the cost of the preliminary infrastructure of sewer mains and interceptors. The Missouri congressional delegation pressed the US Department of Housing and Urban Development (HUD) for a steeper federal commitment, finally winning the "Kinloch Amendment" (named for another of the county's old African American enclaves) to the 1965 Housing Act—that pushed the federal share for qualifying projects to 90 percent.

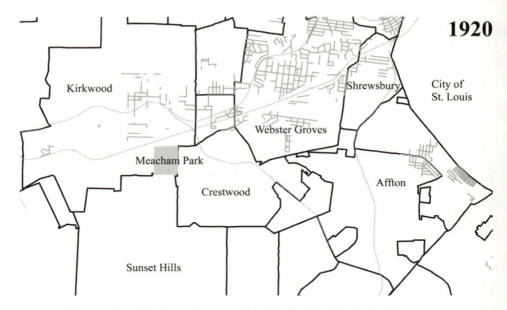

Map 2.4. Sewer Infrastructure in and around Meacham Park, 1920
Sewer mains mapped by date of residential development and street construction.
Source: St. Louis County Department of Planning GIS dataset (2012); US
Census TIGER Line files; Metropolitan St. Louis Sewer District, Meacham
Park Trunk and Lateral Map HUD (WS-MO-120), August 1969.

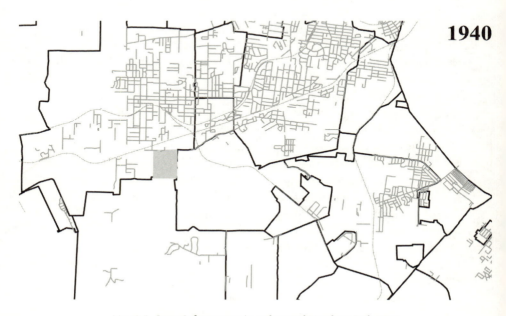

Map 2.5. Sewer Infrastructure in and around Meacham Park, 1940

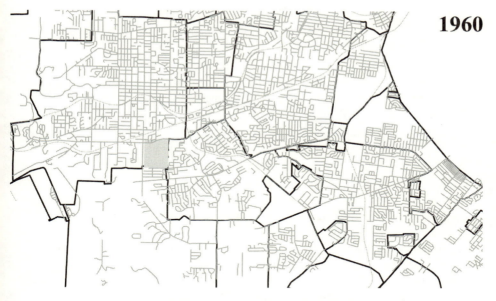

Map 2.6. Sewer Infrastructure in and around Meacham Park, 1960

Map 2.7. Sewer Infrastructure in and around Meacham Park, 1980

Meacham Park residents chartered a sewer-funding bus trip to DC in 1966 and finally won funding of a new sanitary sewer system—including nearly $300,000 from HUD and another $82,000 commitment from the county for completion of the first interceptor line. The new system was completed in 1971. The first interceptor was routed in such a way as to displace four of the five community septic tanks "discharging effluent into creeks," and then new trunks followed the street grid north and west into the neighborhood. "The country had sent a man to the moon twice," as one observer noted, "before it got the roads and sewers fixed in Meacham Park."[102]

The new mains, however, did nothing to address the prohibitive cost of running lateral lines to individual homes. In that first year, the MSD issued only thirteen permits in Meacham Park for individual hookups. Lapses in title and title documentation (not uncommon in such an old rural enclave) slowed the task of establishing easements for sewer work. Those interested in establishing service had to upgrade interior fixtures in addition to paying for the lines to the house. And many found that estimates for that work were much higher than those sketched by HUD and county planners—and much higher than comparable work elsewhere in the county. Local churches (including the First Presbyterian Church of Kirkwood) bridged some of this gap with a low-interest loan program to help cover the cost (usually about $2,500) of connecting homes to new mains. It was not until the early 1980s (pushed along by new development) that all occupied units in Meacham Park were connected to sanitary sewers.[103]

Here, again, as with schooling and policing, the provision of local services reflected the underlying fragmentation of political authority and jurisdiction. Local services reflected uneven local fiscal capacity—both from one county municipality to the next and between county municipalities and the remnants of unincorporated residential development. But services like sewer and water waste removal also reflected the logic of private development and "consumable" public goods. Much of the responsibility for initial water and sewer infrastructure rested on suburban developers, and homeowners were (and are) generally responsible for the costs and maintenance of lateral lines that connect individual homes to municipal water or sewer lines. Uneven provision, in this respect, came at the intersection of political and economic inequality: patterns of development often made such services inaccessible, and if or when access was extended, the service was often unaffordable.

These patterns of schooling, policing, and basic service provision underscored the larger and lasting implications of fragmented municipal governance. In part, the provision of services simply echoed the patchwork of political authority and fiscal capacity. Where property values were high, municipalities or school districts could deliver both robust services and low tax rates. In part, local discretion or discrimination created uneven provision within jurisdictions. Operating from larger assumptions as to who belonged in the suburbs and who did not, the police made choices every day, at every traffic stop, about who to protect and who to punish. And, in part, many public services were not fully "public," and their provision relied on private investments or consumption.

Little wonder that where and when democratic institutions failed, local services were often the flash point. The poverty of citizenship in the Jim Crow South was largely marked by the segregation of public recreation, public education, and public transportation. In the aftermath of the urban unrest of the mid-1960s, the Kerner Commission identified discrimination in policing, education, recreation, and other local services as the most important contributing causes.[104] And in Greater St. Louis, African American residents routinely equated uneven local services with uneven local citizenship. Meacham Park, as the United States Commission on Civil Rights observed in 1977, was "an unincorporated area without a revenue base and with no government of its own," and as a consequence, its residents were "treated as second-class citizens, receiving inadequate police protection and inferior street maintenance and lighting services."[105]

THREE

Bulldozing Citizenship:
Renewal, Redevelopment, and Relocation

In 1997, Susette Kelo bought her dream house, a cottage overlooking the Thames River in New London, Connecticut. New London had seen better days, having suffered through the closing of a major naval-research facility, so when Pfizer announced plans to build a new research facility nearby, city officials hurriedly reactivated the New London Development Corporation (NLDC) and charged it with "renewing" Kelo's neighborhood. In November 2000, the NLDC condemned the properties of Kelo and her neighbors. While many took the NLDC's offer, Kelo and a handful of others stayed put and challenged the premise that padding the local tax base constituted a "public purpose." By June 2005, Kelo's case had wound its way to the Supreme Court, where a 5–4 opinion agreed with New London that a new private use for the property was a sufficiently public purpose and upheld the condemnation. *Kelo v. New London* became one of the most widely discussed and controversial cases in the court's recent history. For the right, this was big-state liberalism at its worst, running roughshod over private-property rights and private markets. For the left, this was corporate liberalism at its most craven, the state hiring out its power for the benefit of developers and business interests and at the expense of a working-class community.[1]

Kelo unfolded a thousand miles and nearly a half century removed from the politics of urban renewal in St. Louis County, but the core legal issues—and the implications for citizenship—had changed little. Indeed, in this respect, the political backlash was surprisingly shortsighted. The exercise of eminent domain condoned and confirmed in *Kelo* was hardly exceptional in redevelopment practice or politics. The basic premises (deference to local legislative authority, private redevelopment as public purpose) had been laid down in the first decade after World War II and scarcely challenged since. The real damage, on this score, was done decades ago, in the heyday of urban renewal that ran from the late 1940s to the early 1970s. In this era, the obstacles to redevelopment were not just "hold out" properties but entire neighborhoods or communities faced with the damning assessment that their very existence posed a "blighted" threat to the general welfare.[2] Redevelopment policies underscored the fragile citizenship of those whose residency was considered a threat or an aberration. In this respect, urban renewal not only undermined property rights, it also—in its calculus of blight, in its administration of land clearance and redevelopment, and in its treatment of dislocated residents—bulldozed any semblance of equal protection.

The Law and Politics of Urban Renewal

Urban renewal was a stepchild of the postwar housing crisis. As the war drew to a close, veterans, labor, and urban interests pressed for a wide array of public and publicly-subsidized housing programs. The Housing Act of 1949 called for new housing but, to appease both realty interests anxious about government competition and downtown business interests anxious about suburban flight, also promised "the elimination of substandard and other inadequate housing through the clearance of slums and blighted areas," ensured that most of the new federal spending would flow as subsidies to private enterprise, and left most of the discretion—as to the meaning of "substandard" or "blighted"—with local governments.[3] Under the new urban-redevelopment program, local planners would identify neighborhoods or areas in need of renewal. States (twenty-five of which had passed urban redevelopment acts between 1941 and 1948) established quasi-public redevelopment corporations and granted them the power to assemble and clear land. And, in 1949, the federal government offered the missing link: the money to pay for the costs of land acquisition and clearance, some of which would be recovered as the cleared land was sold. The redevelopment program was fine-tuned in 1954 and rechristened "urban renewal."[4]

The enterprise was troubled from the start. Program revisions (in 1954 and after) unhitched urban renewal from its original justification. What began as part of an effort to find "a decent home and suitable living environment for every American family" was soon little more than a way for local business and political interests to underwrite sports stadiums, convention centers, downtown parking lots, and university or hospital expansion with federal money.[5] Urban renewal won notoriety, across the political spectrum, for its uneven results, its immense costs, and its callous disregard for those in its path. Jane Jacobs's *The Death and Life of Great American Cities* (1961) sees urban renewal as destructive of urban vitality and variety. Martin Anderson's *The Federal Bulldozer* (1964) blasts the program as an affront to private-property rights and personal liberty. And local observers noted the bitter logic of "Negro removal" in a program that cleared the central city of substandard housing while making little effort to erase economic and racial discrimination in private housing markets elsewhere. This was "not a war on poverty," as opponents argued, "but rather a war on the poor."[6]

Behind growing doubts about the intent and impact of the urban renewal program lay a fundamental legal question: Could the government take the property of a private landowner, run it through the hands of a redevelopment corporation, and sell or lease it to another private party? In the first test of this proposition, *Schneider v. District of Columbia* (1953), the court conceded the right of the government to acquire (by eminent domain if necessary) any property to be used for streets, schools, and parks as such "public use" exceptions were "established beyond question." But it stopped short of what it saw as the government weighing in on aesthetic questions or picking and choosing among private interests. There were, quite simply, no conceivable constitutional grounds for seizing property simply because local boosters could dream up a better use for it.[7] This check on the urban renewal program lasted barely a year. In 1954, the Supreme Court reversed the decision and established the legal foundation for the next half century of urban renewal and redevelopment. *Berman v. Parker* not only flattened the cautionary logic of *Schneider* but also confirmed the lower court's worst fears. The definition of "blight" was now solely a matter of local discretion. "If those who govern the District of Columbia decide that the Nation's Capital should be beautiful as well as sanitary," wrote Justice William Douglas for the majority, "there is nothing in the Fifth Amendment that stands in the way."[8]

In the wake of *Berman*, urban renewal drifted free of any logical or legal restraint. Much local effort and federal money was directed at truly troubled neighborhoods, but scattered successes were overshadowed by mounting criticism of the program's motives and impact. Federal policy now gave local government broad discretion in both identifying "blighted" neighborhoods and determining the "public purpose" served by their redevelopment.[9] Both concepts proved remarkably elastic. A "blighted" property, originally envisioned as a tenement breeding vice and disease, could now be a tony shopping mall lacking a Nordstrom's. And *any* efforts to eradicate blight could now be considered a public purpose—a concept that, under the urban renewal program, slipped from meaning actual public *use* to the more nebulous public *benefit*.[10] It became both legal and routine to condemn properties not because they were blighted but because someone had proposed a private use that would generate more tax revenue.[11]

In turn, blight and its eradication were hopelessly entangled with the racial transformation of the midcentury city. When urban-renewal enthusiasts listed the "things that urban renewal is designed to get rid of," they were often describing the consequences of African American migration into racially restrictive housing markets—the "wretched homes and suffocating neighborhoods in which thousands of families are still forced to live."[12] Urban renewal programs, in their local administration, routinely viewed black occupancy as a form of blight—an assessment that echoed and carried forward the neighborhood surveys conducted by the Federal Housing Administration in the late 1930s and early 1940s. As local governments assembled land and federal money, they disproportionately targeted African American tracts for renewal. While the Housing Act of 1954 and *Berman* both followed *Brown v. Board of Education* by a matter of months, they pushed policy in almost exactly the opposite direction, hardening patterns of residential segregation and deferring blindly to local governments.[13]

Greater St. Louis was a poster child for urban renewal and its limits. Its river-based economy sat at the leading edge of deindustrialization, shedding jobs, economic resources, and tax capacity earlier and more quickly than most of its peers. Patterns of black migration into St. Louis resembled that of other northern settings such as Chicago or Detroit, but the city's race relations were essentially southern. As a result, local administration of federal housing and urban renewal programs yielded even starker segregation.[14] City and suburban planners saw "blight" and black occupancy as essentially synonymous—a view captured as early as the 1915 clearance of riverfront properties for the Jefferson Memorial and maintained through the "big ticket" projects of the 1950s and 1960s.[15] The first run of projects, an effort to "transform costly slums into economically sound industrial and commercial areas"[16] through the commercial core, displaced thousands— many of whom were warehoused in public housing projects.[17] Others moved west and north ahead of the bulldozer, only to find *those* neighborhoods targeted for renewal as the city's attention shifted to the reclamation of West End housing, the expansion of university-based hospital complexes, and the tourism dollars promised by the development of retail, sports, and convention centers.[18]

In St. Louis County, urban renewal efforts were more modest, but the motives and the consequences were much starker—and left no doubt as to whom local authorities considered citizens, and who were interlopers. The only areas targeted for redevelopment (with the exception of a few tracts of flood-prone vacation housing in the far West County) were pockets of historically (or more recent) African American settlement, including Kinloch, Prospect Hill, Robertson, South Maryland Heights, South Richmond Heights, North Olivette, North Webster Groves, the inner suburbs of Wellston and University City, Elmwood Park, and Meacham Park.[19] Indeed, the only check on redevelopment efforts was the obligation, under state and federal programs, to provide relocation housing. Some projects foundered on the unwillingness of the county or local municipalities to house displaced families. Some plowed ahead on the assumption that displaced African Americans would move "back" to the city where public housing was plentiful.[20]

The Law and Politics of Relocation

As the taking of land under the auspices of urban renewal posed a fundamental threat to citizenship, so too did the absence of any substantive relocation assistance for those displaced. The dispossession of one's home undermines the most basic of civil rights. Exercised locally, such "takings" shape the boundaries and membership of local communities. While federal policy, from 1949 onward, has specifically guaranteed "decent, safe and sanitary" housing to displaced families, "the bleakness of the relocation landscape," as one observer noted in 1968, "contrasts strikingly with the rosy picture painted by the urban renewal legislation."[21] The sorry history of this era underscores the threat to citizenship—and to democratic voice—embedded in postwar urban renewal.[22]

The Housing Act of 1949 made it clear that relocation was a "public responsibility and an essential feature of slum clearance" and required local redevelopment agencies to document local rehousing resources and to write into their plans a "feasible method" for relocating displaced families.[23] The Housing Act of 1954 refined the relocation program, requiring local redevelopment authorities to develop a "workable program" for slum clearance, including provision for the relocation of displaced residents.[24] Over the next decade and a half, legislators and administrators continued to tweak federal relocation standards and guidelines.

In 1956, relocation assistance was clarified as a basic right and not just a means of hastening clearance. Further reforms in 1959 required local authorities to maintain a relocation inventory and a narrative description of the local housing supply and to hold public meetings covering relocation plans and options. In 1965, the new Department of Housing and Urban Development (HUD) added the requirement that local agencies set up a formal relocation service and submit a comprehensive relocation report. And in 1966, HUD required that a "substantial number" of units in redeveloped areas be set aside for moderate- and low-income families—a threshold that was raised to "majority" (20 percent of those units for low-income families) in 1968.[25]

On the ground, these requirements and guidelines were largely ignored. Local authorities gave little thought to relocation and simply hoped that low-income housing would "trickle down" as middle-income homeowners moved into redeveloped areas. Yet, as local and federal officials routinely conceded, it didn't work out this way. New housing (and especially public housing) could not keep pace with clearance. Displaced residents were often priced out of standard housing and confounded federal goals by drifting to other substandard units. And local patterns and institutions of racial segregation starkly constrained housing options.[26]

Little wonder that, even as federal requirements expanded, so too did the litany of horror stories, ably documented in local and national media; in the 1965 report of the congressional Advisory Commission on Intergovernmental Relations, *Relocation: Unequal Treatment of People and Businesses Displaced by Governments*; and in a string of legal challenges. Before 1970, as a rule, local and state courts held relocation to be a matter of federal policy and law, and federal courts routinely denied standing to those protesting relocation. The first run of relocation cases all held that the federal housing acts conferred no actual rights on those displaced by redevelopment.[27] It was not until 1968, in *Norwalk CORE v. Norwalk Redevelopment Agency* (an egregious case in which the redevelopment authority willfully ignored a local housing shortage, systematic discrimination in the local housing market, and a long waiting list for public housing), that a federal court finally acknowledged the standing—on equal-protection grounds—of displaced residents.[28] The *Norwalk* decision—and the accumulated grievances that it represented—led, in 1970, to the passage of the Uniform Relocation Assistance and Real Property Acquisition Policies Act, which granted more expansive eligibility to residents in advance of demolition, more extensive allowances for moving expenses, compensation for homeowners and renters, and more elaborate relocation services. However, this came just when the federal government was bowing out of participation in large-scale renewal projects. Noncompliance by local authorities was still the rule, and the damage was already done.[29]

The scale of that damage is hard to pin down—in part because HUD and local redevelopment authorities often failed to track displacement and relocation, and in part because even when and where numbers were generated, they are notoriously unreliable and suspect. As HUD and other audits routinely demonstrated, local redevelopment authorities cooked the numbers by pushing relocatees to the head of the public-housing queue (solving their problems at someone else's expense), using turnover (the rate of exchange, not vacancy) as an index of housing availability, and ignoring the often-systematic segregation of local housing markets. Local authorities were especially lax in reporting the availability of low-income units, which lagged far behind the need created by clearance. Many simply started the reporting process too late, leaving uncounted and unserved those who had moved ahead of the bulldozer. In order to satisfy even meager federal guidelines, as one critic noted, local authorities "resort[ed] to misstatements of fact rare in the annals of official reporting."[30]

With those caveats, what do the numbers look like? Let's start with housing units. Between 1950 and 1975, federal agencies participated in about 2,100 local redevelopment projects (figure 3.1), with most of the activity in the decade from 1958 to 1968. Over this span, the urban renewal program cleared just over 750,000 dwelling units while constructing only 300,000 units on renewal sites—a net loss of over 450,000 units. All of the units destroyed were, under the terms of the national and local programs, blighted or substandard. But only about half of the new units were priced for low-income families—a net loss of low-income units approaching 300,000. By one estimate, the urban renewal program constructed one low-income housing unit for every *six* low-income families it displaced. Under the guise of improving the nation's housing stock, as the comptroller general conceded in 1970, the "effect on housing for low- and moderate-income families in many cities has been the opposite."[31]

Estimates of the numbers displaced vary—again because the reporting was so uneven. In his 1964 jeremiad *The Federal Bulldozer*, Martin Anderson puts the total at close to four million, based on reporting through 1962 and projections for the next decade.[32] The federal Housing and Home Finance Agency's own count, as of 1968, was 291,000 relocated families and 141,000 relocated individuals—a grand total of about 1.2 million.[33] While Anderson's estimate is probably too high (he was working from soft estimates in 1962 and determined to craft a strong indictment), the HHFA tally is undoubtedly dampened by the underreporting of the local agencies on which it relies. A reasonable estimate (allowing for underreporting, and extending across the program's full history) would be about two million displaced and relocated by urban renewal. This, by most accounts, represents only about one-third of property displacements as a result of government action, as the urban renewal numbers are matched by

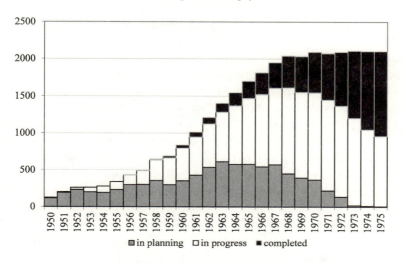

3.1. Federal Urban Renewal Projects, 1950–1975
Source: HHFA and HUD Annual Reports (various years).

displacements due to highway construction, other local improvements, and code enforcement.[34]

The result—in terms of the numbers displaced and the fraction of those who received relocation assistance—was dramatic and devastating. The very logic of local relocation plans was flawed. Priced out of the old neighborhood, the relocated were often steered to public housing. On this score, local authorities offered exaggerated estimates of those eligible for public housing and then assumed that every relocated family would prove eligible *and* choose that option.[35] The challenge was magnified by the duration of projects, in which years often passed between land clearance and project completion. This pace virtually guaranteed that most displaced families would not and could not hold out for the prospect of returning to the redeveloped neighborhood. And, of course, there was often nothing to return to. National housing goals were frustrated by the local determination to sustain racial segregation and to replace cleared residential parcels with higher-cost housing or higher-return commercial or industrial land use. "The dispossessed enjoy as their reward," one observer noted, "a distant view of luxury apartments rising over their old homes."[36]

In city after city, local race relations shaped both renewal planning and relocation policies. In most settings, African Americans were vastly overrepresented among displaced and relocated residents—hardly surprising in a program that routinely equated black occupancy with "blight." Nationally, about two-thirds of families and individuals displaced during urban renewal were nonwhite.[37] These rates were much starker in larger metropolitan settings, where racial segregation was already well-established, and relocation options for displaced African American families and individuals were slim.[38] Little wonder that local activists warned residents, as one Chicago handbill put it, to "Beware of Slum Clearance (Negro Clearance)."[39] Local practice and custom—including steering by realtors, redlining by banks and insurers, and exclusion through deed covenants or zoning—sustained stark shortages of "open" housing.[40] Surveys of local vacancies, hurriedly completed to grease the wheels for redevelopment, ignored all of this.[41] The end result—as redevelopment projects erased pockets of black occupancy, bulldozed transitional neighborhoods, and warehoused the poor at the margins of the old urban core—was that urban renewal actually hardened patterns of local segregation.[42]

As one might expect of a program that destroyed more housing units than it created (especially for those of limited means) and dumped displaced families (with little or meager assistance) into tightly segregated local housing markets, the costs were substantial. Most relocated families faced substantially higher (often nearly doubled) median rents or monthly housing costs, often while reporting no improvement in the quality of their housing.[43] The costs of relocation included not just steeper monthly rents or payments but also refinancing costs, relocation expenses, higher living costs (a longer commute, for example), and condemnation losses.[44] In turn, displacement and relocation impose other, less-tangible costs. Just compensation, as *Kelo* underscored, may be incalculable to one facing the loss of a home and community. Psychologists and sociologists assessing the impact of urban renewal documented this sense of profound loss and dislocation: "the forced disintegration of the social milieu which was theirs in the old [neighborhood]."[45] Such feelings were magnified by the loss of community and family ties and the public spaces of the neighborhood. "Clearance destroys not only housing," as Herbert Gans noted in 1959, "but also a functioning social system, the existence of which is not even recognized by current relocation procedures."[46]

Greater St. Louis offers a stark case study of the logic and limits of relocation policies. There is no clean count of relocations, as local redevelopment authorities routinely underestimated displacements and overestimated the capacity of the public and private housing markets to absorb them. "The scarcity of hard baseline information," as city officials admitted in 1971, "dramatized the information fog in which these agencies frequently operate."[47]

The Mill Creek Valley redevelopment project (1958) alone displaced 4,200 families (about fifteen thousand persons); the Kosciusko project (1959) displaced 1,800 families. The city's housing authority estimated 6,700 family displacements due to slum clearance from 1950 through 1963—a number that more than doubles if displacements due to other government action are taken into account. Once the federal urban-renewal program ended, these numbers tailed off: just under three thousand families were displaced by government action from 1972 to 1977, about six hundred of these due to urban renewal.[48] If we assume that the rate of displacement was constant through the 1960s, the number of families displaced by urban renewal runs close to twenty thousand families or seventy-five thousand persons—fully 10 percent of the city's 1960 population.

Relocation services were haphazard and half-hearted. A scathing 1964 HUD audit found that more than half of the Mill Creek families never appeared on the local authority's relocation workload. And when HUD officials spot-checked relocation units, it found that twenty-one of thirty-five units randomly selected from the Mill Creek caseload and thirty of the thirty-one units randomly selected from the Kosciusko caseload were substandard ("no running water, no heating facilities, doors falling off hinges, infestations with vermin, and leaks in roofs and walls"). Most of those displaced, in other words, got no relocation assistance, and most of those who got assistance saw no improvement in their housing. This reflected both the Land Clearance for Redevelopment Authority's approach to relocation ("federal regulations specifying this obligation were to be considered advisory," as LCRA officials conceded, "to be followed or discarded as necessary") and the fact that many of the displaced wanted nothing to do with the assistance offered by the "Local City Rip-off Artists" that had taken their homes.[49]

Relocation was a persistent riddle for city officials. They justified renewal projects in the hope that they would stem residential flight to the suburbs, but also relied on that flight to open up units for those displaced. They relied heavily on the big downtown public-housing projects to meet federal thresholds for relocation housing, while conceding (by the late 1960s) that "the condition and repute of many public housing projects in St. Louis mitigate against their use as even temporary relocation sites." And they reluctantly admitted that the persistently high ratio of substandard units city-wide meant that urban renewal was pushing people around at great public expense and little public benefit—and might even yield "a net decrease in the housing quality city-wide." Indeed, the exodus from "cleared" tracts—some into local public housing but most into neighborhoods to the west and north—had the effect of both deepening segregation and creating new demands for renewal in neighborhoods overrun by those displaced.[50]

Although its urban renewal program was more modest, these motivations and machinations were even more pronounced in St. Louis County. Like its counterpart in the city, the county LCRA looked to displace pockets of "blighted" black occupancy and convert the land to a "higher use." But residential segregation was much starker west of the city border (even LCRA officials conceded that "St. Louis County has been very closed to the Negro people"), making it harder to make the case for the availability of relocation housing.[51] And county redevelopment plans invariably proceeded from the assumption that blacks displaced from county tracts would and should be accommodated by public or private housing in the city. There was "some concern in Washington for some of the programs in these suburban communities," as the National Association for the Advancement of Colored People (NAACP) noted in 1962, "which in planning seem to indicate a pattern of displacing Negro families back into the city of St. Louis, whether they like it or not."[52] This was a stark and blunt reminder of the citizenship afforded to the county's scattered African American residents; even those who had lived in county enclaves for generations were out of place and—in the eyes of county redevelopment agencies—"belonged" in the city. These same assumptions held but played out in very different ways in Elmwood Park, which was razed and completely redeveloped between 1962 and 1970, and in Meacham Park, where redevelopment planning sputtered through the end of the century.

Redevelopment in St. Louis County

St. Louis County charged its Land Clearance for Redevelopment Authority (LCRA) with defining "blight" and eradicating it. What this meant, in the bargain, was that the LCRA also defined "citizenship"—the boundaries of belonging in the St. Louis suburbs—and sought to relocate those who did not fit the bill. Indeed, at its very first meeting in 1956, the LCRA zeroed in on the county's scattered African American enclaves—Webster Heights, Robertson, Meacham Park, and Elmwood Park—as the first targets for renewal. The principal evidence offered by local officials in support of redevelopment was, of course, the product of their own neglect during a generation of suburban growth. At a follow-up meeting in October, for example, the health commissioner of Olivette told the LCRA that "the portion of Elmwood Park which lies in the City of Olivette is in deplorable condition, having no sanitary facilities whatsoever." In March 1957, the LCRA narrowed its attention to Meacham Park and Elmwood Park (whose residents had also approached the county about local conditions), formally designating each as a "slum, blighted, insanitary, deteriorated or deteriorating area." LCRA officials assumed that "probable reuse would be residential at Meacham Park and industrial at Elmwood Park" and gave little thought to the relocation of displaced residents (a cost it assumed would be borne entirely by the federal government).[53]

Early planning ran along three tracks: the LCRA's redevelopment plans for Elmwood Park and Meacham Park respectively and the city of Olivette's parallel plans for the southern slice of Elmwood Park that fell within its borders. Local voters didn't authorize creation of a separate redevelopment authority for Olivette until November 1960, but city officials had already piggybacked on the county's early efforts and begun planning to "acquire blighted property in the north-central portion of the city which is now occupied by several Negro families."[54] As these plans were being drafted, the county LCRA pressed ahead (in early 1958) with a letter to all "residents of the Meacham Park and Elmwood Park areas, describing the need for information on their families and requesting cooperation on a survey of the areas."[55]

These plans needed to be vetted by the Urban Renewal Agency of the federal Housing and Home Finance Agency (the predecessor to HUD).[56] The agency's regional office in Fort Worth (which had responsibility for Missouri projects), however, immediately raised a series of questions and objections. Their skepticism (echoed by some local planners) stemmed largely from the county's interest in commercial and industrial redevelopment, its indifference to the challenges of relocation, and its thinly veiled opposition to the development of local public housing.[57] Indeed, the Fort Worth office offered a tentative go-ahead to the Meacham Park plan in April 1958 but withheld approval of the Elmwood Park plan, which proposed industrial reuse and the relocation of most residents to public-housing projects in the city of St. Louis.[58]

County planners were torn by the issue of public housing. They conceded, as early as 1958, that "people of the area could not be displaced until the Authority had something to offer them" and that there was a stark shortage of affordable and racially unrestricted properties to accommodate the relocation of Elmwood Park and Meacham Park families. At the same time, however, local officials clearly hoped that public housing outside the redevelopment areas (that is, in St. Louis City) would satisfy federal reviewers. The LCRA worried that private developers would be scared off by on-site public housing. And the LCRA commissioner, while acknowledging the necessity of meeting local needs and federal guidelines, allowed that "he had been instructed from above to oppose public housing of any kind in all localities."[59]

The tug-of-war was simple. Federal programs, however imperfect in design and oversight, were intended to eradicate substandard housing and to accommodate their former residents in better housing—either on the footprint of the redevelopment plan or elsewhere in the locality. St. Louis County and Olivette officials, for their part, wanted to displace African American residents entirely—both because they viewed African American occupancy of the central city (St. Louis) as the natural order of things and because they pined for the higher returns of commercial or industrial redevelopment.[60] The trick was to yield enough on the affordable housing issue to start the flow of federal money, but no further. Embedded in this debate, of course, was the larger logic of urban renewal and relocation in which public housing was not provided or offered as a foundation of social citizenship, as a right to shelter. Instead, public housing became a mechanism for abrogating those rights. What mattered (especially to local authorities) was not their ability to house the poor but their ability to displace them.

Housing, population, and income surveys in 1958 and 1959 did little to help the county's cause. The LCRA's first survey returns on Elmwood Park residents found an average age of fifty-six and an average family income of just over $3,000 (about $28,000 in 2018 dollars, right at the poverty level for a family of four). County officials reluctantly agreed with the federal assessment that fully two-thirds of Elmwood Park and Meacham Park residents could not afford another house in the area—their prospects further dimmed by the irretrievably racial premises of the county's real-estate market. "It seemed almost impossible," as the LCRA conceded in early 1959, "to relocate them without public housing."[61] This issue would dog both projects for years. Throughout the long process of redevelopment, public housing and relocation divided the residents of Elmwood Park: some worked with the LCRA to rehabilitate the area and establish a small public-housing project, others dug in against displacement. And, while the Elmwood Park plan was reworked to satisfy federal rehousing guidelines, public housing—and the larger redevelopment plans—foundered in Meacham Park.

The LCRA's plan for Elmwood Park (maps 3.1 to 3.4), drafted and redrafted in the late 1950s and early 1960s, called for the clearance of "all deteriorated structures which are not capable of rehabilitation," retention of "several structures which are standard or capable of rehabilitation," and the provision of "cleared sites . . . which will be made available for purchase by private redevelopers." In the end, the LCRA judged only three properties

Map 3.1. Redevelopment of Elmwood Park: Aerial View, 1955
Source: St. Louis County GIS Service Center, 1955 Aerials.

Map 3.2. Redevelopment of Elmwood Park: Property Survey, 1962
Source: St. Louis County GIS Service Center, 1955 Aerials; Urban Renewal Plan: Elmwood Park,
Project MO R-10 (October 1962), *Brooks v. LCRA* case file, RG 600, Missouri State Archives.

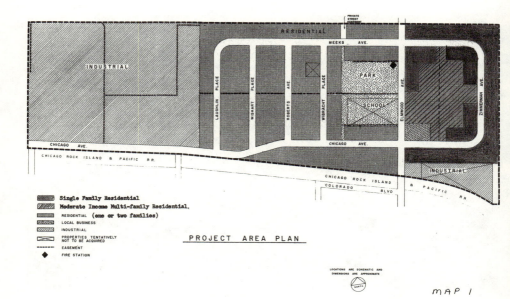

Map 3.3. Redevelopment of Elmwood Park: Project Plan, 1962
Source: Urban Renewal Plan: Elmwood Park, Project MO R-10 (October
1962), *Brooks v. LCRA* case file, RG 600, Missouri State Archives.

Map 3.4. Redevelopment of Elmwood Park: Aerial, 1966
Source: St. Louis County GIS Service Center, 1966 Aerials.

"capable and feasible of rehabilitation." As of a 1962 survey (map 3.2), nearly half (184 of 377) of Elmwood Park properties stood vacant—a rate swollen by families leaving the area ahead of the LCRA's bulldozers.[62]

Under the plan (map 3.3), the western third of the old residential footprint (west of the rerouted Laughlin Road) was replatted for industrial use. The street grid east of Dielman Road was replaced with a perimeter road of single-family lots surrounding a public-housing project. The plan established new lot and building standards: front and rear yards of twenty-five feet, side yards of six feet, a maximum lot coverage of 50 percent, and a maximum building height of three stories or forty-five feet. The new layout also required new street and sewer infrastructure. Lingering concerns about relocation aside, the LCRA largely delivered on its pledge to "provide decent, safe, and sanitary dwellings . . . substantially equal to the number of substandard dwellings to be cleared from the area, at rents within the financial reach of the income groups displaced."[63]

Progress was slow as the LCRA moved ahead with the acquisition or condemnation of properties in unincorporated Elmwood Park. As of early 1962, the LCRA had bought up about a hundred properties, held the option on forty more, and was proceeding with condemnation suits against another sixty.[64] The project hit numerous obstacles, including delays in the approval of a zoning plan, and an inadequate budget for water and sewers (federal money could not be used for the lines that extended beyond the project boundaries, and the LCRA had not budgeted for the extension of sewer and water service to new houses). In turn, "every time we felt we were in a position to start forward," as one LCRA official complained, "the Federal Government has stepped in with restriction that has brought about delays."[65] In 1963, the LCRA awarded the primary redevelopment work to the Reasor Corporation, the contract stipulating that all clearance, filling, grading, leveling, and infrastructure would be completed by the county before turning the project over to the developer. The LCRA kept pushing the completion date forward—to 1963, to 1964, to 1965—and construction did not wrap up until 1970.[66]

Olivette's slice of the project was smaller, and its motives were starker. The plan covered only about twenty acres, bisected by Dielman Road south of the railroad tracks. The area consisted of about forty structures and parcels, including a couple of small businesses and housing for about thirty African American families—at the time the only African Americans living in Olivette.[67] The central goal of Olivette's redevelopment plan was to displace all of the area's residents and rezone for industrial development, "the highest and best use . . . [that] will substantially increase the tax base of the community."[68] The goal was to take an area "predominantly populated by Negro citizens," as local officials argued, and transform it into an "economic asset to Olivette." The plan would include paving Dielman, realigning the River des Peres, replacing the bridge where Dielman crossed the river, and creating a fifteen-acre industrial park. The establishment of public housing on the county's share of the redevelopment only cemented these plans: displaced Olivette residents could move across the tracks into the county. "From all indications," as a local NAACP officer observed, "the intention of the undertaking of this redevelopment is to move Negroes out of the city of Olivette."[69]

Olivette's redevelopment plans also progressed slowly and depended heavily on federal funding (which would cover about three-quarters of the project's roughly $600,000 price tag). The final urban-renewal plan was not approved until 1967, and it took the redevelopment authority another four years to buy up the remaining parcels. Under pressure from federal agencies, the Olivette LCRA added two small residential areas, a total of twenty-four single-family homes on two cul-de-sacs (one running east of Dielman, one west). Ground had not broken on these in 1970, when Olivette's redevelopment plans—and their motives—were made a central exhibit in the St. Louis hearings held by the United States Commission on Civil Rights. Construction on new residential units was finally completed in 1974, and the houses east of Dielman (Rothwell Heights) were reserved for the Olivette Housing Authority.[70] These pockets of housing were far removed from other Olivette neighborhoods, accessible via an industrial collector street, and separated by parkland from the Indian Meadows subdivision—a peculiar planning choice, "especially given the obvious attempt," as one observer noted, ". . . to separate industry from residence in all other sections of the city."[71]

The fate of the Meacham Park project (maps 3.5 and 3.6) was at once simpler and more complicated. From the outset, the county's vision of renewal did not include the area's existing residents. New single-family housing proposed in the 1959 redevelopment plan was crafted to meet Federal Housing Administration (FHA) guidelines—but was also pointedly priced beyond the reach of displaced residents. "For various reasons," local real-estate interests concluded, "these families must be excluded from the market."[72] As redevelopment progressed elsewhere in Greater St. Louis (including Elmwood Park), Meacham Park residents became increasingly convinced that urban renewal meant "black clearance," and offered little cooperation.[73]

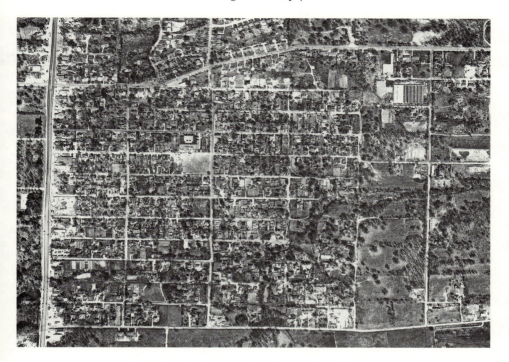

Map 3.5. Redevelopment of Meacham Park: Aerial, 1955
Source: St. Louis County GIS Service Center, 1955 Aerials.

Like Olivette officials, the county LCRA saw the construction of low-income and public-housing units in Elmwood Park as the solution to relocation from Meacham Park. Federal officials were unimpressed by this plan, maintained that the Meacham Park project needed its own relocation plan and relocation housing, and tightened their oversight. As the Elmwood Park redevelopment crept forward, the Meacham Park project bogged down in negotiations with FHA officials in Fort Worth. Unable to overcome local objections to public housing on site and unable to convince the FHA that Elmwood Park could house residents displaced by both projects, the LCRA pulled the plug on Meacham Park redevelopment in June 1964.[74]

These early years of redevelopment in St. Louis County neatly captured the larger limits and logic of urban renewal. While federal money made it all possible, deference to local governments frustrated federal goals—and, in many respects, simply threw resources and legal authority behind the very interests responsible for the housing crisis in the first place. This was underscored in expansive working definitions of "blight" (often baldly equated

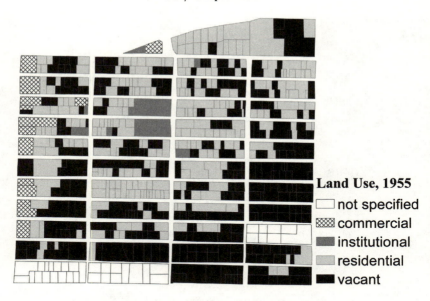

Land Use, 1955
☐ not specified
▨ commercial
▪ institutional
▪ residential
■ vacant

Map 3.6. Redevelopment of Meacham Park: Property Survey, 1955
Source: Market Analysis and Reuse Appraisal of Meacham Park Urban
Renewal Area, Series 4, folder 75; Roy Wenzlick Papers, Western Historical
Manuscripts Collection, University of Missouri–St. Louis.

with black occupancy) and in expansive working definitions of "public use"
or "public purpose." Although enabled by federal housing acts, redevelopment plans for Elmwood Park and Meacham Park proposed and pursued effective reductions in the housing stock. Redevelopment planning in
St. Louis County rested largely on the conviction that these "little ghettos"
were out of place: tar-paper shacks and outhouses did not belong amid the
cul-de-sacs of the modern suburban fringe, and their residents did not belong west of the city's border.

The Elmwood Park Diaspora

As redevelopment sputtered forward in Elmwood Park, the project offered
a telling glimpse into the larger policies and problems of relocation under
urban renewal. Relocation proceeded with little respect for the deep, multigenerational roots of many residents: "People don't want to be displaced because there is something familiar about where they live, despite the fact that
it's a deteriorated area," as relocation officials conceded. "But they feel that
it belongs to them and they belong to it, so they are comfortable there."[75]

As in so many other settings (and St. Louis area projects), the impact was starkly racial: "It's not a land clearance," as one observer put it, "it's a race clearance"—adding that renewal projects in St. Louis and St. Louis County "affected ninety-nine percent Negroes." Relocation policies ignored the starkly racial structure of local real-estate markets. Displaced residents had few choices other than to settle in other blighted neighborhoods or in the city's already notorious public-housing projects.[76]

Elmwood Park residents, with the assistance of the Federated Civic Association of St. Louis County, pushed back, pressing Robert Weaver (the new HHFA administrator) to impose stricter standards. Weaver visited Elmwood Park in March 1961, and officials from the Fort Worth office followed up later that spring.[77] The HHFA's directive was to accommodate those displaced on the footprint of the redevelopment itself. Olivette, which hoped to convert most of its redevelopment area to industrial use, understood this to mean that unincorporated Elmwood Park could serve as the solution to its relocation problems. They worried that their plans would "appear as a conspiracy to rid the community of its Negro population" but made little effort to disguise the fact that this was exactly what they had in mind.[78]

The circumstances in the county's share of the project were more complicated. In early 1962, three Elmwood Park residents (Willis Corbett, Leo Wallace, and Clifford Surgener) began talking to a lawyer about contesting the redevelopment. The HHFA sent staff from Fort Worth to put out the fire but readily conceded that the relocation plan was inadequate. HHFA directed local officials that "unless the Elmwood residents prefer relocating outside of the Elmwood Park area . . . that they be relocated in temporary relocation quarters until new homes are available." The county LCRA responded defensively ("Residents of Elmwood Park," they argued, "have been relocated in good homes wherever they could be found within a resident's budget, mostly in North St. Louis"). But they also grudgingly conceded the point: "Federal representatives from the Washington level have requested that the authority discontinues this method, stating that many letters have been received by the Senators and Congressmen from this district claiming that the minority group in St. Louis County are being pushed out of St. Louis County."[79]

At this point, Elmwood Park residents, the LCRA, and the HHFA struck a deal: for the county's share of the project, the LCRA would make a commitment to staged redevelopment, so that the first phase of completed houses could be used to relocate residents from the later phases. No properties west of Dielman Road, by this agreement, would be acquired or condemned until those east of Dielman had been rebuilt. Given the extent of vacancies throughout Elmwood Park, the HHFA also hoped that those east of Dielman could temporarily relocate to empty houses on the west side—essentially shuffling families back and forth across Dielman in such a way that none would have to leave the area. The regional director of the HHFA made sure that local officials understood: he "pointed his finger at Mr. Reichert [from the LCRA]," as one observer recalled, "and he says 'This is what I want done and I want this carried out. . . . I have given my word on this.'" A week later, the terms of the deal were outlined in a public meeting in Elmwood Park and adopted by the county council. In a flurry of meetings after taking office, the new county commissioner, Lawrence Roos, reaffirmed the county's commitment.[80]

The commitment to staged redevelopment (managed so that "almost all relocation . . . will be within the project area") was followed in short order by a formal relocation plan, adopted by the LCRA in November of 1962. The plan called for a survey of site residents, dissemination of information about project progress and relocation options and resources, aid and counsel, standards for relocation housing (and provisions for inspection), assistance for those eligible for public housing, and assistance in obtaining mortgages or home-improvement loans. And it elaborated a new commitment to multifamily, low-income housing on at least a portion of the project.[81] The plan was more ambitious on paper than in practice. Much of it relied on boilerplate provisions, some of which were irrelevant and some of which were woefully optimistic given the area's deeply racialized housing market. On closer look, the plan outlined a relocation effort that, "aside from keeping statistics and the preparation of reports, involve[d] nothing more to be done for the inhabitants than they could do for themselves by merely perusing the 'For Rent' and 'For Sale' columns in the newspapers." And staffing the relocation effort itself was a challenge, given the deep distrust of the LCRA's motives. The county hired Ida Scott, a resident who had deep roots in the community but—by her own admission—no relevant experience or training.[82]

The relocation agreement did not last long. In early 1963, the LCRA began acquiring properties west of Dielman, long ahead of any schedule that would allow residents to relocate east of Dielman. Redevelopment contracts specified that "displaced residents in the Elmwood Park area shall be given priority in the renting or purchasing of apartments or new homes or lots in the area," but in the absence of staged redevelopment, no such new homes existed. In October of 1963, the Federated Civic Association again pulled together officials from the HHFA and the county LCRA, but the latter were uncooperative and clearly resentful of the federal standards. A little over a year later, the LCRA director made it clear that "her understanding of urban renewal is that it is for the general benefit of the entire community," and that "nowhere in the contract, nor in the urban renewal plan, was it stated that this project is for the specific purpose of the residents of Elmwood Park, nor that these residents were not to be relocated anywhere else. At no time has the Authority been charged with the responsibility of providing housing for any person, and specifically low-income housing. This is the responsibility of the County or private citizens."[83] The statement was at once candid and jarring: the "entire community" was clearly something other than Elmwood Park and, in any respect, the displaced residents were clearly not its citizens.

In its initial planning, the county did what it could to placate federal officials with the promise of staged redevelopment while sticking to its original assumption that most of the Elmwood Park families would never return. But, even on this score, its efforts were patently insincere. The LCRA argued publicly that displaced families had many options, but admitted privately that such options were limited. Assessing the relocation prospects for African American families in 1958, realtor Roy Wenzlick counted 155 rental units and 240 sale properties "available to non-whites" in the city and only six sale properties and no rental units in the county. Urban renewal officials in Olivette assumed that displaced families would relocate "across the track in Elmwood Park," but were at a loss when Elmwood Park itself was slated for redevelopment: this "poses quite a relocation problem for St. Louis County," a 1958 HUD memo notes, "since housing available to Negroes is very limited in the County."[84]

As redevelopment progressed, it continually ran up against formal and informal institutions of discrimination and segregation. It was not easy, as the Olivette LCRA admitted in 1963, to come up with a relocation plan that "will meet Federal requirements while simultaneously considering local conditions."[85] Those working with displaced families underscored the problem. "Even our experience in the frustrations of community relations work," staff of the American Friends Service Committee concluded in 1967,

> did not fully prepare AFSC staff workers for the webs of obfuscation that have been encountered by them and by homeseekers with whom they have worked in attempts to secure housing. . . . Prospective buyers have found salesmen who are not authorized to sell, unsold homes that are not for sale, prices that suddenly rise, GI certificates and sales contracts that get lost, routine business transactions that spin into months of delay, credit companies that find unpaid bills that were never incurred, and questionable expressions of concern by builders and sales agents that their clients not move into a neighborhood where they "wouldn't be happy."[86]

The other lingering issue facing redevelopment officials was the role of public housing in the redevelopment plans. The starting assumption here was that public housing in the city of St. Louis was appropriate and sufficient. Olivette and county officials saw the established city projects (especially Pruitt-Igoe) as the best destination for those unable to afford market housing in the county, at the same time holding those projects up as failures of public policy not to be replicated. It was this conviction that sank the prospect, floated half-heartedly in the late 1950s, of refitting the recently decommissioned Jefferson Barracks in South County as a public-housing project. Local officials, especially in Olivette, rebuffed federal programs and even put off creating local housing authorities for as long as possible. As late as 1970, Olivette lacked a housing authority and the county boasted fewer than 150 units of public housing (there were over eight thousand in the city), all of them in Kinloch.[87]

The countywide strategy was to grudgingly build just enough low-income units to ensure that the federal funds kept flowing. Under HHFA pressure to accommodate displaced low-income families, county planners gave a little. Unable to avoid public housing altogether, they worked to contain it on a few sites, so that Kinloch—and later Elmwood Park—might serve the relocation needs of the entire county.[88] In late 1963, Bishop Howard Thomas Primm of the African Methodist Episcopal Church took the lead in sponsoring an application for Section 221(d) assistance (a federal program offering mortgage insurance to nonprofits building or rehabilitating multifamily units). A separate relocation-demonstration grant set aside twenty of the planned 210 units (forty-seven townhomes, and 160 one- to three-bedroom apartments) for rent subsidies.[89] At its completion in 1972, Primm Gardens was one of only three apartment complexes in all of St. Louis County to offer a three-bedroom apartment for under $150 per month. By 1973, there were over six hundred families on a waiting list for the subsidized units.[90]

Given the insincerity of the LCRA's commitment to rebuild for the former residents, and given the paucity of options—in private and public housing—elsewhere, relocation proceeded fitfully. Ida Scott's own account of the relocation program underscores the widespread bitterness and resentment of families facing the upheaval of their lives, the condemnation of homes that many had held for generations, and often substantial financial losses. The accounting (of displacement and relocations) was haphazard. The relocation assistance was meager. And the relocation office was undertrained and understaffed.[91]

Much of the resentment hinged on the financial burden. For the county, the ramshackle homesteads of Elmwood Park were of little value. But the residents, of course, saw things differently. For those with deep generational ties to Elmwood Park, their homes were worth much more than the assessed value. And the meager options for African Americans elsewhere in the county dramatically inflated the replacement value. In this light, the LCRA's offers were insulting. Clara Burden, a resident of Elmwood Park for over fifty years, was offered $2,200 for a house she had inherited from her parents. Mary Bryant, who had lived at 9941 Chicago for twenty-four years, got an early offer of $7,000 but no follow-up. Ida Scott and her husband, whose holdings included a salvage yard on eleven lots adjoining 9917 Meeks, were offered $14,000 for everything.[92] The average LCRA settlement (for the subset of properties recording sales or condemnations) was $3,400; the average price paid by displaced families for new housing outside of Elmwood Park was about $10,000.[93]

These losses were magnified by uneven title documentation. Those who did not own their homes outright often held informal or contract mortgages. Many purchase offers (and later condemnations) by the LCRA ended up in court, with much of the housing value disappearing in contractual disputes and legal fees.[94] Not surprisingly, given these conditions, many homeowners rebuffed the LCRA entirely. In the end, almost 80 percent of the properties in Elmwood Park were transferred to county control through condemnation proceedings, which began in December of 1961. Because the project took so long to complete, many displaced owners remained in their homes as tenants of the LCRA, their home equity whittled away in rent on houses they used to own.[95] Those who received early payment for condemned properties were caught: "there was no property available to absorb this payment . . . and by receiving this very payment they became ineligible for [other forms of public assistance]."[96]

In violation of federal standards and its own relocation plan, the LCRA routinely offered displaced families substandard housing—sometimes in other African American enclaves in the county, sometimes in North St. Louis, and sometimes on-site. The irony of the latter was bitter. Residents were told to leave because their "blighted" homes were substandard threats to the public welfare. The solution, more often than not, was to shuffle them into other blighted homes in order to clear the way for redevelopment. When Lillie Lemmons was forced out of her home, she was offered a short-term rental at 9824 Rebie, a house with no running water and broken windows that was itself scheduled for condemnation in a few months. When Fannie White was forced from her home, she was offered a temporary rental west of Dielman that "wouldn't even [be] fit for an animal to live in, much less a human being."[97] In their 1967 assessment of the Elmwood Park project, the American Friends Service Committee found that redevelopment had hardened patterns of local discrimination, and that the LCRA had neglected to inform residents of their options or their rights, and—in response to the inevitable complaints—offered "clumsy and grossly inadequate remedial tools."[98]

While some residents were shuffled in and out of substandard dwellings, often one step ahead of the bulldozer, others were discouraged by the "runaround" they faced in their efforts to rebuild—to actually participate in the redevelopment. The LCRA was reluctant to inform residents of the option to purchase and rebuild on their own lots, because it feared that piecemeal rebuilding would discourage developers from bidding on larger chunks of the project. Willis Corbett (who lived at 9823 Chicago and owned the lots at 9623 and 9617 Roberts) was offered $12,000 for his lots on Roberts. When he approached the LCRA about rebuilding, he was given the same contract drafted for large developers and told that he would have to either bid on the contract to redevelop multiple properties or strike a deal with a developer that had won such a contract. For a time, he worked with the Reasor Corporation (the lead developer of the residential properties), but, unsatisfied with the result, he pulled out of the deal in 1966.[99]

The glacial pace of redevelopment also frustrated the efforts of those who wanted to stay—or at least return. The redevelopment plan itself, of course, shaped the choices made by residents and shaped the value of their homes. Initial letters—outlining the plans and residents' options—went out in 1960 and 1961. Within a year, fifty-five of 146 families and thirteen of thirty-nine householders had left Elmwood Park, most with minimal contact with (or assistance from) the LCRA. By the end of 1963, fully three years after the buyouts and condemnations had begun, only one house had been built, and development of the multifamily project (Primm Gardens) was still being hashed out. As of June 1965, the developer had completed and sold a grand total of eleven houses.[100] On the Olivette side of the project, planning commenced in 1961, funding was not assembled until 1967, and the first contract for new development was not tendered until 1972.[101] This pace alone (especially given the demographics of those displaced) made resettlement in a redeveloped Elmwood Park a distant prospect.

Finally, for those who left, relocation assistance was meager (although the half-heartedness of the effort also means that the records on who got what and when are scattered and incomplete). The city of Olivette provided relocation assistance to a total of twelve families and nine individuals (about two-thirds of the households displaced), but almost all of this came after new federal relocation guidelines were introduced in 1970.[102] On the

Bulldozing Citizenship / 105

county side, many refused all assistance. Of the 102 relocations recorded
as of 1962, more than three-quarters (sixty-three families and sixteen individuals) were listed as "self-relocated"—many with the annotation that they
had "refused help," had "no desire to return," or "wants nothing to do with
[LCR]Authority."[103] This, of course, was especially burdensome for a population that was largely poor and elderly. The average annual income of those
facing displacement (sixty-three owners and tenants) in 1963 was $2,667,
less than half of the median household income for 1963 ($6,249) and
barely three-quarters of the median black household income ($3,645).[104]

By the early 1960s, the politics and practice of redevelopment had begun to unravel the social fabric of Elmwood Park. Some residents clung to
the original promise of the redevelopment plan, which—despite its many
problems—would modernize basic public services (sewer, water, roads) and
(once the Primm Gardens project was complete) expand housing options.
But others felt that the burden and uncertainty borne by displaced residents
was too much. "The Elmwood Park owners," as the emerging legal challenge
put it, ". . . naturally resented the taking of their homes for public use"—a
sentiment exaggerated by the ham-handedness of local authorities. Relocation options were poorly thought-out, and relocation assistance was meager. And the prospect of return seemed both impractical and unaffordable—
especially given local demographics, the pace and staging of redevelopment,
and the options presented to residents.[105]

In early 1963, residents began complaining that any equity they had
realized from sale or condemnation was disappearing in rent to the LCRA
and asked that rental payments (often on homes they had once owned) be
at least partially set aside for down payments on new homes in Elmwood
Park. But the LCRA would not budge. By that fall, the LCRA had—by its
own estimate—lost all constructive contact with residents. It worked with
Ida Scott and others to revamp a local citizen's committee. But rather than
assuage residents' anxieties, these efforts widened the gap between local
supporters and opponents. Many viewed those who were working with the
county as Elmwood Park's "most favored" residents—with the implication
that they were getting a better deal. Three of the five members of the community liaison committee (Ida Scott, Wallace West, and Grace Howard)
were employed by the county, and opponents accused West of being "the
fair-haired boy for the Land Clearance Authority."[106]

By early 1964, the split seemed unmendable. There were now compet-
ing local committees: the official Elmwood Park Citizens' Committee (led
by Wallace West), and the dissident Elmwood Park Improvement Association. Ida Scott advised the LCRA to not even bother printing a newsletter

updating residents on the redevelopment, arguing that it would do little to change the minds of residents who fell into three factions: "those who don't care," "those who care," and the troublemaking "Willis Corbett group."[107]

The dissidents succeeded in getting their case before a grand jury in early 1965. The grand jury's June 1965 report offers a scathing indictment of the project, dubbing it an "evasion of responsibility and intent" that had destroyed a stable and long-standing community in one of the few pockets "where there was never any question of the right of Negroes to buy, own and rent property." The jury argued that a project promising "to raise standards and improve the living conditions of the residents of this area" had instead resulted in unrelenting "hardship and inequity." The "apathy and indifference of the entire County Community," it concluded, had allowed the project to proceed without "an honest commitment to the original intent of the Urban Renewal Plan" or the "firm and realistic intention of using the project, first and foremost, for the area residents' benefit."[108]

The extent of the grand jury's recommendation was that such a mistake not be repeated. But the core of its argument was carried forward in a lawsuit launched by Elmwood Park residents seeking a declaratory judgment and a restraining order prohibiting the LCRA from proceeding with the urban renewal plan. The circuit court dismissed the claim in 1966, and the Missouri Supreme Court, finding no constitutional questions at stake, referred it to the Court of Appeals, where it was tried in 1967.[109] The case, *Esther Brooks et al. v. the Land Clearance Authority of St. Louis County*, painstakingly documented the patterns of redevelopment and relocation outlined above. And the unhappy resolution, as we have seen, was the cruel finding that—with the redevelopment and its accompanying displacement now complete—former residents lacked the standing to sue.[110]

Redevelopment drove the residents of Elmwood Park from their homes. The initial hope and presumption of local redevelopment officials, that erasing blight meant erasing black occupancy, was haphazardly and begrudgingly succeeded by a relocation program that offered little assistance and meager options. The resulting diaspora was shaped by the pace and character of the redevelopment, by the demographics of the displaced population, and by deep and persistent segregation in the metropolitan labor market. Owners were compensated for their homes but not for the high cost of a split housing market. "I can't get land for that," complained one resident, "at least where they got it for colored people." "Because of the lack of a feasible relocation plan," as the plaintiffs in *Brooks v. LCRA* argued, "the greater number of Elmwood Park residents has been dispersed indiscriminately throughout widely separated slum areas in the City and County of

St. Louis in complete frustration of the avowed purpose and intent of the redevelopment project."[111]

This dispersal, in turn, eroded the local and family ties that might have facilitated return. "It's no longer a community," observed Brooks's lawyer, "but it's individuals as far away as the City of St. Louis, near the river, public housing. Some of them in Wentzville, some of them in Kirkwood, some of them in Kinloch. It's about as wide a dispersal of a formerly cohesive community as anybody could think of."[112] The prospect of resettlement was further eroded by the age of many of those displaced. Many moved out of the area, as Ida Scott recalled, and "many of the elderly had passed on or moved on to live with relatives out of the area."[113] The average age of those facing displacement (sixty-three owners and tenants) in 1964 was fifty-six years old. Many of those appearing on the early relocation ledgers had died before the project was completed, and many others, in their sixties or older before 1970, were unlikely or reluctant to make another move.[114]

Relocation was also frustrated by the character of the redevelopment. At the onset of planning in the late 1950s, there were about 185 residential housing units (most of them family residences) in the county portion of Elmwood Park, and about as many vacated lots. On the Olivette side, there were another forty structures housing some thirty families. Redevelopment bulldozed all but a handful of structures, upward of 220 housing units in all. New construction included thirty-two single-family homes built under HUD's Section 235 Program, another seventy-six privately developed single-family homes, and 210 townhouse and apartment units in Primm Gardens.[115] While Elmwood Park (as of 1970) counted over three hundred housing units and a population (at 1,120) slightly larger than it was in 1960, the underlying housing stock had changed markedly.[116] The new residential footprint was substantially smaller, ceding most of the land south of Chicago and west of Elmridge to industrial use. This, in effect, sustained the older practice of quarantining African American neighborhoods with buffer areas of nonresidential land use. And redevelopment virtually erased a large swath of African American homeownership. As of the 1940 census, eighty-nine of 118 heads of household in Elmwood Park owned their homes. The 1962 survey (preliminary to redevelopment) found a similar rate of homeownership (about 70 percent) and noted that most of those claimed full equity. After redevelopment, the housing stock now dominated by the multifamily units at Primm Gardens, the homeownership rate plunged to 14 percent.[117]

If the LCRA neglected the task of relocation, it at least tracked some of the choices made by former residents (map 3.7). Of one hundred relocations

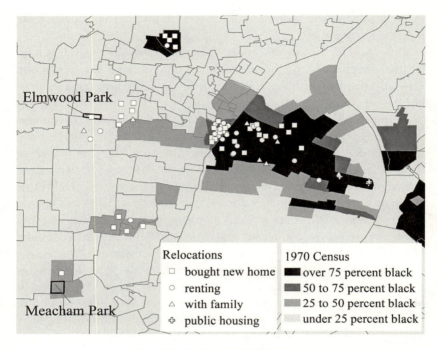

Map 3.7. The Elmwood Park Diaspora
Source: Relocation Ledger, *Brooks v. LCRA* case file, Missouri State Archives; National
Historical Geographic Information Systems (NHGIS), Minnesota Population Center.

recorded though 1964, five had moved out of state and six to other counties in Missouri. The remaining eighty-nine relocated across the metropolitan area—the vast majority moving to largely African American tracts on the city's north side, public housing downtown, transitional neighborhoods in the inner suburb of Wellston, or other pockets of African American settlement in the county, such as Kinloch and Webster Groves. This reflected both the options available and the persistent recommendation of relocation officials that displaced residents look to public housing in the city or "predominantly negro ghettoes" elsewhere in the county.[118]

The longer-term record was only a little bit better. "When this came along, when their properties were sold," as Ida Scott recalled, "some of them moved out altogether . . . some of them didn't do any better and then some just bought homes right here. They thought they couldn't afford it but they did."[119] But the reconstitution of Elmwood Park fell far short of the assurance—from the St. Louis County Housing Authority—that, as of the

1970s, "the vast majority who had lived there before are back living in Elm-wood Park."[120]

We have three overlapping records for the pre-redevelopment population. The 1940 manuscript census lists ninety-nine families in the county (unincorporated) portion of Elmwood Park. The property survey completed early in the redevelopment planning (circa 1960) lists 120 occupied parcels. And the 1964 relocation ledger tracks one hundred families and individuals. The latter is almost certainly an undercount, since the LCRA did not track families who left Elmwood Park after redevelopment plans were announced in the late 1950s but before work got underway in 1961. So we can assume a displacement of between one hundred and 120 households (most of them families) as a direct result of redevelopment. As of 1974, fifteen families who had lived in Elmwood Park before redevelopment (according to the 1940 census and the LCRA record) had returned and bought homes. At least five others returned to rental housing in the new Primm Gardens complex. In other words, no more than one in six of the pre-redevelopment homeowners returned to the site as homeowners, and no more than one in four pre-redevelopment residents returned at all.[121]

The Best-Laid Plans: Meacham Park, 1965–2000

As plans for Elmwood Park pressed ahead, those for Meacham Park languished. The source of this divergence was a seemingly small detail: the county LCRA was able to strike a deal for public housing that satisfied federal agencies for Elmwood Park, but was unable or unwilling to do so for Meacham Park.[122] The consequences of this divergence were huge. For more than a decade, Elmwood Park and its residents went through the throes of redevelopment—a process that split the community, relocated its residents, and transformed the local urban landscape. For the next decade, redevelopment plans across the county were stunted by the paucity of public housing.[123] And over that same span, Meacham Park was further isolated and quarantined by adjacent development and then slowly chipped away at by the next (post–urban renewal) generation of redevelopment.

In the early 1970s, the county's redevelopment priorities had changed little. Taking due note of ongoing renewal efforts in Elmwood Park and elsewhere, county planners identified (as they had since the 1950s) pockets of African American settlement as persistent blights on the suburban landscape.[124] Redevelopment planning for Meacham Park was shaped by the annexation and development aspirations of neighboring Kirkwood and by the growth and development of the county's infrastructure (including the Metropolitan Sewer District and I-44). At the same time, federal support for large-scale renewal projects was in full retreat. If the priorities had not changed, the tools at the disposal of local planners had. Redevelopment of Meacham Park, as a result, would proceed much more fitfully and haphazardly.

In 1972, the county launched a new survey of substandard housing conditions in unincorporated areas. Foremost among these was Meacham Park, still largely cut off from basic services, its western border set by Kirkwood's 1957 annexation of commercial frontage on Kirkwood Road, its southern and eastern borders set by I-44 (completed in 1965) and by commercial zoning in neighboring Crestwood. In some respects, Meacham Park reflected suburban norms: fully 93 percent of its structures were single-family homes, and just under two-thirds of the residents of those were homeowners. But, in other respects, Meacham Park posed a stark contrast: Its population was 95 percent black. Only 17 percent of Meacham Park adults were high-school graduates (the rate in the rest of the county was over 60 percent). Nearly one in seven housing units were dilapidated or vacant, and almost half (42 percent) were considered either beyond repair or in need of major structural work (map 3.8). Only 15 percent of dwelling units had sanitary sewer hookups. Although they viewed the causes very differently, few residents disagreed as to the assessment: "Most Whites have run and left the already rundown conditions. Although the Whites were poor, they were able to find better housing available to them. They handed down the difficulties of the community to the deprived people of Black color and became the slumlords of the Blacks, collecting outstanding rents for horrid houses."[125]

Based on this inventory of blight, the county secured $8 million in federal redevelopment funding. Federal assistance was targeted for street repairs, sewer hookups, curbs and gutters, park development, and new housing—some of which was financed under the Housing Act of 1968's Section 235 Program, which subsidized and insured private mortgages to low-income homebuyers. Redevelopment plans featured eighty townhouse public-housing units and upward of two hundred new single-family homes, but progress was slowed both by local conditions and by a January 1973 federal moratorium on subsidized housing. In the end, about fifty public-housing units were built on a seven-acre site in southeast Meacham Park (map 3.9), bounded by Tolstoi Street to the east, Orleans to the west, Chicago to the south, and Electric to the north. By 1975, only twelve new homes had been built under Section 235.[126]

The redevelopment efforts of the 1970s brought some improvement (most noticeably in infrastructure), but substandard conditions persisted.

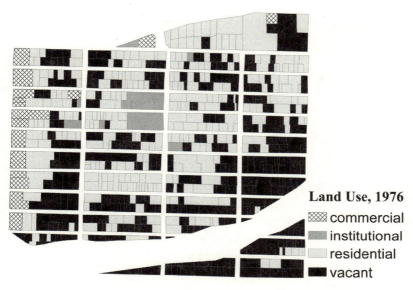

Land Use, 1976

- ▨ commercial
- ▨ institutional
- ☐ residential
- ■ vacant

Map 3.8. Meacham Park, Land Use and Vacancies, 1976
Source: St. Louis County, *Meacham '76: A Community Plan* (1976).

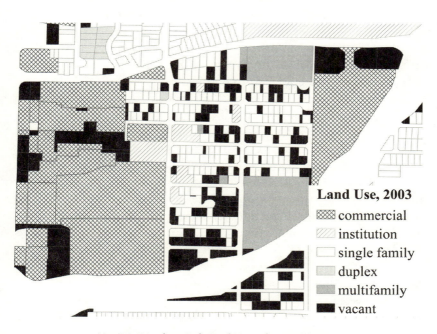

Land Use, 2003

- ▨ commercial
- ▨ institution
- ☐ single family
- ▨ duplex
- ▨ multifamily
- ■ vacant

Map 3.9. Meacham Park, Land Use and Vacancies, 2003
Source: St. Louis County Department of Planning GIS dataset (2003).

Meacham Park residents remained bitter about Kirkwood's annexation of their commercial frontage in the late 1950s and feared that county-funded improvements would spark another push for full or further annexation. Taking note of the shrunken residential footprint of redeveloped Elmwood Park and the commercial focus of post-1974 renewal programs, locals feared that any redevelopment would come at the expense of the old residential base. "Some of the citizens in Meacham Park have about lost hope for the plan," as one observer noted, and "some are even worried that the area will be re-zoned for commercial use."[127]

The next push for redevelopment came just over a decade later, along-side and tangled up with Kirkwood's annexation of Meacham Park in 1992. Kirkwood's goals were clear. After annexation, it wanted to push "big box" commercial development across the western half of Meacham Park, from the frontage on Kirkwood Road that it had claimed in 1957, all the way to Milwaukee Street. "We could not justify the annexation," as then–Kirkwood mayor Herbert Jones put it simply, "if we did not feel commercial develop-ment would pay the bills." The new commercial area, Kirkwood officials hoped, would dress up the "entrance to the community" at I–44 and South Kirkwood Road. Redevelopment would be underwritten with tax-increment financing, a budgetary innovation that allows developers to capture the in-crease ("increment") in sales- and property-tax revenues and dedicate it to paying off the costs of improvements. The project would not only build the local commercial-tax base but also upgrade the residential base—improving lots and erasing a tract of Section 8 housing.[128]

For their part, many residents of Meacham Park supported annexation on the assumption that commercial development—extending no further east than Shelby Street—would entail minimal disruption to residential areas. The proposed extension of Kirkwood's zoning regulations into Mea-cham Park, negotiated by the two communities, set Shelby as the eastern edge of the commercial zone fronting Kirkwood Road. Although it was clear that this boundary would have made the proposed development (which was already negotiating terms with several large retailers) impossible, Kirk-wood city administrator Michael Brown assured Meacham Park residents that "we don't plan on going east of Shelby," although he hastened to add that "if the developer says it's best to go, we're committed to make [Mea-cham Park residents] a part of the process changing that plan."[129]

Plans pushed ahead over the next couple of years, led by the Minnesota-based Opus Corporation. Not surprisingly, the Opus development spilled well beyond Shelby Street and broke the promises made in 1991 and 1992. The new commercial area would swallow over fifty acres, displacing a hundred houses—about a third of Meacham Park's residential base. Opus promised tax revenues of between $2 and $3.5 million annually for an area that currently generated less than $300,000.[130] Opus estimated its costs at just under $40 million for the commercial redevelopment. In late 1994, Kirkwood City Council approved creation of the project's tax-increment financing (TIF) district, which would raise another $15 million that could be used to clear land and relocate displaced residents. Under the terms of the TIF, the revenue from the increase in the tax base (the difference between the predevelopment revenues of $300,000 and the post-development promise of ten times that) would be used to retire $15 million in bonded debt.[131]

For many, the development was a sign of "long-awaited, long-overdue progress." Even some in Meacham Park—Cookie Thornton prominent among them—lauded the project and the economic opportunities it promised. And some were assuaged by the developer's commitment to build at least eighty-five single-family houses for Meacham Park residents displaced by the project and to pay relocation allowances of $12,000 for homeowners and $6,000 for renters.[132] But others dug in their heels. Opponents could muster little enthusiasm for the benefit conferred by a smattering of low-wage, no-benefit retail jobs—especially given the immense public costs of the project. And, more importantly, they objected fiercely to the project's expansive commercial footprint. "I am opposed to the project," as Harriet Patton, a longtime community activist and president of the Meacham Park Post-Annexation Association, put it bluntly, "because it dismantles the community."[133]

For the developer, this controversy was both embarrassing and expensive. It put Opus in the line of fire in a long-standing confrontation, with deep racial overtones, between Kirkwood and Meacham Park. And it promised years of legal battles over property acquisition. In the spring of 1995, Opus decided to pull out. Many saw the announcement as a stunt designed to light a fire under local authorities or to scare residents into accepting offers made on condemned parcels. But Opus was clearly concerned by the project's intractable racial politics and wanted out. The legal and financial hurdles (the annexation, zoning revisions, project financing) were one thing. The local politics of race and space were quite another.[134] "Can anything be learned from this tale of trouble?" asked the *St. Louis Post-Dispatch* as Opus left town in 1995. Its answer was unsurprising. The history between the two communities was already a bitter one. Assurances about the scale of redevelopment made during the annexation process were almost immediately discarded: "The Opus development would have demolished much, if not all, of Meacham Park. That was bound to spark anger, suspicion and dissent." Rather than representing the concerns and interests of its newest citizens, Kirkwood, "perhaps entranced by the potential tax revenue," as the newspaper's editors concluded, "seemed to represent Opus against the concerns of residents."[135]

About a year later, Kirkwood managed to interest a new developer in the project. The DESCO group, based in nearby Clayton, was the only firm to respond to a request for proposals issued after the departure of Opus. DESCO's plan for "Kirkwood Commons" differed little from that sketched out a year earlier: fifty-one acres bounded by Big Bend to the north, I-44 to the south, Kirkwood Road to the west, and Milwaukee Street to the east. The mall would feature nine buildings ranging from 35,000 to 125,000 square feet. Tenants included Walmart, Lowe's, and a Target that would relocate about a mile south from its current location on Kirkwood Road. The only concession to the objections that had scuttled the Opus version was a small park sketched in for the eastern halves of Meacham, Saratoga and New York Streets between Milwaukee and Shelby.[136] But even this shrank as the plans progressed, ending up as little more than a thin, grassy right-of-way behind the Target and T.J. Maxx buildings (map 3.10).

The financing of Kirkwood Commons rested on the original TIF plan, now almost three years old. Kirkwood would put up about $21 million, initially through the sale of public improvement notes to the developer that would then be replaced by longer-term bonds. The bonds, in turn, would be paid off with the sales- and property-tax revenues (estimated at about $2 million annually) from the TIF district (under Missouri's TIF law, the district could claim half of the increase in sales and utility taxes and all the increase in property taxes). The repayment period was twenty-three years, a clock that had started with the establishment of the TIF district in 1994. About $17 million of Kirkwood's investment was slated for acquisition, relocation, and infrastructure costs on the footprint of the project itself. But the TIF district was drawn more expansively, allowing reinvestment of the remaining $4 million in the rest of Meacham Park.[137]

The mall development would bulldoze 170 parcels, including twenty-seven owned by the St. Louis County Housing Authority. DESCO's relocation plan would provide displaced homeowners up to $40,000 toward the purchase of a new home in Meacham Park, and displaced renters up to $6,000. The developer, in turn, would make new housing available in the eastern half of Meacham Park—replacing all of the displaced housing authority units, and redeveloping vacant lots as needed (including a large vacant tract, bounded by Big Bend Road, Tolstoi Street, Attucks Street, and Milwaukee Street, in Meacham Park's northeast corner). In addition, DESCO proposed to pay for improvements (up to $15,000 per house) on

Map 3.10. Meacham Park, 2012
Gray parcels show remaining single-family lots in Meacham Park. Source: City of St. Louis
Planning and Urban Design Agency, Tiled Orthoimagery, http://dynamic.stlouis-mo.gov
/citydata/aerials.cfm; St. Louis County Department of Planning GIS dataset (2012).

the remaining residential stock, and ancillary costs (closing costs, moving
costs, security deposits) for displaced owners and renters.[138]

Finally, nearly eight years after the 1992 annexation, Kirkwood Commons opened for business. The mall included four major retailers (Lowe's,
Walmart, Target, and T.J. Maxx) and a range of smaller outlets. Just as important, the $4 million in TIF revenues spent in the neighborhood east of the
mall yielded lasting and tangible improvements. Kirkwood upgraded lighting, roads, and sidewalks throughout Meacham Park. A tired public-housing
complex in Meacham Park's southeast corner was replaced by Stonecrest
Townhomes (a complex built by the county housing authority but not as
public housing), and a largely vacant block in the northeast corner was redeveloped as Kingsgate Apartments. New single-family homes were financed
from the developer's relocation budget and through low-interest second
and third mortgages secured by the city. "This is the rebirth of Meacham

Park," boasted Kirkwood mayor Mike Swoboda in early 2002. "This is city government keeping its promises."[139]

Swoboda and other Kirkwood officials had reason to celebrate. Planning for what eventually became Kirkwood Commons gave the city the incentive to finally annex Meacham Park. Once developed, the shopping center yielded Kirkwood a lucrative new tax base. And, the terms of that development peeled off new investment for Meacham Park's remaining neighborhoods. But resentment lingered. Some Meacham Park residents saw Kirkwood Commons as the culmination of a long-standing plan to displace or isolate Meacham Park entirely—a process that began with the annexation of Kirkwood Road commercial frontage in 1957 and pushed aggressively east after 1992. Many who had championed the redevelopment plans came to doubt Kirkwood's sincerity in implementing them. And, at the intersection of these views, fantastic and conspiratorial versions of events flourished.[140]

The thorniest issue, considering both the areas' long history and the controversy that embroiled the Opus proposal, was the displacement of homes and residents. The plan to build or renovate homes in the eastern half of Meacham Park for everyone displaced by the mall proved much harder to implement than DESCO or Kirkwood (both of whom viewed the terms as generous) had anticipated. Negotiations with the federal government, which had paid for the original construction of the lots owned by the St. Louis County Housing Authority, dragged on for almost two years. Few displaced property owners expressed any interest in swapping houses. In the end, only six of the sixty-two homeowners took DESCO up on its offer to build elsewhere in Meacham Park. By March 1998, DESCO had failed to reach an agreement with twenty-six of the property owners in the development area and launched the first of a series of condemnation suits. The use of eminent domain (DESCO lawyers handled the suits, but since they relied on Kirkwood's power of eminent domain, the city was the plaintiff of record) in a historically black neighborhood evoked the "Negro clearance" of the earlier urban-renewal era.[141]

Even many who took advantage of the TIF-financed improvement programs (about $4 million was spent in Meacham Park outside of the footprint of Kirkwood Commons) grew skeptical of the city's motives. Homeowners tapping into this program (twenty-five to thirty received grants of up to $35,000 for home improvements and code compliance) also participated in a secondary mortgage program under which Kirkwood held deeds of trust against the improved properties. If the owner sold inside of five years, the conditional deed guaranteed Kirkwood a return on the costs of improvement. Many saw this as an invasion of property rights or as a threat with which Kirkwood could silence community dissent.[142]

Most profound, however, was the irretrievable loss of the older neighborhood and community. In 1957, Meacham Park residents watched as Kirkwood annexed a thin slice of lucrative commercial property on Kirkwood Road, leaving the rest of the area unincorporated and underserviced. In the 1960s, I-44 lopped off the neighborhood's southeast corner and created a hard boundary to the south and to the east. In the 1970s, Kirkwood added insult to injury by blocking through access from Meacham Park to Kirkwood Road. After 1992, Meacham Park residents watched as post-annexation commercial development swallowed housing stock well beyond the promised Shelby Street line. "I get this feeling," as one resident noted in 1999, "that eventually they'll creep farther and farther until they get it all."[143]

Through all of this, Meacham Park shed population. Most homeowners on the development footprint moved ahead of the bulldozers—60 to 80 percent, depending on the estimate, moving out of Meacham Park permanently. In 1992, at the moment of annexation, Meacham Park's population hovered at just over one thousand people. By the time redevelopment was underway in the late 1990s, this number had fallen to just over seven hundred. "Every day, a little bit more of Meacham Park disappears," the *Post-Dispatch* noted in 1999. "Ground. Trees. Houses. Bulldozed, uprooted and churned to make way for the $56 million Kirkwood Commons shopping center. . . . And exactly what's left? A little more than half of what was Meacham Park. For now, the western half is wide open, like a gaping, brown wound."[144]

Finally, Meacham Park residents were disappointed by the economic spillover from redevelopment. It is, of course, routine to pepper such redevelopment proposals with wildly optimistic projections of job growth and leveraged private investment. Indeed, promotional material circulated in 1999 and 2000 promised upward of a thousand new jobs and preferential hiring for area residents. But there were reasons to suspect these numbers. Kirkwood Commons' big-box retailers employ about 250 to 300 people per store, many of them part-timers. Studies of the labor-market impact of new big-box stores suggest that these gains are largely—if not entirely—offset by losses elsewhere in local retail and wholesale employment. Because these were largely "poverty wage" jobs, their impact on the local economy was negligible.[145] And, the Target jobs at Kirkwood Commons could hardly be claimed as "new jobs," since the company had simply moved its outlet a mile south from the older Kirkwood Road location. Little wonder, as one observer noted, that "the number of jobs that went to neighborhood residents is in the scores, not hundreds."[146]

The other implicit promise in all of this was that a share of the redevelopment work itself would go to local workers and contractors. For Cookie Thornton—as we saw in the opening pages—the expectations on this score were impossibly high, and the disappointment, when contracts failed to materialize, was starkly irrational. "I believe that's where the disillusionment started," as one observer noted. "[Thornton] said the mayor and council members had told him that, but the contract was up to the developer. We encouraged him to go sit down with the developer, but he just expected that the phone was going to ring. Things didn't happen the way he expected them to—and it just went downhill from there."[147]

Redevelopment cost the residents of Elmwood Park and Meacham Park their homes and their communities. They were, from the outset, the targets and not the beneficiaries of "renewal." If a "public purpose" was served, they were, from the outset, never considered a member of that public. The exercise of eminent domain threatened the sanctity of their homes—this sanctity a property right, Margaret Radin argues, that forms "the moral nexus between liberty, privacy, and freedom of association." Involuntary relocation threatened another foundation of local citizenship: the right to move or to stay—a right already attenuated, for the county's most marginal residents, by the poor resale value of unevenly serviced homes and the paucity of alternatives in deeply-segregated local housing markets. Residents of unincorporated areas had no voice in the political decision-making of neighboring municipalities and, as a result, had little input into planning for redevelopment, little capacity to alter or slow plans once underway, and little recourse once forced from their homes.[148] Being told to move by the Land Clearance for Redevelopment Authority and being offered a pittance in compensation and relocation assistance only set such unequal citizenship in stark relief. Little wonder that African Americans viewed urban renewal, like policing, as a public policy that conceived of them as targets rather than beneficiaries.[149]

Urban renewal, in this sense, became yet another mechanism of exclusion and segregation, another blunt reminder of unequal protection and unequal citizenship. The first generation of suburban development accomplished this through direct legal means, especially race-restrictive deed covenants. Local incorporation, annexation, and zoning policies (as we saw in chapter 1) were employed to the same end. If these policies of exclusion and quarantine were insufficient, urban renewal offered expulsion and displacement as the next option. "Most cities are engaged in urban renewal, which means moving Negroes out: it means Negro removal," as James Baldwin observed in 1963. The implications for citizenship, and for civic engagement, extend beyond the mere fact of displacement or relocation. "We are talking about human beings," as Baldwin continued. "These are Negro boys and girls who at 16 and 17 don't believe the country means anything it says and don't feel they have any place here on the basis of the performance of the entire country. Am I exaggerating?"[150]

FOUR

Arresting Citizenship:
Segregation, Austerity, and
Predatory Policing

In St. Louis County's long-established African American enclaves, citizenship was fragmented and truncated. The political rights and public goods that accompanied new development and municipal incorporation scarcely penetrated. And when municipal or county authorities decided to address these pockets of "blight," the resulting process of condemnation, demolition, relocation, and redevelopment cleared the landscape of both substandard structures and any vestige of local citizenship for those displaced. In areas of the county undergoing racial transition, especially the inner suburbs of North County, citizenship was stratified in different ways and by different means. In Elmwood Park and Meacham Park, white flight and suburban development overran—and ultimately displaced—the original inhabitants. In settings like Ferguson, by contrast, black migration from north St. Louis filtered into the housing stock built by the first generation of white flight. At issue here was not the jarring contrast between older enclaves and new development but the east-west boundary between white and black occupancy in Greater St. Louis.

In the early and middle decades of the last century, realtors, developers, and white property owners across Greater St. Louis erected elaborate obstacles to black property ownership and occupancy. These restrictions were, over time, adopted and formalized as an ethical obligation of private realtors, lenders, and insurers; as the organizing principle of both local zoning and federal housing policies; and as the key determinant of value whenever property was taxed, "blighted" for redevelopment, or redeveloped.[1] In some respects, these tactics were perfected in the suburbs, where legal restrictions and private discrimination were buttressed by exclusionary development and zoning. Over the middle years of the twentieth century, inner suburbs like Ferguson employed many of the same discriminatory and exclusionary tactics but, in the long haul, less successfully. Disinvestment in north St. Louis, the dislocation caused by urban renewal in the city and in St. Louis County, and the yawning racial gap in local wealth created immense pressures on the older, relatively affordable, and less exclusively zoned housing stock of the inner suburbs.

The private and public policies that shaped the urban crisis in Greater St. Louis, in the inner suburbs of north St. Louis County, and in Ferguson both entrenched patterns of residential segregation and disrupted them. The inner St. Louis County suburbs crowded between the city's western border and the airport (an area known locally as North County) became a logical and necessary zone of racial transition. Here, educational and employment opportunities were much better than those in the city's crumbling north-side neighborhoods. And here, the older housing stock was more affordable—and the local zoning less exclusive—than it was in the outer and central county suburbs. The net result in settings such as Ferguson was both racial transition and an uneasy balance—reflected in local politics, local schooling, and local policing—between past practices and present realities.

Making St. Louis

In order to understand Ferguson, we first need to understand the broader metropolitan context of racial segregation, political fragmentation, population flight, and economic decline. As a border city, Greater St. Louis bears a dual legacy: its race relations are essentially Southern, rooted in the institutions and ideology of Jim Crow, but its organization of property—reflected in private realty and in public policy—follows a Northern pattern in which the institutions and mechanisms of local segregation are particularly stark. The national pattern of white flight and inner-city decay, as one observer noted, could be found in St. Louis "in somewhat purer and less ambiguous form than almost anywhere else." St. Louis retained (decade after decade) its dubious distinction as one of the nation's most segregated metropolitan areas.[2]

Segregation in Greater St. Louis was accomplished and enforced by private and public strategies of exclusion that overlapped and reinforced one another. At the center of this story is the local realty industry, which lobbied for explicitly racial zoning in the World War I era, pursued and enforced race-restrictive deed covenants into the middle years of the century, pioneered the practice of residential security rating that governed both private mortgages and public mortgage guarantees, and—as a central precept of industry practice—actively discouraged desegregation of the private housing market.

At a time when cities were first exploring the politics and legality of zoning, St. Louis was one of a handful of cities to propose formalizing racial segregation. The St. Louis racial zoning ordinance (1916) and others like it were subject to immediate political challenge—both on "equal protection" grounds and as an unwarranted intrusion of the local police power onto private-property rights. The St. Louis law sat in legal limbo for about a year until it was struck down when the Supreme Court ruled against a similar Louisville law in *Buchanan v. Warley* (1917).[3] In the wake of *Buchanan*, local property and realty interests moved to segregate by other means. The solution was a combination of private realty practices and race-restrictive deed covenants that eventually formed a ragged, defensive quadrangle at the western boundary of the city's traditionally African American wards.[4]

In the mid-1940s, a flurry of challenges to restrictive agreements culminated in a St. Louis case that would ultimately end up in the Supreme Court: *Shelley v. Kraemer*. While the Missouri courts had sustained the agreement in question, the Supreme Court disagreed and decided in 1948 that "judicial enforcement by state courts of such covenants is inhibited by the equal protection clause." In the wake of the decision, private parties were free to draft such agreements but could not turn to the courts for their enforcement.[5] Local interests instead turned to the practice of private realty to sustain segregation, and the boundary between black occupancy and white occupancy moved north as white homeowners abandoned neighborhoods now "unprotected."[6]

The practices and assumptions of private realtors distorted not only the market for housing but also the local and federal public policies that subsidized and regulated that market. In the 1930s, the new Home Owners Loan Corporation (HOLC) and Federal Housing Administration (FHA) established the basic framework (low down payment, long-term amortization) for modern homeownership by offering federal insurance on qualifying mortgages. To rate local properties and neighborhoods, the FHA and HOLC turned to the architects of racial zoning and restrictive deed covenants—local realtors and lenders—and echoed their assumption that neighborhoods "invaded" or "infiltrated" by African Americans had lost all value. At the core of the FHA rating system, parroting the same juxtaposition of "nuisances" found in many St. Louis deed covenants, was the prohibition of "undesirable buildings such as stables, pig pens, temporary dwellings, and high fences" and the *prohibition of the occupancy of properties except by the race for which they are intended* (italics added).[7]

All of this had a lasting and decisive impact on residential patterns and opportunities in Greater St. Louis. During the peak years of African American migration to the St. Louis area, all but a handful of the city's neighborhoods were off-limits. "Housing is desperately short-handed in St. Louis as it is in most other large cities," the St. Louis Urban League noted in the wake of World War II, "but the lack of housing facilities for Negroes in St. Louis is critical for peculiar reasons. Approximately 97% of the Negro population in St. Louis lives at the geographical heart of the city, surrounded on the east by commerce and business, and on the south, west, and north by neighborhood covenant agreements. There are no outlets to the open county for any kind of expansion. There is a complete circle of restriction."[8]

Segregation was abetted by local zoning. Local governments, as we saw in the opening chapter, have every incentive to sort the population by race and class in such a way as to maximize tax returns and minimize other demands on the public purse.[9] Where local governance is fragmented (the St. Louis metropolitan statistical area includes over 260 incorporated municipalities, almost a hundred of which are in St. Louis County alone), there is an exaggerated incentive and opportunity to use property zoning as a means of sorting and segregating populations. Outside the central city, the dominant practice (emerging in the mid-twentieth century) was "exclusionary zoning," land-use controls that ensured a pattern of predominantly low-density, single-family settlement through a combination of outright prohibitions (no heavy industry, no manufactured housing), effective prohibitions (no land zoned for multifamily housing), and area or density standards (for lot size, setbacks, and building size). Older cities, by contrast, did not have the power to zone until long after local land use had been determined by private restrictions and market forces. Unable to compete with the suburbs for high-end residential development, central cities often ran in the other direction—designating large areas for commercial or industrial use and often "clearing" low-return residential tracts as part of the bargain.[10] From a metropolitan perspective, the results have not been pretty. Exclusive and fragmented zoning in the suburbs erased any semblance of residential diversity, sorting the white middle class into income-specific single-family enclaves on the periphery and leaving African Americans, the elderly, and the poor to filter into older and higher-density housing stock (much of it unprotected by local zoning) in the central city and inner suburbs.[11]

The net effect of political fragmentation, real-estate restrictions, and exclusionary zoning was the virtual devastation of north and central St. Louis. City planners began taking stock of these conditions (substandard housing, abandoned commercial property, aging infrastructure) as early as World War I, but all that really changed over the following decades were the terms— "obsolescence," "decadence," "blight," "ghettoization," "decay"—used to

label them. The prescription, in St. Louis and elsewhere, was urban renewal—a tangled combination of federal money, state-enabling laws, local initiative, quasi-public redevelopment corporations, and private investment.[12] Between 1954 and 2000, the city of St. Louis "blighted" hundreds
of areas under Chapter 353, the Missouri Urban Redevelopment Law, and
Chapter 99, the Missouri Land Clearance Act.[13] Although the condition of
the residential north side was often used to make the case for urban renewal,
those neighborhoods received virtually none of the subsequent political
attention, private investment, or public subsidies. Most of the attention
instead flowed to commercial development—stadiums, retail, convention
centers—in the city's central corridor.

Urban renewal in the city, as we saw in chapter 3, displaced thousands
of families—some of whom were accommodated in new public-housing
projects, most of whom simply moved west and north ahead of the bulldozer. Urban renewal in St. Louis County was both more modest and more
pointed—blighting and razing pockets of African American settlement now
surrounded by new suburban development. Underinvestment, underzon-
ing, and the erosion of public services on the city's north side also encouraged population flight—although the outmigration of African Americans
did not really take off until civil-rights jurisprudence began to pry open
county housing markets. And the abject failure of "big-box" public housing (the city's infamous Pruitt-Igoe towers were razed in 1972) created yet
another anxious diaspora.

On balance, federal housing and renewal policies did little to address the
paucity of safe, affordable housing in Greater St. Louis and actually deepened
patterns of residential segregation. FHA mortgage insurance flowed primarily
to the suburbs, subsidizing white flight. Federal public-housing assistance
flowed primarily to the inner city, cementing the region's spatial organization of race and poverty. Indeed, when the federal government—in the context of protracted litigation over school desegregation—set out to prove that
the St. Louis Board of Education was defying the mandate of the 1954 *Brown*
decision, both local officials and expert witnesses identified federal housing
policies as the prime culprit. "The segregated black community was left to
fester," as a city official observed, "while developers aided by the federal government rushed out to build new white enclaves on the city's edge."[14]

Making Ferguson

If we re-center our attention from broader metropolitan patterns to the inner suburbs of north St. Louis County—including Ferguson—four elements

of the story stand out: First, systematic discrimination and disinvestment in black neighborhoods produced a stark (and growing) disparity between black wealth and white wealth. Those barred from equal access to housing, federal subsidies, and home finance in the middle years of the twentieth century also lost the ability to pass housing equity on to the next generation. Second, in the developmental and demographic history of Greater St. Louis, the inner suburbs of North County (including Ferguson) had an uncertain and liminal status. They were, as early enclaves of white flight, much like the other suburbs that sprawled west from the city border. But they were, in the timing and pattern of their residential development and zoning, more like the city itself. Third, decline and disinvestment on the north side and redevelopment projects in the city and in the county generated immense pressures on affordable housing stock in the inner suburbs. And finally, the racial premises of both development and redevelopment created and sustained a particular pattern of population movement in Greater St. Louis, marked by "white flight" into St. Louis County (and beyond) beginning in the 1940s and by black flight into North County a generation later. As a result, the black-white divide between north and south St. Louis extended out into St. Louis County, and local segregation was replicated in transitional neighborhoods—like Ferguson—in North County. Let's look at each of these elements in turn.

By almost any economic metric (unemployment, job quality, wages, incomes) the gap between white Americans and black Americans is sustained and substantial,[15] but the starkest gap, in this respect, is in wealth. While the median black worker earns about three-quarters of the wages of his or her white counterpart and the median black household claims about two-thirds the income of its white counterpart, the gap in wealth—with black net worth stuck at about 10 percent of white net worth—is dramatically wider.[16] The racial gap in wealth reflects gaps in the rate of homeownership,[17] in the tenure of homeownership,[18] and in the terms of homeownership.[19] Facing systematic discrimination in both private realty and private lending, fewer African Americans entered the housing market, they entered it later in life, and they entered it on relatively unfavorable terms. Federal incentives and subsidies sorted opportunity by race—not only for homeownership but also for the intergenerational accumulation of equity and wealth and for the other advantages (public services, good schools) that flow from homeownership.[20]

Income, wealth, and inequality are embedded in places—in the neighborhoods (deeply segregated across our history) where families buy homes, raise families, and pass assets and opportunities to the next generation.[21]

Even as civil-rights and fair-housing legislation and litigation curbed the worst of these practices, substantial hurdles—including continued discrimination, systematic disadvantage, and late access to housing markets—slowed progress. What this meant, in St. Louis and its suburbs, was that a long history of discrimination and segregation effectively "lived on" in the form of the black-white wealth gap. This gap was widened both by discriminatory obstacles to homeownership and by the dismal returns on homeownership for those who overcame those obstacles.[22] As a result, when housing markets did open up after the 1970s, segregation by wealth (and income) both displaced and sustained segregation by race. Where African Americans would or could live was determined less by the legal triumphs of the civil-rights era than by the limited supply of affordable housing—much of it abandoned by white flight and rapidly depreciating in value.

Where was that affordable housing? Private development pressed westward, especially after World War II, relatively unconstrained by local or state limits on what we now call "sprawl." Like most Midwestern cities, St. Louis faced few geographic obstacles to growth. And, among Midwestern settings, Missouri was notoriously lax in exerting any regulatory control over the incorporation of new municipalities. Against a backdrop of systematic segregation, as we traced in chapter 1, this pattern of suburban development had three important consequences: First, it meant that private development generally preceded municipal incorporation, so that, when it came, incorporation (and zoning) simply cemented private development patterns and choices. Second, it meant that such patterns sustained segregation—hardly surprising given that municipal incorporation was largely animated by the desire to seal exclusionary patterns of land use. And third, it meant that the municipal organization (especially in St. Louis County) was remarkably fragmented, with each of those fragments playing a particular role in sustaining and regulating patterns of land use and occupancy.

But Ferguson, just to the northwest of the city border in St. Louis County, occupies a precarious spot in St. Louis's hierarchy of places. It was incorporated in 1894, an outgrowth of rail-based development, and grew dramatically in the mid-twentieth century. One of the county's few municipalities to have incorporated before the turn of the twentieth century, Ferguson's residential stock was older and its lots were smaller than those in the cul-de-sacs sprouting up in the cornfields of West County. In the postwar decades, in a suburban landscape in which the prohibition of multifamily housing became the norm, Ferguson permitted construction of a series of apartment complexes. Affordable and accessible, the suburb became an early target of working-class "white flight" and, a generation later, an attractive option for black families leaving Kinloch, Wellston, and the city of St. Louis. In 1970, at its peak population of just over twenty-eight thousand, Ferguson was 99 percent white and just 1 percent black. By 1980 its black population had grown to 14 percent, by 1990 it was over 25 percent, and by 2000 it was over 50 percent. Ferguson, Missouri, was on its way to becoming a "secondhand" suburb marked by aging infrastructure, growing public-service needs, and persistent fiscal troubles.

All of this occurred amid a starkly uneven pattern of housing development and housing opportunity. Median home values in North County, at $88,000 in 2012, are almost 40 percent less than the figure for the whole of St. Louis County ($144,000). From 2005 to 2011 (including the housing crash and recovery), most properties in Central, West, and South County showed a slight increase in assessed values; in most areas of North County, assessed values fell. Of the county's twenty-four thousand foreclosures (2005–2012), fully 70 percent (seventeen thousand) were in North County.[23] And just as low values, foreclosures, and vacancies are concentrated in North County, so too are the region's multifamily rental units. This is an artifact of both early and uneven suburban development, and of less-exclusionary zoning in North County's inner suburbs—characterized by the rental complexes strung along Maline Creek in south Ferguson and in Kinloch.[24] As a result, much of the region's affordable housing and rental housing is concentrated in North County: of the 6,600 tax-credit units that are part of large properties (fifty or more units) in the county, 63 percent are in North County.[25]

All of this left Ferguson in an unusually vulnerable position. Much of its midcentury residential development rested on the same motives and restrictions and subsidies that marked "white flight" suburbanization elsewhere in the region. But because such development was crowded next to the city, it proved less exclusive and more transitional. Because these municipalities were older and their footprints generally smaller (especially in North County), they suffered both higher costs and lower fiscal capacity as they aged. And because land use was less exclusive and lots were smaller in these inner suburbs, they served as the logical destination not just for the white working class fleeing the city in the 1940s and 1950s but also for African Americans displaced by disinvestment and urban renewal a generation later. In St. Louis County, 83 percent of public-housing units and 93 percent of housing-voucher units are occupied by African Americans (the rate for both is only 3 percent in outlying Franklin and Jefferson Counties).[26]

This uneven development was accompanied by unrelenting pressures on the region's affordable housing stock. The population of the city of St. Louis peaked at just over 850,000 in 1950, at which point it claimed just under half (47.9 percent) of the population of the metropolitan area. With each new census, the city's population dropped further (750,000 in 1960, 622,000 in 1970, 453,000 in 1980, 397,000 in 1990, 348,000 in 2000, 318,000 in 2010), as did its share of the metropolitan area. The city lost an average of just under ten thousand persons a year between 1950 and 2013. The housing shortage of the 1940s and 1950s gave way to chronic vacancy and abandonment: by 1978, St. Louis had the highest vacancy rate (just under 10 percent) of all central cities. More important than the dimensions of this decline was its racial profile: in the 1940s, 1950s, and 1960s, the city experienced dramatic "white flight" to the suburbs. In the 1970s and after, this was followed by an equally dramatic pattern of black flight as civil-rights victories began to open county housing markets and whites began moving west again from the inner suburbs.

Just as blacks fled the residential north side (for the same reasons as whites but a generation later), they were also being expelled from neighborhoods targeted for urban renewal. As we have seen, the city's first major projects were accompanied by cynical and haphazard plans for relocated residents. The haphazard movement of African Americans from cleared tracts—some into local public housing, but most into neighborhoods to the west and north—deepened segregation in many central city neighborhoods, created new demands for redevelopment in neighborhoods accommodating the refugees from the latest round of renewal, and encouraged white residents of north St. Louis out into the inner and outer suburbs.[27]

While the city's redevelopment and public-housing policies hardened segregation within St. Louis, those of the county and its municipalities hardened the racial divide between the city and its suburbs. Urban renewal in St. Louis County, as we have seen, was often designed and pursued as a means of relocating suburban pockets of African American settlement "back" into the city. Among these pockets was Kinloch, bordering Ferguson to the west. Kinloch had a peak population of over 6,500 at the 1960 census but was targeted by surrounding municipalities (which worked to quarantine African American students into a separate and unequal school district), St. Louis County (which was looking to erase the last pockets of older African American occupancy in the name of redevelopment), and the St. Louis Airport (which was looking to expand in the Kinloch area). While the county's "Maline Creek" redevelopment scheme never got off the ground (in part because the county refused to contemplate building affordable housing for those displaced), airport expansion did eventually erase much of Kinloch—whose population had shriveled to fewer than three hundred people by 2016.

Taken together, uneven metropolitan development, disinvestment in the central city, and city and county redevelopment policies drove racial transition and segregation in the inner suburbs of North County. Initially developed and populated by white working-class migrants from north St. Louis, Ferguson now became the logical frontier for black flight—and for those displaced by urban renewal to the west and the east. In part, this transformation and transition reflected the tangle of factors traced above. In part, it reflected the slow erosion of formal restrictions on black occupancy, especially after *Jones v. Mayer* extended civil-rights protections to private realty and the institutions of home finance (after the 1975 passage of the Home Mortgage Disclosure Act) followed suit. And in part, it reflected the evolution of public housing from large-scale central city projects (like St. Louis's Pruitt-Igoe towers) to portable "Section 8" vouchers.[28]

The impact and implications of these patterns were dramatic and, in some respects, devastating. Disparate patterns of white and black settlement, of white and black wealth, and of white and black flight hardened racial segregation and isolation. Black flight from the north side opened a class rift in the black community, concentrating poverty in the central city and eroding the middle-class institutions (hospitals, schools, churches) on which that community depended. By the 1980s and 1990s, these losses were underscored and exaggerated by dramatic patterns of local economic decline, disinvestment, vacancy, and property abandonment. Taken together, these trends began to exact tremendous social costs—captured by any regional assessment of educational attainment, public safety, or public health.[29]

The fragile line between white and black occupancy at the city-county line eroded over time as white settlement looked farther west and the collapse of formal racial restrictions finally opened county housing markets. But the north-south divide between black and white occupancy largely held, so that whites leaving the city (or its inner suburbs) moved south and west, while blacks leaving the city (including the diaspora from the failure of the city's public-housing projects) settled largely in North County. In effect, the "Delmar Divide" between north and south St. Louis pushed across the county, splitting University City and marking everything to the north—the twenty-five postage-stamp municipalities between the city boundary and Highway 170 and south of Lindbergh—as a zone of racial transition (see map 4.1).

At the same time, the patterns and mechanisms of segregation invented and sustained in the city of St. Louis migrated along this north-south line out into St. Louis County. This extended the contours of segregation so ingrained in the city's history and also reinvented them in new settings (including Ferguson) in the inner suburbs. Here, segregation was spatial:

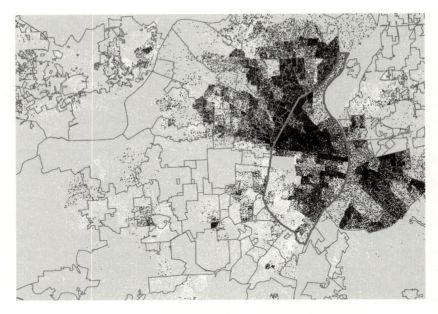

Map 4.1. Racial Occupancy by Block Group, Greater St. Louis, 2010
Source: HUD data (Segregation Patterns 2010), courtesy of Metropolitan
St. Louis Equal Housing and Opportunity Council.

African Americans settled overwhelmingly in the apartment complexes
(Suburban Heights, Northwinds, Canfield) along Maline Creek in south
Ferguson and Kinloch, and in pockets of single-family housing east of West
Florissant Avenue and south of I-270. And it was also political, especially in
settings where the previous generation of white residents retained a stran-
glehold over local employment, local politics, and local services such as
education or policing.

And with racial transition came a replication and extension of the tangled disadvantages long faced by African Americans on the city's north side.
Income inequality, measured as a share of the metropolitan median, spread
out into North County after the 1970s. Inflation-adjusted average earnings
(for those employed) fell by one-third between 2000 and 2012. In 1990,
median household income for North County was 3 percent greater than
that of the region as a whole; now it is 13 percent lower.[30] Poverty rates
rose dramatically: between 2000 and 2013, the poor population of Ferguson doubled, by which point about one in four residents lived in poverty.[31]
Ferguson's unemployment rate almost doubled between 2000 and 2010

and was 11.2 percent as of 2017—nearly double the unemployment rate (5.9 percent) for the whole county. Localized inequality, racial segregation, and concentrated poverty multiply the problems faced by both communities and poor families.[32] Such circumstances underlie social disorganization, increased crime, threats to public health, and further flight of population, investment, and resources. As population flees and property values plummet, local tax capacities collapse—a combination that yields baser public services, deteriorating public schools, *and* higher tax rates, all of which make new investment less likely and old investment less secure. The school districts of North County, including Ferguson-Florissant, combine property values well below the metropolitan average with tax rates well above the county average. To add insult to injury, the collapse of the local property-tax base has also encouraged struggling North County communities to backfill public coffers with court costs and fines—a tactic that underlies the dismal state of community-police relations in North County and created the backdrop for the shooting of Michael Brown.

Killing Michael Brown

In early August 2014, Michael Brown was shot by Officer Darren Wilson on Canfield Drive in Ferguson, Missouri. Brown's death soon became a marker, shorthand for an array of urban and suburban ills, including persistent economic and racial segregation, a racial divide in economic opportunity and outcomes, police violence, and the uneven—carceral, custodial, disciplinary—citizenship claimed by African Americans. "One group of people in this country can expect the institutions of government to bend in their favor," as John Lewis wrote in the wake of Brown's death, but in what Martin Luther King Jr. called the "other America," "children, fathers, mothers, uncles, grandfathers, whole families, and many generations are swept up like rubbish by the hard, unforgiving hand of the law."[33]

Brown's death represented all of this. But as the Department of Justice and local activists (including Arch City Defenders and Better Together St. Louis) pulled back the veil on policing in Ferguson and St. Louis County, other conspirators emerged. The first of these was fragmented local government—the very fact that a sliver of development like Ferguson claimed the authority to police Michael Brown in the first place. The second culprit was segregation's moving boundary in North County; race relations are always most fragile on the frontier of racial transition. And when that frontier sits in a struggling inner suburb—its citizens mostly black, its police almost exclusively white—the fuse is always lit. And the third was the ongoing fiscal crisis of local government—the desire to exercise home rule without the capacity to pay for it. In this context, the confrontation on Canfield Drive was as unsurprising as it was tragic.[34]

The jurisdictional fragmentation of the St. Louis metropolitan region, which by 2010 sprawled across over two hundred incorporated municipalities and eighteen counties in two states, is, first and foremost, an artifact and a mechanism of segregation. In the city of St. Louis itself, during the second half of the twentieth century, the east-west "Delmar Divide" separated North City from South City, while north-south Skinker Boulevard, at the city's western edge, was what planners dubbed a "Berlin Wall" between the predominantly black city and its wealthy, white western suburbs. These physical borders marked racial boundaries that had been established by race-restrictive covenants and maintained by decades of racist practices in private real estate.[35]

A similar marker of racial division was the steel barrier that blocked access to the city of Ferguson from Kinloch at the municipal boundary line on Suburban Avenue. In the spring of 1968, following the assassination of Martin Luther King Jr., hundreds of local activists marched to the Ferguson-Kinloch barricade, demanding its removal. When the Ferguson City Council voted to dismantle it, local property owners, along with their alderman, responded by temporarily erecting a series of new barriers (a wooden board, a "No Trespassing" sign, a car and a truck that blocked the roadway), each of which the city removed in turn. But this was not the end of efforts by whites in Ferguson to wall off their community from Kinloch. In 1975, when, as part of a school desegregation order, US District Judge James Meredith compelled the merger of the adjoining districts of Ferguson-Florissant, Berkeley, and Kinloch, Ferguson council member Carl Kersting responded by proposing that the city build a ten-foot wall between the communities or, alternatively, relax the building code to allow homeowners to erect such a barricade parcel-by-parcel.[36]

These physical borders and barriers reflect the larger logic of municipal boundaries as guarantors of racial and economic segregation in Greater St. Louis. In Missouri, as in most American states, over the course of the twentieth century, local governments were granted significant legal authority, including the authority to decide and to enforce zoning laws, to collect taxes, and to fund public services that they made available to their residents only. Across St. Louis County, developers and homeowners took advantage of these powers to engage in what Charles Tilly calls "opportunity hoarding," by incorporating dozens of new municipalities, passing zoning regulations aimed at excluding unwanted uses—and unwanted people—and gerrymandering local school districts along racial lines.[37]

By century's end, Ferguson was a monument to both the persistence of local segregation and its failure. Developed as a bastion of white flight, it now lay squarely in the path of racial transition as disinvestment in north St. Louis (and with it the failure of local public goods like schools) and the dislocation caused by urban renewal (shouldered overwhelmingly by African Americans) in the city and in St. Louis County created immense pressures on the older, relatively affordable housing stock of the inner suburbs.

As segregation eroded in settings like Ferguson, so too did the fiscal logic that sustained the proliferation of the region's postage-stamp suburbs. The midcentury premise was pretty clear: small municipalities composed of (and zoned for) mostly single-family, owner-occupied homes could provide a modicum of local services and rely on the local residential-property-tax base to cover the costs. Where homes and lot sizes were large, the books were easy to keep as revenues were stable and demands on public services (including schools) were slight. In settings (like Ferguson) where homes were more modest, fiscal viability depended on new construction, steady appreciation of property values, generous state and federal aid, and regional investments in infrastructure. And none of that would last.

Across the last generation, shrinking national commitments and haphazard devolution have pared back public goods and services, as political authority—or just the fallout and wreckage—is passed through to smaller jurisdictions that are uninterested or unwilling or unable to pick up the pieces. "What Washington does to the states," as Jamie Peck observes, "the states do to cities, and cities do to low-income neighborhoods."[38] In a setting like Greater St. Louis, that burden fell hardest on struggling inner suburbs like Ferguson. And in response, Ferguson turned to its police department—not just to discipline and control its most marginal citizens but also to extract from them, one busted taillight or jaywalking fine at a time, the revenue to keep the lights on at City Hall. "Such austerity," as Peck concludes glumly, "is the means by which the costs of macroeconomic mismanagement, financial speculation, and corporate profiteering are shifted onto the dispossessed, the disenfranchised, and the disempowered."[39]

The weakness of local finance in the United States has deep historical roots. Unmentioned in our founding documents, local government enjoys only the authority—and taxing power—extended by the uneven "home rule" provisions in state codes. In the South, as Robin Einhorn shows, local fiscal power was further eroded by an aggressive disinterest in public goods

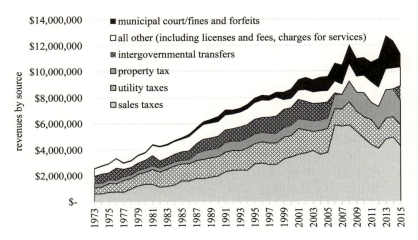

4.1. General Fund Revenues by Source, Ferguson, MO, 1973–2015
Source: Ferguson Combined Annual Financial Reports, 1973–2015.

and deep anxieties over slaves as taxable property.[40] In only seventeen states (as of 2013) does the property tax account for less than 40 percent of local revenue; ten of these (including Missouri, where property taxes account for 36.9 percent of local revenues) are from the former Confederacy. In almost all of these states, regressive sales taxes make up most of the slack.[41]

For Ferguson, this was but a dismal starting point. In 1984, in the city's Combined Annual Financial Report (CAFR), officials wrote, "Because Ferguson is a fully developed community, only an increase in the city's general taxing effort will provide significant growth in revenues."[42] But this strategy was vexed. The 1980 "Hancock Amendment" to the state constitution constrains local fiscal capacity by requiring voter approval for all property-tax levies and sales-tax increases.[43] What is more, analysis of Ferguson's CAFRs since 1973 (the earliest year for which they are available) shows that although estimated actual property values held steady through the 1970s and grew from the mid-1980s until the crash in 2007, assessed property values remained low and flat. Indeed, from 1973 until 2015, local property taxes sustained, on average, barely 10 percent of Ferguson's general fund revenues (see figure 4.1).

It gets worse. Between 1930 and 1970, a full seventy-eight municipalities incorporated in St. Louis County, thrusting Ferguson—one of just six municipalities in the county at the turn of the century—into a fierce interjurisdictional competition for local revenues. Municipalities waged annexation battles over pockets of unincorporated land that promised any return, including a prolonged and bitter showdown (eventually won by Ferguson) over which North County municipality would add the footprint of the Fortune 500 firm Emerson Electric to its tax rolls. But these were often hollow victories, as the most common strategy for luring commercial ratepayers was to promise them that you wouldn't collect. Indeed, Ferguson relied on rolled-back property-tax assessments, real-estate tax abatements, and public-construction subsidies in a series of attempts (some successful, some not) to attract new investment.[44]

Such gambits, in part, rested on the hope that money forgone in property taxes could be made up in local sales taxes, which, the CAFRs show, are consistently the single largest contributor to Ferguson's general fund (see figure 4.1). Indeed, Ferguson has been quick to forgo revenues on commercial property. Some of its largest ratepayers, including Walmart and Home Depot, sit in tax-increment financing (TIF) districts, where growth in property-tax revenues—and, in the case of the most recent TIF district, growth in sales-tax revenues as well—is siphoned off to pay back the bonds the city used to finance development. Ferguson's reliance on large commercial properties as sources of revenue is undermined by the ability of property owners (including Emerson Electric) to appeal—often successfully—to St. Louis County to roll back their assessments (figure 4.2). In 2011, a single reassessment for Emerson cost the municipality over $50,000 in forgone revenue in the next fiscal year.

This is a scramble for revenue that municipalities like Ferguson are forced to join but virtually guaranteed to lose. Indeed, the revenue profiles

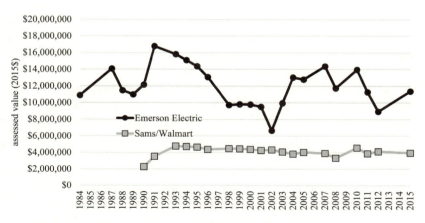

4.2. Major Commercial Assessments, Ferguson, 1984–2015
Source: Ferguson Combined Annual Financial Reports, 1984–2015.

of St. Louis County municipalities vary widely. Property taxes account for between a half and a quarter of local revenues where property values are high and stable (Huntleigh, Glen Echo Park, Ladue) but fall well below that level where property values are slipping. Sales taxes account for between 83 percent and 6 percent of local revenues across St. Louis County. The state of Missouri allows municipalities to opt in or out of a statewide sales-tax pool, with those that opt in dividing the total and those that opt out keeping a share of locally generated revenue. This system presents an easy choice for municipalities rich in commercial development. Not so for older suburbs like Ferguson, where the retail base is weak and faltering and the concessions made to attract (or retain) commercial development ensures that any gains are hollow or short-lived. Ferguson's CAFRs show that, since the early 1970s, officials have closely monitored sales-tax revenues, opting in and out of the state pool year to year in a largely futile attempt to game the system.

This scramble for local investment—what we used to call "smokestack chasing" but now involves mostly big-box retail—is dismally unproductive. As the work of Good Jobs First and others have underscored, whoring after Walmart yields nothing but diminished revenues and destructive sprawl.[45] This pattern is especially acute in suburban St. Louis, given the proliferation of local governments and the stark inequality among them. As Ferguson doles out tax abatements and low commercial assessments, of course, every other municipality is doing the same thing—effectively playing musical chairs with scarce retail investment and sales-tax revenues. In 1994, Ferguson's finance director noted glumly that a dip in sales-tax revenues was "attributable in part to the opening of more outlets in the St. Louis area by one of our major businesses [Walmart] which tends to draw customers to the new locations."[46]

This is a dismal, but not uncommon, feature of American local government. Where the need is the greatest, conventional revenue streams are the least reliable. Where property values and commercial development are robust, so too are public goods and public services. Consider school funding. In the Ferguson-Florissant School District, the local school levy (at 5.3 percent) is near the upper limit allowed by the state and generates about $6,200 per student. In nearby Clayton, the levy (at 3.7 percent) is one of the lowest in the county and generates nearly three times the local revenue ($17,155) per student.[47]

Such gaps are partially filled by transfers from other levels of government. Indeed, after the sales tax, the largest single source of revenue for Ferguson from the early 1970s through the early 2000s was transfers from the state of Missouri (for example, the city's share of the state gas, road and bridge, motor vehicle, and cigarette taxes) and from the federal government (for example, housing and community development grants). But these transfers were fickle. State and federal aid to local governments have declined sharply in the past decade. In 2013, for example, state and federal aid to Missouri local governments was less than $4,000 per capita. Because much of this aid is targeted or constrained (the local share of road taxes, for example, can only be spent on roads), intergovernmental transfers contribute little to the city of Ferguson's general fund. What is more, because many state and federal transfers are calculated on a per capita basis, they have declined with Ferguson's population.[48]

At the same time, the city's costs were rising. Adjusted for inflation, the per capita cost of all city services rose by more than 50 percent between the early 1970s and the early 2000s. The cost of "public safety" alone more than doubled, as policing (in Ferguson and elsewhere) was pressed to fill the gaps created as austerity savaged other public goods and services. Resources for local policing were buoyed by new concerns for "law and order" in the wake of the uprising of the 1960s,[49] by the withering of local social services,[50] and by heightened concern for the protection of property as municipalities and homeowners alike rode the housing boom.[51] These conditions—declining revenues and rising costs, tax breaks and other subsidies for the well-heeled, the erosion of public goods alongside the bolstering of public authority—suggest a local neoliberalism that was both intense and haphazard. In some respects, local actors mimicked the larger political priorities of market deference and market discipline. In other respects, local actors were just flailing in the wreckage.

In this dismal context, and especially when local revenues and intergovernmental aid were squeezed further by the Great Recession, the solution in Ferguson—part design and part desperation—was to look for some other way to backfill the city coffers. In the absence of stable revenues from conventional sources, local authorities in Ferguson resorted to fiscal fracking of the lowest economic strata of their citizenry.[52] Racial transition alone, as we have seen, led to a pattern of local policing marked by regulatory intensity and racial bias. This now became nakedly predatory as well. "Perversely," as Whitney Benns and Blake Strode observe, "these tiny municipalities maintain their ability to continue offering subpar city services by extorting and caging the very people they are meant to serve."[53] Figures 4.3 through 4.6 summarize this pattern, plotting revenue from local courts against local poverty rates, median household income, and revenue from property and sales taxes. Where poverty rates are high (figure 4.3) and median income low (figure 4.4), municipalities lean more and more on revenue from the courts. Where revenues from local property (figure 4.5) and sales (figure 4.6) taxes lag, again the courts begin to take up the slack.

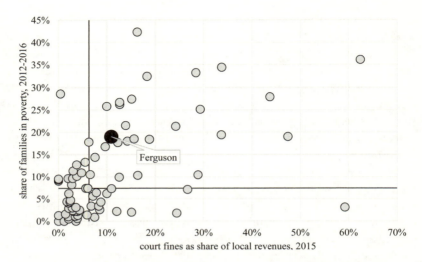

4.3. Revenues from Fines and Poverty Rates, St. Louis County Municipalities (2015)
Source: Revenues from Better Together St. Louis, General Administration Study, Report #2,
Table 3 (December 2015), https://www.bettertogetherstl.com/generaladministration;
local family poverty rates from American Community Survey (2012–2016).

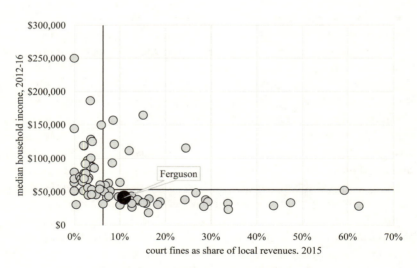

4.4. Revenues from Fines and Household Income,
St. Louis County Municipalities (2015)
Source: Revenues from Better Together St. Louis, General Administration Study, Report #2,
Table 3 (December 2015), https://www.bettertogetherstl.com/generaladministration;
local median household incomes from American Community Survey (2012–2016).

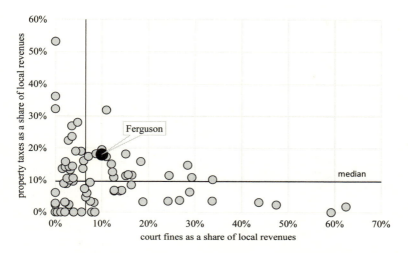

4.5. Revenues from Fines and Property Taxes, St. Louis County Municipalities (2015)
Source: Revenues from Better Together St. Louis, General Administration Study, Report #2,
Table 3 (December 2015), https://www.bettertogetherstl.com/generaladministration.

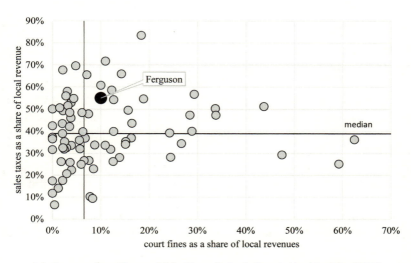

4.6. Revenues from Fines and Sales Taxes, St. Louis County Municipalities (2015)
Source: Revenues from Better Together St. Louis, General Administration
Study, Report #2, Table 3 (December 2015); data online at
https://www.bettertogetherstl.com/generaladministration.

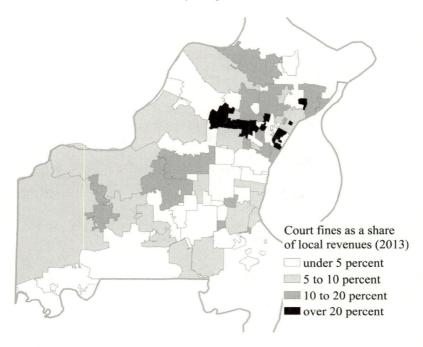

Map 4.2. Revenue Policing in St. Louis County, 2013
Source: Better Together St. Louis, General Administration Study, Report #2, Table 3
(December 2015), https://www.bettertogetherstl.com/generaladministration.

If the county's patchwork municipal structure (as well as its attendant
fiscal weaknesses) makes this form of revenue extraction necessary, it also
makes it possible. As of 2017, St. Louis County alone counted eighty-nine
municipalities, eighty-one municipal courts, and sixty-one police departments. This fragmentation multiplied the potential points of contact between African American residents and revenue-thirsty local jurisdictions
and magnified the costs for those targeted. "Sometimes you take the long
route," as one correspondent told the Ferguson Commission, "because
you don't want to drive through the municipalities."[54] The political and
economic consequences of municipal fragmentation in Greater St. Louis
make plain the structural context within which public officials developed
these predatory policing practices and this exploitative system of municipal
courts. Such practices, in fact, were starkest in the transitional and fiscally
strapped inner suburbs of North County (see map 4.2).

In Ferguson, fines and forfeitures surpassed the property tax as a source
of general-fund revenues in 2001, and by 2013, they made up a full 20 per-

cent of municipal revenues (see figure 4.7). The shift was not lost on local officials, who noted in 2006 that "policing efforts [had] contributed
$313,138 in additional revenue over 2005–06 budget figures" and listed
"enhanced policing efforts" as a key cause of that year's increase in the city's
general-fund balance. "Fines and forfeitures," they noted approvingly, "were
$365,221 over budgeted figures due to the increased efforts of the Police
Department."[55]

In practice, this predatory policing compromised local citizenship in
two ways. First, much local policing in Greater St. Louis is aimed at enforcement of trivial violations of the municipal code—including such threats to
the public safety as "Manner of Walking along Roadway" (the pretext for
stopping Michael Brown), and a long litany of "failure to comply" offenses
that make it easy to manufacture an arrest out of virtually any police stop.
In the larger picture, it is unclear how many of these local ordinances, or
their enforcement, served any clear or legitimate municipal purpose. Fines
for broken taillights, sagging pants, improperly storing drywall, insufficient
window coverings, or jaywalking do little to enhance public safety or welfare. These laws are designed and enforced to extract revenue rather than to
moderate or change behavior.[56]

In its 2015 report, the Department of Justice emphasized that "the City
budgets for sizeable increases in municipal fines and fees each year, ex-
horts police and court staff to deliver those revenue increases, and closely

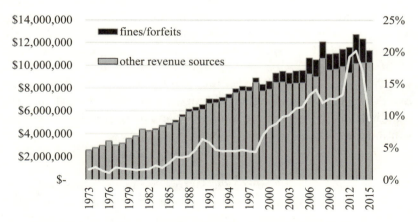

4.7. Fines and Forfeits as Share of General Fund Revenues, Ferguson, 1973–2015
Total revenue (bars) on left axis; share of revenue (line) on right axis.
Source: Ferguson Combined Annual Financial Reports, 1973–2015.

monitors whether those increases are achieved." For example, in 2010, Ferguson's finance director wrote to the city's police chief, warning him that, "unless ticket writing ramps up significantly before the end of the year, it will be hard to significantly raise collections next year." "Given that we are looking at a substantial sales tax shortfall," the finance director continued, "it's not an insignificant issue." According to the Department of Justice, the following year the acting prosecutor of the municipal court "talked with police officers about assuring all necessary summonses are written for each incident, i.e. when DWI charges are issued, are the correct companion charges being issued, such as speeding, failure to maintain a single lane, no insurance, and no seat belt, etc." The goal, the prosecutor underscored, was to ensure "that the court is maintaining the correct volume for offenses occurring within the city."[57] By 2013, the Ferguson Municipal Court was processing almost twenty-five thousand warrants and more than twelve thousand court cases annually: a rate of three warrants and 1.5 cases for each household in its jurisdiction.[58] What Ferguson's acting prosecutor called the "correct volume" of charges was a measure that had little to do with public safety. Instead, its "correctness" was a function of the capacity, in the words of Ferguson's finance director, "to fill the revenue pipeline."[59]

Second, the distribution of this burden—"the simple fact . . . that violations of these ordinances only lead to jail time for certain people in certain places"—left little doubt as to their underlying racial logic and animus.[60] As the US Department of Justice made clear in its scathing March 2015 report, by the time Darren Wilson confronted Michael Brown in August 2014, members of Ferguson's police department and officials of its municipal court had, for years, systematically targeted the city's black residents, extracting from them exorbitant fines for minor infractions and gratuitously arresting and jailing them when they proved unable to pay.[61] The thrust of these policies, as well as the discretion exercised in their enforcement, was starkly and unabashedly racial; they disproportionately targeted African Americans, and—by playing out assumptions of who belonged where—drew indelible distinctions between white and black places and between white and black citizens.

The fragmented political structure of St. Louis County was designed to cement racial and economic segregation and to enable the privileged to hoard local resources and opportunities. Many municipalities succeeded in the competition to attract commercial development and middle-income and wealthy residents. But many others—like Ferguson—failed. In some of the earliest and fiercest outposts of suburban segregation—which, due to fair-housing legislation, continued white flight, and the racial wealth gap, are now majority black—a combination of declining property values, the erosion of support from higher levels of government, and a beggar-thy-neighbor scramble for sales- and property-tax revenue has produced a severe and intractable fiscal crisis. The result is a yawning gap between local authority and local capacity. Municipal policies sharpen local inequalities and bear heavily on the most vulnerable among us. In this sense, the predatory policing that cost Michael Brown his life underscores both the repressive character of local policing and the regressive burden of local taxation. The wicked logic of Ferguson was that these could be pursued in tandem: that policing could backfill the budget so that the budget could sustain more policing.

The murder of Michael Brown and its aftermath shed a spotlight on these practices and their implications for local citizenship but did little to ease the underlying causes. Indeed, Ferguson's fiscal woes deepened as it struggled to comply with the Justice Department's consent decree on one hand and to meet the costs of policing protests (and prosecuting protesters) on the other.[62] Negotiations between Ferguson and the Justice Department proceeded fitfully, slowed by the city's fiscal anxieties ("We feel that what they are asking would financially ruin the city," as one city councilor complained just before the anniversary of Brown's death[63]). In January 2016, Ferguson officials finally agreed to a settlement that would bolster community policing and meet the modest expectation that municipal code enforcement be animated by a concern for public safety rather than the city's budget.[64]

A month later, that deal crumbled when the Ferguson City Council unilaterally amended the consent decree, most notably pulling back on commitments to raise police salaries and asserting that the terms of the deal would not apply to outside agencies if the city decided to contract out policing or collections.[65] The Justice Department wasted no time filing suit, citing the city's "routine violation of constitutional and statutory rights, based in part on prioritizing the misuse of law enforcement authority as a means to generate municipal revenue over legitimate law enforcement purposes," and the unlikelihood "that the City will remedy these patterns and practices of unlawful conduct absent judicial mandate."[66]

A parallel effort at the state level to reign in predatory municipalities followed a similar path. In July 2015, just under a year after Brown's death, Missouri Senate Bill 5 capped court fines as a share of municipal revenues in St. Louis County at 12.5 percent.[67] The county and twelve of its municipalities immediately challenged the law, and in May 2016 they won a partial victory when the state's supreme court held that St. Louis County municipalities could not be held to a different standard than the rest of the state—raising the revenue cap back to the statewide threshold of 20 percent.[68] And, since this cap applied only to revenue from traffic stops, municipalities simply shifted their attention to other forms of predation, such as code violations.[69]

And, through all of this, the logic and limits of local citizenship remained the same. "At first glance, issues of local governance appear more bureaucratic than political, more administrative than ideological," as the Arch City Defenders underscored. "However, the history of St. Louis and the surrounding county make clear that many of the region's cities—with their municipal charters, departments and ordinances—were established with the explicit intent of keeping out undesirable black residents threatening to upset the racial order. Such places were never meant to be hospitable to such people."[70]

Conclusion

The death of Michael Brown was both tragic and unsurprising. In the immediate aftermath, our attention was drawn to the causal chain of that morning, to the motives and actions of both Brown and Officer Wilson on the stretch of Canfield Drive between the spot where Wilson stopped his cruiser just after noon on August 9, 2014, and the spot where Brown lay lifeless just minutes later. Brown's death, in turn, was not an isolated event but took its place among the growing "canon of the wrongfully dead" that catalyzed both the "Black Lives Matter" movement and a searching reexamination of the nexus between race and justice in contemporary America.[1] In March 2015, when the Department of Justice released its devastating indictment of policing in Ferguson, our compass widened further, taking in not just the Ferguson Police Department's naked racial animus but also its charge to bolster local revenues through predatory policing and the municipal courts. "The residents of Ferguson do not have a police problem," as Ta-Nehisi Coates notes acidly. "They have a gang problem."[2]

To fully understand the death of Michael Brown (and the response to it), we need to broaden our view even further. At issue, as I have argued in these pages, is not just the treatment of African Americans by the police or the courts but also their treatment by the state—and their status as citizens in their own communities. For many, encounters with the police are their most substantial and routine interaction with the state, especially in an era in which other local services have withered. Such encounters, in turn, send powerful messages about citizenship—about who deserves protection and who deserves suspicion. For those at the suspicious end of that scale, as Bennett Capers notes, police discretion tramples not just due process but also the very "promise of equal treatment, the most tangible marker of equal citizenship."[3] Predatory policing, in this respect, is but the bluntest example of unequal treatment and unequal protection hardwired into local politics, schooling, housing, social policy, service provision, and economic opportunity. African American citizenship in the St. Louis suburbs was compromised or discounted whenever municipal or school-district boundaries were drawn, whenever private developers and local governments extended public services, and whenever choices were made about development or redevelopment.

And at issue is not just our recent history, the potent combination of neoliberal austerity and state violence on display in Ferguson and elsewhere, but also the long shadow of systematic segregation and discrimination in the urban north. Assumptions about African Americans—as workers, as neighbors, as criminal threats—were quite pointedly invented and elaborated in response to the Great Migration north in the first decades of the last century.[4] Private and public interests in northern cities, most starkly throughout the industrial Midwest, erected an elaborate and unprecedented system of residential apartheid sustained by private markets, by public policies, and by the law.[5] And because (in the American context) so many other goods and opportunities flow from housing, that segregation became the keystone for a much broader pattern of racial stratification. Constraints on housing and neighborhood choice led to a cascade of disadvantages in schooling, employment, health, safety, and mobility.[6]

As the formal and legal instruments sustaining these patterns fell to equal-protection challenges, patterns of segregation persisted—especially in settings like Greater St. Louis where the local economy and demographics had changed little across the last half century. Segregation lasted because people continued to act on its core assumptions as to what constitutes a good neighborhood or one to be avoided.[7] It lasted because, even in the absence of explicit racist intent, African Americans lacked the means and white Americans lacked the incentive to overcome or erase the original inequality or disadvantage.[8] It lasted because many of the public policies and private practices on which it depended, including local land-use zoning and discrimination in realty and credit markets, remained in place.[9] And it lasted because uneven opportunities in the past lived on in the form of a yawning and stubborn gap between black wealth and white wealth. In the wake of the Great Recession, the median net worth of white families with children was just under $78,000; the median wealth of black families with children was zero.[10] This gap ensured that, as racial segregation was slowly eclipsed by economic segregation, in many settings the two remained essentially synonymous.[11] And wealth (home equity for most Americans) is not just a distributional marker; it also buttresses all of the other things—economic security, mobility, and opportunity—that help to ensure substantive and meaningful citizenship.[12]

In one respect then, segregation and its consequences are persistent and sedimentary—a "socially layered accumulation of disadvantages," as Oliver and Shapiro put it, "passed on from generation to generation."[13] But in other respects, there is a new ferocity to those disadvantages and to the politics that sustain them. The long civil-rights movement lasted about fifty years, from the Great Migration into the late 1960s; the backlash against that movement is now about the same age.[14] The policing of African American citizens and African American communities became more pointed and more intense in the aftermath of the civil disturbances of the mid- and late 1960s.[15] School-level segregation scarcely budged until the Civil Rights Act of 1964 and formal desegregation orders gave teeth to *Brown*, and then it slowly returned as those orders expired or were lifted in the 1980s.[16] Openly partisan and racial constraints on the right to vote are now commonplace across the states.[17] African Americans were pointedly excluded by the original design and administration of most social programs, and once they won a semblance of equal protection, their "deservedness"—and the legitimacy of the programs themselves—became increasingly suspect.[18]

Against this backdrop, insidious racial distinctions between the worthy and the unworthy, the deserving and the undeserving, the makers and the takers, increasingly infect politics and political conversation. Race "takes over the imagination," as Barbara and Karen Fields note; "it shrinks well-founded criticisms of inequality to fit crabbed moral limits, leaving the social grievances of white Americans without a language in which to frame them." As discerning observers of the 2016 US election and its aftermath underscored, economic anxieties easily become racial resentments, animating inchoate attacks on public programs and their presumed beneficiaries.[19] All that was new about this "new racism" was its preference for "ostensibly nonracial" markers—family values, work ethic, social behavior, market outcomes—of worth or citizenship.[20]

The motives behind and consequences of these political choices, and the assumptions underlying them, are especially stark and striking when we watch them play out in a particular setting. This is not just because a local "case study" offers unique insights or details but also because much of the substance and meaning of citizenship is negotiated in local settings and local spaces. The fragmentation of political responsibility and authority in the St. Louis suburbs, as we saw in chapter 1, was a purposeful and intentional project—pursued largely to create or sustain patterns of residential segregation. Local planners drew municipal and school-district boundaries to sort the population by race and by class. This determined, as we traced in chapter 2, the scope and quality of local public services. Suburban schools reflected the demographics and fiscal capacity of their gerrymandered districts. Suburban law enforcement was largely animated by race and space, by the exercise of discretion as to who was protected and who was scrutinized, and by the task of policing hard and soft boundaries. Suburban infrastructure (sewers, water lines, sidewalks), which largely followed the contours of private development and investment, was barely a public good at all.

The powerful and persistent subtext across all of this, across the long, segregated century, was that African Americans were "out of place" in the suburban patchwork that sprawled west across St. Louis County. This conviction, as we saw in chapter 3, extended even to those who had owned and occupied homes in St. Louis County long before the mid-twentieth-century suburban boom. Municipal incorporation, explicit racial restrictions, and exclusive residential zoning isolated and quarantined the county's scattered black enclaves. Urban renewal projects, under the pretense of eradicating "blight," then targeted those communities for removal and relocation. And this conviction, as we saw in chapter 4, shaped the response to racial transition in older inner suburbs like Ferguson. The urgency of policing the boundaries between white spaces and black spaces hardened even as the boundaries themselves moved or became less distinct.

The experience of African Americans in the suburbs of St. Louis is illuminating not because it is exceptional but because it is so ordinary. Fragmented governance, often fueled by exclusionary impulses, is an engine of local inequality in any setting. Local land-use policies arrange market inequalities in space and then ensure that a combination of uneven service provision, neighborhood effects (the cascade of disadvantage that flows from place-based poverty), and opportunity hoarding will make them worse.[21] More than a half century after *Brown*, battles over school-district boundaries or school catchment zones remain the most common and most intense confrontations over local space and resources.[22] All local governments scramble for new investment and the "highest use" of the land within their borders, while most are routinely indifferent to the fates of those displaced by gentrification or redevelopment.[23] And local policing, whether in 1968 or in 2018, has cast a harsh spotlight on local political and economic inequalities. As the Department of Justice plodded through reports on race and policing in Ferguson, Baltimore, Chicago, Cleveland, and Newark, the conclusions and condemnations about each city were distressingly similar. "Toss this damning collection into the air," as Jelani Cobb notes, "and it would be nearly impossible to determine which pages belong where."[24]

We can (and should) understand the death of Michael Brown alongside the deaths of so many other victims of police violence in the era of mass incarceration. But we should also understand the life of Michael Brown alongside the lives of Cookie Thornton, Esther Brooks, the Hurst family, and other African American residents of St. Louis County across the last century, for whom full and meaningful citizenship was so elusive. For these Americans, the promise of equal protection unraveled in local settings. They were pointedly excluded from local political communities or jurisdictions. They could not be sure that the fire department would show up when needed or that sewers or water lines would be extended into their neighborhoods. In local planning and redevelopment, their property rights were routinely discounted or discarded. On the streets and in the courts, they had little protection against unreasonable searches or excessive fines.

In 1968, at the legal high-water mark of the modern civil-rights movement, the Kerner Commission sounded a famously discordant note: "Our nation is moving towards two societies, one black, one white, separate and unequal."[25] The prevailing explanation for this gap between promise and reality has been that a dearth of economic opportunity—both across the postwar boom and especially as deindustrialization took hold—undercut the impact of changes in the law. Yet, as the commission's running narrative of unrest in city after city made clear, the real and lasting damage (of which uneven economic opportunity was a part) could be traced to the institutions, assumptions, and practices of local citizenship. Here—in neighborhoods and in schools, in local politics and in local courts—the impact of national policy and law was thin or fleeting. And here, the mechanisms of segregation and discrimination and unequal protection were scarcely challenged, easily reinvented, and willfully sustained.

ACKNOWLEDGMENTS

This book has a circuitous history. It began as an effort to delve deeper into the story of an African American enclave in St. Louis County (Elmwood Park) that had made a brief appearance in my book *Mapping Decline: St. Louis and the Fate of the American City*. Just as *Mapping Decline* was going to press in early 2008, Cookie Thornton of Meacham Park (another old African American enclave) killed five people in the city-council chambers of nearby Kirkwood, Missouri. As I (and many others) struggled to understand the context and backstory of the Kirkwood shootings, I also began working on a series of death-penalty cases, all of which asked me to use my St. Louis research to sketch the life circumstances and mitigating factors faced by young African American men growing up in Greater St. Louis. Then, in August 2014, Michael Brown died at the hands of the police in Ferguson, Missouri—another, albeit quite different, "suburban" setting. In the aftermath, I wrote extensively on the larger context for Brown's death. I was also asked to provide an expert opinion in *NAACP et al. v. Ferguson-Florissant School District*, a voting-rights case concerning African American representation on the local school board.

All of this is to say that, in drawing on my St. Louis research to make sense of current events, support litigation, and address local audiences, I thought a lot more and learned a lot more about the nexus of race and citizenship in the modern American city, and I incurred many debts. So here goes. Thanks to the lawyers I worked with on the capital cases and on the Ferguson-Florissant schools case: Maria Pulzetti, Elizabeth Unger Carlyle, Derek Verhagen, Kim Newberry, Julie Ebenstein, and Sophia Lakin. These experiences taught me a lot about the law and its limits, and about the art of employing historical evidence in legal argument.

I could not have pulled this together without the help of many St. Louis–based scholars, journalists, librarians, archivists, correspondents, collaborators, confidants, and activists. Special thanks to Clarissa Rile Hayward, Todd Swanstrom, D. J. Wilson, Romona Williams, Frank Kovarik, Paul Fehler, Mary Delach Leonard, Will Jordan, Marilyn Merritt, Kayla Reed, Nick Reding, Vince Bantu, Reverend Mike Jones, Melanie Adams, Sylvester Brown, Elisabeth Risch, the late Maggie Garb, Kim Norwood, Sarah Siegel, Taylor Desloge, Clark Randall, Jeannette Cooperman, Jason Purnell, Mary Rocchio, Carolyn Nolan, and the late Doris Wesley.

I was fortunate to be included in an interdisciplinary "Ferguson Working Group," which met twice after the death of Michael Brown. These workshops (one in New Haven, one in Camden) introduced me to an extraordinarily rich body of scholarship and an extraordinarily smart and generous group of scholars: Clarissa Hayward, Tracey Meares, Ben Justice, Joe Soss, Josh Page, Daria Roithmayr, Melissa Nobles, Meira Levinson, Donna Murch, Tom Sugrue, Gerald Torres, Vesla Weaver, Bennett Capers, Devin Fergus, Issa Kohler-Hausmann, Michael Sierra-Arevalo, Andrew Papachristos, Megan Quattlebaum, and Tom Tyler. An essay cowritten with Clarissa Hayward, "The Murder of Michael Brown," came out of these conversations.

This book has been shaped by friends and scholars I encountered in other settings, including the workshop on "Multi-level Government and Sub-National Inequalities" held at CUNY's Advanced Research Collaborative in April 2016, and a raft of academic meetings and panels plumbing the historical and political implications of Ferguson and its aftermath. For their insights, their encouragement, and their skepticism, thanks to Joel Rogers, Patrick Barrett, David Roediger, Clarence Lang, Shawn Alexander, Walter Johnson, Diane Davis, Nathan Connolly, Keona Ervin, Catherine Rymph, Joseph Heathcott, Alexander von Hoffman, Todd Michney, Amy Hillier, Jodi Rios, Richard Rothstein, Robin Bachin, Kim Norwood, Phil Ethington, Jelani Cobb, Heather Thompson, Khalil Gibran Muhammad, and Marcia Chatelain.

My academic interests, across the past decade, have been shaped and focused by collaboration and conversations with friends in the policy world. Their example has pressed me to make my work relevant and accessible; any failure on that score is my own. Special thanks to Mike Owen, David Osterberg, Peter Fisher, Beth Pearson, Christine Ralston, Amy Hanauer, Laura Dresser, Annette Bernhardt, Joel Rogers (again), Steve Hertzenberg, Mark Price, John Schmitt, Donald Cohen, Greg LeRoy, and David Cooper.

Thanks, of course, to my wonderful colleagues at Iowa, especially Landon Storrs, Ty Priest, Leslie Schwalm, Shel Stromquist, Linda Kerber, Jen Sherer,

Matt Glasson, and John McKerley. A special shout-out to Sarah Bruch, a colleague and collaborator whose insights and suggestions are all over these pages—and whose own work sets the bar for critical and engaged social science.

Thanks to Tim Mennel and Rachel Kelly Unger at the University of Chicago Press for both believing in the project and shepherding it along. Serene Yang's virtual blue pencil made this a better book.

Over the last few years, portions of the text appeared, in a different form, in commentary for *Dissent*. Some of the material covered in chapter 1 can also be found in "Patchwork Metropolis: Fragmented Governance and Urban Decline in Greater St. Louis" (*St. Louis University Public Law Review* 34, no. 1 [2014]: 51–70). Earlier versions of the material presented in chapter 4 were published as "Making Ferguson: Segregation and Uneven Development in Greater St. Louis" (in *Ferguson's Fault Lines*, edited by Kimberly Norwood, 75–97 [Chicago: American Bar Association, 2016]), and (with Clarissa Rile Hayward) "The Murder of Michael Brown" (*Jacobin*, August 2016). Thanks to my editors in these settings—especially Colin Kinniburgh and Nick Serpe at *Dissent* and Shawn Gude at *Jacobin*—for their help and support.

NOTES

INTRODUCTION

1. This account draws on "Battery Was Dead: Five Children Die before Help Comes,"
    St. Louis Argus, January 22, 1965; "Five Children Die in County Home Fire," *St. Louis
    Globe-Democrat*, January 18, 1965; "Delay by Firemen Reported in Fire that Took
    Five Lives," *St. Louis Post-Dispatch* (hereafter cited as *SLPD*), January 18, 1965; "Tragic
    Fire Spurred Kirkwood Interest in Meacham Park," *Webster-Kirkwood Times*, Novem-
    ber 14–20, 1986, reprinted March 21, 2008; William H. Freivogel, "Kirkwood's
    Journey: Separating Myths and Realities about Meacham Park, Thornton, Part 2,"
    St. Louis Beacon, February 7, 2010; and Lonnie Speer, *Meacham Park: A History* (self-
    pub., 1998), 4.

2. Testimony of Esther Brooks, Transcript on Appeal, vol. 1, p. 139, *Brooks et al. v. LCRA*,
    Supreme Court of Missouri (September 1966), Supreme Court file 52147, *Brooks v.
    LCRA*, Missouri State Archives, Jefferson City.

3. Appellant's Brief, *Brooks v. Land Clearance for Redevelopment Authority* (1966), RG 600,
    Supreme Court Judicial Case Files; Elmwood Park Urban Renewal Plan, October
    1964, in *Brooks v. Land Clearance for Redevelopment Authority* (1966), RG 600, Su-
    preme Court Judicial Case Files; Final Report of the Grand Jury of St. Louis County
    (January 1965), in *Brooks v. Land Clearance for Redevelopment* (1966), RG 600, Su-
    preme Court Judicial Case Files.

4. Appellant's Brief, *Brooks et al. v. LCRA*, Supreme Court of Missouri (January 1967),
    Supreme Court file 52147, *Brooks v. LCRA*, Missouri State Archives.

5. Final Report of the Grand Jury of St. Louis County (January 1965); Appellant's Brief;
    and Transcript on Appeal, 156, all in *Brooks v. Land Clearance for Redevelopment Au-
    thority* (1966), RG 600, Supreme Court Judicial Case Files.

6. Testimony of Esther Brooks, Transcript on Appeal, vol. 1, p. 137, *Brooks et al. v. LCRA*,
    Supreme Court of Missouri (September 1966), Supreme Court file 52147, *Brooks v.
    LCRA*, Missouri State Archives.

7. *Esther Brooks et al. v. Land Clearance for Redevelopment Authority of St. Louis County*,
    No. 52147, Supreme Court of Missouri, Division One, 414 S.W.2d 545, 1967 Mo.
    LEXIS 978 (March 13, 1967); *Esther Brooks et al. v. Land Clearance for Redevelopment Au-
    thority of St. Louis County*, No. 32916, Court of Appeals of Missouri, St. Louis District,
    425 S.W.2d 481, 1968 Mo. App. LEXIS 769 (February 1968).

8. This background is drawn from Stephen Deere and Doug Moore, "Charles Lee 'Cookie' Thornton: Behind the Smile," *SLPD*, May 4, 2008; and Jeannette Cooperman, "The Kirkwood Shootings," *St. Louis Magazine*, May 2008.

9. "Defendant's Memorandum in Opposition to Plaintiff's Motion," *Thornton v. City of Kirkwood*, United States District Court, Eastern District of Missouri (March 26, 2007), 3, original complaints and summons reproduced on pages 39 and 48; Deere and Moore, "Charles Lee 'Cookie' Thornton."

10. "Defendant's Memorandum in Opposition to Plaintiff's Motion," *Thornton v. City of Kirkwood*, United States District Court, Eastern District of Missouri (March 26, 2007), 1, 5; Cooperman, "The Kirkwood Shootings": Doug Moore, Stephen Deere, and Steve Giegerich, "A Smile That Gave In to Anger," *SLPD*, February 9, 2008; Heather Ratcliffe and Greg Jonsson, "Kirkwood Starts Long Road to Recovery," *SLPD*, February 9, 2008; Steve Giegerich, "City Attorney: 'I Had to Fight for My Life,'" *SLPD*, February 9, 2008; Deere and Moore, "Charles Lee 'Cookie' Thornton"; Heather Ratcliffe, "6 Dead in Shooting Rampage at Kirkwood City Council," *SLPD*, February 8, 2008.

11. This narrative is drawn from "Anatomy of a Rampage," *SLPD*, February 9, 2008, A11; Ratcliffe and Jonsson, "Kirkwood Starts Long Road to Recovery"; Deere and Moore, "Charles Lee 'Cookie' Thornton"; Nancy Cambria, "Thornton Moved Fast, Used Two Guns," *SLPD*, February 9, 2008; Giegerich, "City Attorney: 'I Had to Fight for My Life'"; "Racial Tensions Might Have Sparked Kirkwood Shooting," *Columbia Missourian*, February 11, 2008; and Stephen Deere, Elizabeth Holland, and Doug Moore, "1 Year Later: Recollections, and Pain, from Those Who Survived Kirkwood Shootings," *SLPD*, February 1, 2009.

12. John Elgion, "Michael Brown Spent Last Weeks Grappling with Problems and Promise," *New York Times*, August 24, 2014; "A Youth, an Officer and 2 Paths to a Fatal Encounter," *New York Times*, August 15, 2014.

13. "A Youth, an Officer and 2 Paths"; Ferguson Mun. Code §§ 44–344; US Department of Justice, Civil Rights Division, *Investigation of the Ferguson Police Department* (Washington, DC: Department of Justice, March 2015), 7, 11.

14. Elgion, "Michael Brown Spent Last Weeks Grappling"; "A Youth, an Officer and 2 Paths"; Testimony of Darren Wilson to the Grand Jury (September 16, 2015), and Testimony of Dorian Johnson to St. Louis County Police Department (August 13, 2014), both available in "Documents Released in the Ferguson Case," *New York Times*, November 25, 2014, https://www.nytimes.com/interactive/2014/11/25/us/evidence-released-in-michael-brown-case.html; "Why Was Michael Brown's Body Left There for Four Hours?," *SLPD*, September 14, 2014.

15. Reim quoted in William H. Freivogel, "Meacham Park Residents Demand Changes in Mediation Agreement," *St. Louis Beacon*, February 2, 2010.

16. William H. Freivogel, "Kirkwood Agreement Looks toward Better Race Relations," *St. Louis Beacon*, January 22, 2010.

17. US Department of Justice, Community Relations Division, "Mediation Agreement between the City Team of Kirkwood and the Community Team of Kirkwood" (January 22, 2010), http://www.kirkwoodmo.org/mm/files/Mediation%20Agreement.pdf, 1; Tim O'Neil, "Meacham Park Meeting Discusses Race," *SLPD*, February 8, 2008; Freivogel, "Kirkwood Agreement Looks toward Better Race Relations"; Minutes of MPNIA-DOJ Meeting (April 28, 2008), and Meacham Park NIA to William Whitcomb (March 28, 2008), both in Supporting Documents to Mediation Agreement (April 2010), http://www.kirkwoodmo.org/mm/files/Mediation-Agreement-Supporting-Documents.pdf; Jeremy Kohler, "As City Recovers, Racial Tension Remains," *SLPD*, February 15, 2008.

18. US Department of Justice, "Mediation Agreement between the City Team of Kirkwood and the Community Team of Kirkwood," 2–8; Freivogel, "Kirkwood Agreement Looks toward Better Race Relations"; Freivogel, "Meacham Park Residents Demand Changes."

19. See "Former Mayor Swoboda's Death Casts Pall on Kirkwood Healing Meeting," *St. Louis Beacon*, April 2008; William H. Freivogel, "Kirkwood's Journey: Separating Myths and Realities about Meacham Park," *St. Louis Beacon*, February 5, 2010; William H. Freivogel, "Kirkwood Debates Role of Race in Shootings," *St. Louis Beacon*, March 20, 2008; Cooperman, "The Kirkwood Shootings"; complaints submitted to MPNIA (April 2008), in Supporting Documents to Mediation Agreement (April 2010), http://www.kirkwoodmo.org/mm/files/Mediation-Agreement-Supporting -Documents.pdf; O'Neil, "Meacham Park Meeting Discusses Race"; Adam Jadhav, Jake Wagman, and Tim O'Neil, "Shooting Reactions Reveal Racial Divide," *SLPD*, February 9, 2008; "Editorial: Evil Comes Home," *SLPD*, February 10, 2008.

20. "Observations on Social Justice Issues" (n.d.), in Supporting Documents to Mediation Agreement (April 2010), http://www.kirkwoodmo.org/mm/files/Mediation-Agreement-Supporting-Documents.pdf; "Meacham Park: Past, Present, Future," *Webster-Kirkwood Times*, March 21, 2008; Community for Faith and Healing, "Executive Summary of Dialogue Sessions (February–May, 2008)," August 2008, at http://www.cfuh .org/execSummary.pdf (website no longer exists); Kohler, "As City Recovers, Racial Tension Remains"; Freivogel, "Meacham Park Residents Demand Changes."

21. See Nikole Hannah-Jones, "School Segregation, the Continuing Tragedy of Ferguson," *ProPublica*, December 19, 2014.

22. Monica Davey, "Lawsuit Accuses Missouri City of Fining Homeowners to Raise Revenue," *New York Times*, November 4, 2014.

23. Missouri NAACP et al. v. Ferguson-Florissant School District and St. Louis County Board of Elections, United States District Court for the Eastern District of Missouri, Civ. No. 4:14 cv02077.

24. On the recasting of citizenship in the postbellum South, see Eric Foner, *Reconstruction: America's Unfinished Revolution, 1863–1877* (New York: Harper, 2002); C. Vann Woodward, *The Strange Career of Jim Crow* (New York: Oxford University Press, 1955); J. Morgan Kousser, *The Shaping of Southern Politics: Suffrage Restriction and the Establishment of the One-Party South, 1880–1910* (New Haven, CT: Yale University Press, 1974); Robin Einhorn, *American Taxation, American Slavery* (Chicago: University of Chicago Press, 2008).

25. See Khalil Gibran Muhammad, *The Condemnation of Blackness: Race, Crime, and the Making of Modern Urban America* (Cambridge, MA: Harvard University Press, 2011); Ira Katznelson, *Black Men, White Cities: Race, Politics, and Migration in the United States, 1900–30, and Britain, 1948–68* (London: Oxford University Press, 1976); Joseph Heathcott, "Black Archipelago: Politics and Civic Life in the Jim Crow City," *Journal of Social History* 38, no. 3 (Spring 2005): 705–36; David Roediger, *The Wages of Whiteness: Race and the Making of the American Working Class* (London: Verso, 1991); and Matthew Frye Jacobson, *Whiteness of a Different Color: European Immigrants and the Alchemy of Race* (Cambridge, MA: Harvard University Press, 1998). On the roots of housing segregation, see Colin Gordon, *Mapping Decline: St. Louis and the Fate of the American City* (Philadelphia: University of Pennsylvania Press, 2008); Kevin Fox Gotham, *Race, Real Estate, and Uneven Development: The Kansas City Experience, 1900–2000* (Albany, NY: SUNY Press, 2002); Joe Trotter, *Black Milwaukee: The Making of an Industrial Proletariat, 1915–45* (Urbana: University of Illinois Press, 2006).

26. I draw here on George Lipsitz, "The Possessive Investment in Whiteness: Racialized Social Democracy and the 'White' Problem in American Studies," *American Quarterly* 47, no. 3 (September 1995): 369–87; Ira Katznelson, *When Affirmative Action Was White* (New York: W.W. Norton, 2005).

27. See Michelle Wilde Anderson, "Cities Inside Out: Poverty and Exclusion at the Urban Fringe," *UCLA Law Review* 55 (2007–2008): 1095–160.

28. See Andrew Wiese, "Black Housing, White Finance: African American Housing and Home Ownership in Evanston, Illinois, before 1940," *Journal of Social History* 33, no. 2 (Winter 1999): 429–60; and Wiese, "The Other Suburbanites: African American Suburbanization in the North before 1950," *Journal of American History* 85, no. 4 (March 1999): 1495–524.

29. Elizabeth Kneebone and Alan Berube, *Confronting Suburban Poverty in America* (Washington, DC: Brookings, 2014); Scott Allard, *Places in Need: The Changing Geography of Poverty* (New York: Russell Sage, 2017); Margaret Weir, "Creating Justice in the New American Metropolis," in *Justice and the American Metropolis*, ed. Clarissa Rile Hayward and Todd Swanstrom (Minneapolis: University of Minnesota Press, 2011), 251.

30. See Gordon, *Mapping Decline*; and interactive maps at "Mapping Decline," Harvard WorldMap Project, http://worldmap.harvard.edu/maps/866.

31. See Andrew Wiese, "Racial Cleansing in the Suburbs: Suburban Government, Urban Renewal, and Segregation on Long Island, New York, 1945–1960," in *Contested Terrain: Power, Politics, and Participation in Suburbia*, ed. Marc Silver and Martin Melkonian (Westport, CT: Greenwood, 1995); and Donald Clairmont and Dennis William Magill, *Africville: The Life and Death of a Canadian Black Community* (Toronto: McClelland and Stewart, 1974).

32. Jodi Rios, "Everyday Racialization: Contesting Space and Identity in Suburban St. Louis," in *Making Suburbia: New Histories of Everyday America*, ed. John Archer, Paul J. P. Sandul, and Katherine Solomonson (Minneapolis: University of Minnesota Press, 2015), 195.

33. See Gordon, *Mapping Decline*, 71–83; Robert Fogelson, *Bourgeois Nightmares: Suburbia, 1870–1930* (New Haven, CT: Yale University Press, 2005).

34. See Richard Rothstein, *The Color of Law* (New York: Liveright, 2017).

35. *Hearing Before the United States Commission on Civil Rights. Hearing held in St. Louis, Missouri, January 14–17, 1970*, United States Commission on Civil Rights (hereafter cited as USCCR), 304 (1970) (testimony of Adel Allen).

36. US Department of Justice, *Investigation of the Ferguson Police Department*, 2. See also Ta-Nehisi Coates, "The Gangsters of Ferguson," *Atlantic*, March 5, 2015.

37. See Julilly Kohler-Hausmann, *Getting Tough: Welfare and Imprisonment in 1970s America* (Princeton, NJ: Princeton University Press, 2017), 14–16.

38. Charles Tilly, "Democracy Is a Lake," in *The Social Construction of Democracy, 1870–1990*, ed. George Reid Andrews and Herrick Chapman (New York: New York University Press, 1995), 369.

39. T. H. Marshall, *Citizenship and Social Class* (Cambridge: Cambridge University Press, 1950), 47, 18–21.

40. For example, John Rawls, *A Theory of Justice* (Cambridge, MA: Harvard University Press, 1971), 303.

41. Margaret Somers, *Genealogies of Citizenship: Markets, Statelessness, and the Right to Have Rights* (New York: Cambridge University Press, 2008), 6, 136–40. See also Jean Cohen, "Changing Paradigms of Citizenship and the Exclusiveness of the Demos," *International Sociology* 14, no. 3 (September 1999): 245–68.

42. Joe Soss and Suzanne Mettler, "The Consequences of Public Policy for Democratic Citizenship: Bridging Policy Studies and Mass Politics," *Perspective on Politics* 2, no. 1 (March 2004): 56.
43. Marshall, *Citizenship and Social Class*, 24.
44. Sarah Bruch, Myra Marx Ferree, and Joe Soss, "From Policy to Polity: Democracy, Paternalism, and the Incorporation of Disadvantaged Citizens," *American Sociological Review* 75, no. 2 (2010): 205–6.
45. I draw here on Anne Schneider and Helen Ingram, "Social Construction of Target Populations: Implications for Politics and Policy," *American Political Science Review* 87, no. 2 (June 1993): 334–348 (quote on 334). See also Linda Gordon and Nancy Fraser, "Contract vs. Charity: Why Is There No Social Citizenship in the United States?," *Socialist Review* 22 (1992): 45–68.
46. See Joe Soss, "Lessons of Welfare: Policy Design, Political Learning, and Political Action," *American Political Science Review* 93, no. 2 (1999): 363–80; Joe Soss, "Making Clients and Citizens: Welfare Policy as a Source of Status, Belief, and Action," in *Deserving and Entitled: Social Constructions and Public Policy*, ed. Anne Schneider and Helen Ingram (Albany: State University of New York Press, 2005), 291–328; Suzanne Mettler, *Soldiers to Citizens: The GI Bill and the Making of the Greatest Generation* (New York: Oxford University Press, 2007); Gordon and Fraser, "Contract vs. Charity," 45–68; Andrea Campbell, *How Policies Make Citizens: Senior Citizen Activism and the American Welfare State* (Princeton, NJ: Princeton University Press, 2003); Joe Soss, Richard Fording, and Sanford Schram, *Disciplining the Poor: Neoliberal Paternalism and the Persistent Power of Race* (Chicago: University of Chicago Press, 2011); and Bruch, Ferree, and Soss, "From Policy to Polity," 205–6.
47. Charles Epp, Steven Maynard-Moody, and Donald Haider-Markel, *Pulled Over: How Police Stops Define Race and Citizenship* (Chicago: University of Chicago Press, 2014), 5–17.
48. Vesla Weaver, "The Only Government I Know: How the Criminal Justice System Degrades Democratic Citizenship," *Boston Review*, June 2014. See also Vesla Weaver and Amy Lerman, *Arresting Citizenship: The Democratic Consequences of American Crime Control* (Chicago: University of Chicago Press, 2014); Kohler-Hausmann, *Getting Tough*, 13–14.
49. Lee Alston and Joseph Ferrie, "Labor Costs, Paternalism, and Loyalty in Southern Agriculture: A Constraint on the Growth of the Welfare State," *Journal of Economic History* 45, no. 1 (March 1985): 95–117; Gavin Wright, "Postbellum Southern Labor Markets," in *Quantity and Quiddity: Essays in U.S. Economic History in Honor of Stanley Lebergott*, ed. Peter Kilby (Middletown, CT: Wesleyan University Press, 1987); Evelyn Nakano Glenn, *Unequal Freedom: How Race and Gender Shaped American Citizenship and Labor* (Cambridge, MA: Harvard University Press, 2004); Cybelle Fox, *Three Worlds of Relief: Race, Immigration, and the American Welfare State from the Progressive Era to the New Deal* (Princeton, NJ: Princeton University Press, 2012).
50. Judith Shklar, *American Citizenship: The Quest for Inclusion* (Cambridge, MA: Harvard University Press, 1991), 13.
51. On the limits of the Social Security Act, see Ira Katznelson, *Fear Itself: The New Deal and the Origins of Our Time* (New York: Liveright, 2014), 156–94; Gordon and Fraser, "Contract vs. Charity"; Linda Gordon, *Pitied But Not Entitled: Single Mothers and the History of Welfare* (Cambridge, MA: Harvard University Press, 1994); Robert Lieberman, *Shifting the Color Line: Race and the American Welfare State* (Cambridge, MA: Harvard University Press, 2001); Jennifer Klein, *For All These Rights: Business, Labor,*

and the Shaping of America's Public-Private Welfare State (Princeton, NJ: Princeton University Press, 2004); and Colin Gordon, *Dead on Arrival: The Politics of Health Care in Twentieth-Century America* (Princeton, NJ: Princeton University Press, 2004).

52. Jennifer Mittelstadt, "Reimagining the Welfare State," *Jacobin*, July 2015.

53. See Robert Westbrook, "Fighting for the American Family: Private Interests and Political Obligation in World War II," in *The Power of Culture: Critical Essays in American History*, ed. Richard Wightman Fox and T. J. Jackson Lears (Chicago: University of Chicago Press, 1993), 194–221.

54. Somers, *Genealogies of Citizenship*, 1, 132–134.

55. Shklar, *American Citizenship*, 64; see also Nancy MacLean, *Freedom Is Not Enough: The Opening of the American Workplace* (Cambridge, MA: Harvard University Press and Russell Sage, 2006).

56. See Joe Soss and Josh Page, "The Predator State: Race, Class and the New Era of Indentured Citizenship" (prepared for the 2015–2016 Neoliberalism Seminar at CUNY–Hunter College; revised for the Deconstructing Ferguson Meeting at Rutgers, Camden campus, May 2016).

57. See Gordon and Fraser, "Contract vs. Charity," 45–68; Gordon, *Dead on Arrival*, 90–135.

58. See Gerald Frug, "City Services," *New York University Law Review* 73, no. 1 (April 1998): 29–35; and Camille Walsh, *Racial Taxation: Schools, Segregation, and Taxpayer Citizenship, 1869–1973* (Chapel Hill: University of North Carolina Press, 2018).

59. Michael Katz, *The Price of Citizenship: Redefining the American Welfare State* (New York: Henry Holt, 2001), 342–48.

60. See Jacob Hacker, *The Great Risk Shift: The New Economic Insecurity and the Decline of the American Dream* (New York: Oxford University Press, 2008); Arne Kalleberg, *Good Jobs, Bad Jobs: The Rise of Polarized and Precarious Employment Systems in the United States, 1970s–2000s* (New York: Russell Sage Foundation, 2011); and Eva Bertram, "Doors, Floors, Ladders, and Nets: Social Provision in the New American Labor Market," *Politics and Society* 41, no. 1 (2013): 29–72.

61. Somers, *Genealogies of Citizenship*, 2–3. See also Fred Block and Margaret Somers, *The Power of Market Fundamentalism: Karl Polanyi's Critique* (Cambridge, MA: Harvard University Press, 2014); and Soss, Fording, and Schram, *Disciplining the Poor*, 18–52.

62. See Eva Bertram, *The Workfare State: Public Assistance Politics from the New Deal to the New Democrats* (Philadelphia: University of Pennsylvania Press, 2015), 210–41; Elizabeth Anderson, "Welfare, Work Requirements, and Dependant-Care," *Journal of Applied Philosophy* 21, no. 3 (2004): 243–56; Robert Moffitt, "The U.S. Safety Net and Work Incentives: The Great Recession and Beyond," *Journal of Policy Analysis and Management* 34, no. 2 (Spring 2015): 458–66; and Moffitt, "The Deserving Poor, the Family, and the U.S. Welfare System," *Demography* 52, no. 3 (June 2015): 729–49.

63. Martin Gilens and Benjamin Page, "Testing Theories of American Politics: Elites, Interest Groups, and Average Citizens," *Perspectives on Politics* 12, no. 3 (September 2014): 564–81; Jacob Hacker and Paul Pierson, "Winner-Take-All Politics: Public Policy, Political Organization, and the Precipitous Rise of Top Incomes in the United States," *Politics and Society* 38, no. 2 (2010): 152–204; Amy Widestrom, *Displacing Democracy: Economic Segregation in America* (Philadelphia: University of Pennsylvania Press, 2014).

64. Loïc Wacquant, *Punishing the Poor: The Neoliberal Government of Social Insecurity* (Durham, NC: Duke University Press, 2009), 195–208.

65. Soss, Fording, and Schram, *Disciplining the Poor*, 4–9.

66. On the 1930s, see Katznelson, *Fear Itself*, 156–94, and Lieberman, *Shifting the Color Line*. On the modern era, see Michael Brown, *Race, Money, and the American Welfare State* (Ithaca, NY: Cornell University Press, 1999), and Sanford Schram, "Putting a Black Face on Welfare: The Good and the Bad," in *Deserving and Entitled*, ed. Schneider and Ingram, 261–90.

67. See Thomas Sugrue, "The Structures of Urban Poverty: The Reorganization of Space and Work in Three Periods of American History," in *The "Underclass Debate": Views from History*, ed. Michael Katz (Princeton, NJ: Princeton University Press, 1993), 95–117; Somers, *Genealogies of Citizenship*, 63–117; and Joe Soss, "Food Stamp Fables," *Jacobin*, January 16, 2017.

68. See, for example, Marshall, *Citizenship and Social Class*, 12.

69. See Kafui Attoh, "What Kind of Right Is the Right to the City?," *Progress in Human Geography* 35, no. 5 (2011): 669–85; Michael Peter Smith and Michael McQuarrie, "Remaking Urban Citizenship," in *Remaking Urban Citizenship: Organizations, Institutions, and the Right to the City*, ed. Smith and McQuarrie, Comparative Urban and Community Research, vol. 10 (New York: Routledge, 2017), 3–5, 12–15; Anderson, "Cities Inside Out," 1135; and T. Blokland, C. Hentschel, A. Holm, H. Lebuhn, and T. Margalit, "Urban Citizenship and Right to the City: The Fragmentation of Claims," *International Journal of Urban and Regional Research* 39, no. 4 (July 2015): 655–65.

70. Gregory Weiher, *The Fractured Metropolis: Political Fragmentation and Metropolitan Segregation* (Albany: SUNY Press, 1991), 53–59; Richard Thompson Ford, "The Boundaries of Race: Political Geography in Legal Analysis," *Harvard Law Review* 107, no. 8 (June 1994): 1845, 1857–60.

71. Fogelson, *Bourgeois Nightmares*.

72. Nancy Burns, *The Formation of American Local Governments: Private Values in Public Institutions* (New York: Oxford University Press, 1994), 7–9, 19–21, 86–95.

73. Margaret Weir, "Urban Poverty and Defensive Localism," *Dissent*, Summer 1994; Kendra Bischoff and Sean Reardon, "Residential Segregation by Income, 1970–2009," in *Diversity and Disparities: America Enters a New Century*, ed. John R. Logan (New York: Russell Sage, 2014), 208–33; Richard Briffault, "Our Localism: Part I—The Structure of Local Government Law," *Columbia Law Review* 90, no. 1 (January 1990): 1–115; Colin Gordon, "Patchwork Metropolis: Fragmented Governance and Urban Decline in Greater St. Louis," *St. Louis University Public Law Review* 34, no. 1 (2014): 51–71; Widestrom, *Displacing Democracy*, 142–84.

74. Iris Marion Young, "Residential Segregation and Differentiated Citizenship," *Citizenship Studies* 3, no. 2 (1999): 241–42.

75. Michael Danielson, "Differentiation, Segregation, and Political Fragmentation in the American Metropolis," in *Governance and Population: The Governmental Implications of Population Change*, ed. A. E. Keir-Nash (Washington, DC: Government Publishing Office, 1972), 156–57.

76. Susan Bickford, "Constructing Inequality: City Spaces and the Architecture of Citizenship," *Political Theory* 28, no. 3 (June 2000): 360.

77. Patrick Sharkey, *Stuck in Place: Urban Neighborhoods and the End of Progress toward Racial Inequality* (Chicago: University of Chicago Press, 2013); Clarissa Rile Hayward and Todd Swanstrom, "Introduction: Thick Injustice," in *Justice and the American Metropolis*, ed. Hayward and Swanstrom, 6–8.

78. Tony Roshan Samara, "Citizens in Search of a City: Towards a New Infrastructure of Political Belonging," in Smith and McQuarrie, *Remaking Urban Citizenship*, 46–47.

79. Sarah Bruch and Joe Soss, "Schooling as a Formative Political Experience: Authority Relations and the Education of Citizens," *Perspectives on Politics* 16, no. 1 (January 2018): 36–57; Campbell Scribner, *The Fight for Local Control: Schools, Suburbs, and American Democracy* (Ithaca, NY: Cornell University Press, 2016); Annette Lareau, "Schools, Housing, and the Reproduction of Inequality," in *Choosing Homes, Choosing Schools*, ed. Annette Lareau and Kimberly Goyette (New York: Russell Sage, 2014), 169–206; Soss and Mettler, "Consequences of Public Policy for Democratic Citizenship," 56.

80. The classic account is Charles Tiebout, "A Pure Theory of Local Expenditures," *Journal of Political Economy* 64, no. 5 (October 1956): 416–24. For an incisive critique, see Frug, "City Services."

81. Michael Stoll, *Job Sprawl and the Spatial Mismatch between Blacks and Jobs* (Washington, DC: Brookings, 2005); William Julius Wilson, *When Work Disappears: The World of the New Urban Poor* (New York: Vintage, 1996).

82. See L. Owen Kirkpatrick, "Graduated Sovereignty and the Fragmented City: Mapping the Political Geography of Citizenship in Detroit," in *Citizenship and Place*, ed. C. Lyon and A. Goebel (Latham, MD: Rowman and Littlefield, 2018), 71–104.

83. See Richard Thompson Ford, "The Color of Territory: How Law and Borders Keep America Segregated," in *Justice and the American Metropolis*, ed. Hayward and Swanstrom, 223–27.

84. Suzanne Mettler, *Dividing Citizens: Gender and Federalism in New Deal Public Policy* (Ithaca, NY: Cornell University Press, 1998), 12–15.

85. Soss, Fording, and Schram, *Disciplining the Poor*, 83–111 (Theodore Lowi quoted at 83); see also Rachel E. Dwyer and Lora A. Phillips, "The Great Risk Shift and Precarity in the U.S. Housing Market," *Annals of the American Academy of Political and Social Science* 660, no. 1 (July 2015), 199–216.

86. Katherine Newman and Rourke O'Brien, *Taxing the Poor: Doing Damage to the Truly Disadvantaged* (Berkeley: University of California Press, 2011); Institute on Taxation and Economic Policy, *Who Pays? A Distributional Analysis of the Tax Systems in All Fifty States* (Washington, DC: Institute on Taxation and Economic Policy, 2015), https://itep.org/whopays/.

87. Albert Meehan and Michael Ponder, "Race and Place: The Ecology of Racial Profiling African American Motorists," *Justice Quarterly* 19, no. 3 (September 2002): 399–430; Rios, "Everyday Racialization," 192–200.

88. Joel Rogers and Richard Freeman, "The Promise of Progressive Federalism," in *Remaking America: Democracy and Public Policy in an Age of Inequality*, ed. Joe Soss, Jacob Hacker, and Suzanne Mettler (New York: Russell Sage Foundation Press, 2007), 205–27.

89. Linda Lobao and Lazarus Adua, "State Rescaling and Local Governments' Austerity Policies across the USA, 2001–2008," *Cambridge Journal of Regions, Economy and Society* 4, no. 1 (2011): 419–35; Jamie Peck, "Pushing Austerity: State Failure, Municipal Bankruptcy, and the Crises of Fiscal Federalism in the USA," *Cambridge Journal of Regions, Economy and Society* 7, no. 1 (2014): 17–44; Mark Carl Rom, Paul Petersen, and Kenneth Sheve, "Interstate Competition and Welfare Policy," in *Welfare Reform: A Race to the Bottom?*, ed. Sanford Schram and Samuel Beer (Washington, DC: Woodrow Wilson Center Press, 1999), 21–42; Nicholas Johnson, *Laboratories of Underfunding* (Center on Budget and Policy Priorities, 2010); Jiri Jonas, *Great Recession and US Fiscal Squeeze at Subnational Government Level* (New York: International Monetary Fund, 2012): Alex Hertel-Fernandez, "Dismantling Policy through Fiscal Constriction," *Social Service Review* 87, no. 3 (September 2013): 438–76.

90. Dwyer and Phillips, "Great Risk Shift and Precarity in the U.S. Housing Market."
91. See C. Vann Woodward, *The Strange Career of Jim Crow* (New York: Oxford University Press, [1955], 2002); Glenn, *Unequal Freedom*, 52–53; Douglas S. Massey and Nancy A. Denton, *American Apartheid: Segregation and the Making of the Underclass* (Cambridge, MA: Harvard University Press, 1993); Arnold Hirsch, "Choosing Segregation: Federal Housing Policy Between *Shelley* and *Brown*," in *From Tenements to the Taylor Homes: In Search of an Urban Housing Policy in Twentieth-Century America*, ed. John F. Bauman, Roger Biles, and Kristin Szylvian (University Park: Pennsylvania State University Press, 2000), 206–25.
92. Young, "Residential Segregation and Differentiated Citizenship," 238–41; Paul Jargowsky, "Segregation, Neighborhoods, and Schools," in Lareau and Goyette, *Choosing Homes, Choosing Schools*, 97–136; Kendra Bischoff, "School District Fragmentation and Racial Residential Segregation: How Do Boundaries Matter?," *Urban Affairs Review* 44, no. 2 (November 2008): 182–217.
93. Clarissa Hayward, *How Americans Make Race: Stories, Institutions, Spaces* (New York: Cambridge University Press, 2013), 68–69, 192–94. See also Ford, "Boundaries of Race," 1861; and Stephen Macedo, "Property-Owning Plutocracy: Inequality and American Localism," in *Justice and the American Metropolis*, ed. Hayward and Swanstrom, 50.
94. Somers, *Genealogies of Citizenship*, 2–3.
95. Richard Hill, "Separate and Unequal: Governmental Inequality in the Metropolis," *American Political Science Review* 68, no. 4 (December 1974): 1557–68.
96. Ford, "Boundaries of Race," 1852.
97. See Wendy Cheng, *The Changs Next Door to the Diazes: Remapping Race in Suburban California* (Minneapolis: University of Minnesota Press, 2013), 10–11 (quote); and Douglas Massey, "Residential Segregation is the Linchpin of Racial Stratification," *City and Community* 15, no. 1 (March 2016): 4–7.
98. Margaret Jane Radin, "Property and Personhood," *Stanford Law Review* 34, no. 5 (May 1982): 957–1015; Dianne Harris, *Little White Houses: How the Postwar Home Constructed Race in America* (Minneapolis: University of Minnesota Press, 2013); Hayward, *How Americans Make Race*, 111–50.
99. This echoes our understanding of the punitive turn in social policy, in which changing economic circumstances yield new strategies for regulating, disciplining, or punishing the poor. See, for example, Loïc Wacquant, "Crafting the Neoliberal State: Workfare, Prisonfare, and Social Insecurity," *Sociological Forum* 25, no. 2 (June 2010): 197–220; and Wacquant, "Class, Race and Hyperincarceration in Revanchist America," *Daedalus* 139, no. 3 (Summer 2010): 74–90.

CHAPTER ONE

1. Margaret Somers, *Genealogies of Citizenship: Markets, Statelessness, and the Right to Have Rights* (Cambridge: Cambridge University Press, 2008), 21. See also Richard Briffault, "The Local Government Boundary Problem in Metropolitan Areas," *Stanford Law Review* 48, no. 5 (May 1996): 1115–71.
2. *Milliken v. Bradley*, 418 U.S. 717 (1974), overturned a lower court decision that had held that city and suburban school districts were culpable in the segregation of Detroit-area schools. See Richard Thompson Ford, "The Boundaries of Race: Political Geography in Legal Analysis," *Harvard Law Review* 107, no. 8 (June 1994): 1874–76.
3. Quoted in Michael Danielson, "Differentiation, Segregation, and Political Fragmentation in the American Metropolis," in *Governance and Population: The Governmental*

Implications of Population Change, ed. A. E. Keir-Nash (Washington, DC: Government Printing Office, 1972), 151; see also Bryan Ellickson, "Jurisdictional Fragmentation and Residential Choice," *American Economic Review* 61, no. 2 (May 1971): 334–39.

4. Stephen Macedo, "Property-Owning Plutocracy: Inequality and American Localism," in *Justice and the American Metropolis*, ed. Clarissa Rile Hayward and Todd Swanstrom (Minneapolis: University of Minnesota Press, 2011), 46–47, 50; see also Margaret Weir, "Urban Poverty and Defensive Localism," *Dissent*, Summer 1994.

5. See Michelle Wilde Anderson, "Cities Inside Out: Poverty and Exclusion at the Urban Fringe," *UCLA Law Review* 55 (2007–2008): 1113–14; Daniel T. Lichter, Domenico Parisi, Steven Michael Grice, and Michael Taquino, "Municipal Underbounding: Annexation and Racial Exclusion in Small Southern Towns," *Rural Sociology* 72, no. 1 (March 2007): 47–48, 51.

6. E. Terrence Jones, *Fragmented by Design: Why St. Louis Has So Many Governments* (St. Louis: Palmerston and Reed, 2000), 2–3; Truman Port Young, "The Scheme of Separation of City and County Government in St. Louis—Its History and Purposes," *Proceedings of the American Political Science Association* 8 (1911): 100; US Advisory Commission on Intergovernmental Relations, *Local Government Autonomy: Needs for Constitutional, Statutory, and Judicial Clarification* (Washington, DC: The Committee, 1993), 41.

7. Port Young, "Scheme of Separation of City and County Government."

8. For the pace of development within the 1876 boundaries, see the Wayman map, which documents each subdivision, addition, and re-subdivision of property made in the city of St. Louis after 1816. Washington University Libraries, http://omeka.wustl .edu/omeka/exhibits/show/wayman_map/wayman_map_home.

9. Henry Schmandt, "Municipal Home Rule in Missouri," *Washington University Law Review* 4 (1953): 385; Missouri Constitution, art. VI (local government), § 19.

10. In 1920, the African American population of St. Louis was about seventy thousand, or 10 percent of the city's total population; in 1950 it was over 150,000, almost 20 percent of the city's population. Census county totals from Steven Manson, Jonathan Schroeder, David Van Riper, and Steven Ruggles, IPUMS National Historical Geographic Information System (database), version 13.0 (Minneapolis: University of Minnesota, 2018), http://doi.org/10.18128/D050.V13.0.

11. David Freund, *Colored Property: State Policy and White Racial Politics in Suburban America* (Chicago: University of Chicago Press, 2007), 48–53.

12. See Colin Gordon, *Mapping Decline: St. Louis and the Fate of the American City* (Philadelphia: University of Pennsylvania Press, 2008), 35–46, 129–31.

13. Jon Teaford, *City and Suburb: The Political Fragmentation of Metropolitan America, 1850–1970* (Baltimore: Johns Hopkins University Press, 1979), 5–31; Ford, "Boundaries of Race," 1863–64.

14. In 1900, the incorporated municipalities were Bridgeton, Fenton, Ferguson, Florissant, Kirkwood, and Webster Groves; in 1930, these six had been joined by Brentwood, Clayton, Glendale, Huntleigh, Maplewood, Oakland, Olivette, Richmond Heights, Rock Hill, Shrewsbury, University City, and Valley Park. See E. Terrence Jones, "The Municipal Market in the St. Louis Region, 1950–2000," in *St. Louis Metromorphosis: Past Trends and Future Directions*, ed. Brady Baybeck and Terrence Jones (St. Louis: Missouri Historical Society Press, 2004), 276–77.

15. Land Clearance for Redevelopment Authority of University City, "A New Vision for University City," 1963, 4, box 24, S0074, St. Louis County Municipalities Collection (hereafter cited as SLCMC), 1930–1976, Western Historical Manuscripts Collection,

State Historical Society of Missouri, University of Missouri–St. Louis (hereafter cited as UMSL); Terrence Jones and Donald Phares, "Missouri," in *Home Rule in America: A Fifty State Handbook*, ed. Dale Krane, Platon Rigos, and Melvin Hill (Washington, DC: Congressional Quarterly Press, 2001), 243.

16. "Problems Involved in Annexation of Unincorporated Area to the North [Webster Groves]," 1950, vol. 64, ser. 2 (Black), Harland Bartholomew Papers, Washington University Archives; St. Louis County Planning Department, "Kinloch Phase 1: Sketch for Community Development," October 1970, folder 506, ser. 4 (roll 21), James Symington Papers, Western Historical Manuscripts Collection–St. Louis (hereafter cited as WHMC), UMSL; Elwood Street, "Community Organization in Greater St. Louis," *Social Forces* 6, no. 2 (December 1927): 249 (quote).

17. Richard Briffault, "Our Localism: Part I—The Structure of Local Government Law," *Columbia Law Review* 90, no. 1 (January 1990): 18–72; Bernard Frieden, *Metropolitan America: Challenge to Federalism* (Washington, DC: Advisory Committee on Intergovernmental Relations, 1966), 17; Kenneth Jackson, *Crabgrass Frontier: The Suburbanization of the United States* (New York: Oxford University Press, 1987), 116–218; Jane Jacobs, *The Death and Life of Great American Cities* (New York: Random House, 1961), 141–51; Richard Briffault, "Our Localism: Part II—Localism and Legal Theory," *Columbia Law Review* 90, no. 2 (March 1990): 346–49.

18. For this history, see Freund, *Colored Property*; Amy Hillier, "Searching for Red Lines: Spatial Analysis of Lending Patterns in Philadelphia, 1940–1960," *Pennsylvania History* 72, no. 1 (Winter 2005): 25–47; Jackson, *Crabgrass Frontier*, 190–208; Kenneth Jackson, "Race, Ethnicity, and Real Estate Appraisal: The Home Owners Loan Corporation and the Federal Housing Administration," *Journal of Urban History* 6, no. 4 (August 1980): 431–32; Thomas Hanchett, "The Other 'Subsidized Housing': Federal Aid to Suburbanization, 1940s to 1960s," in *From Tenements to the Taylor Homes: In Search of an Urban Housing Policy in Twentieth-Century America*, ed. John Bauman, Roger Biles, and Kristin Szylvain (University Park: Pennsylvania State University Press, 2000); and Gordon, *Mapping Decline*, 88–98.

19. Rose Helper, *Racial Policies and Practices of Real Estate Brokers* (Minneapolis: University of Minnesota Press, 1969); Briffault, "Our Localism: Part I," 1–3, 21–22, 42–56, 58; Howard Lee McBain, *American City Progress and the Law* (New York: Columbia University Press, 1918), 98–115; Lyle Schaller, "Home Rule—A Critical Appraisal," *Political Science Quarterly* 76, no. 3 (September 1961), 409–10; Myron Orfield, *Metropolitics: A Regional Agenda for Community and Stability* (Washington, DC: Brookings Institution Press, 1997), 58–63; Jackson, *Crabgrass Frontier*, 206–8.

20. See Gordon, *Mapping Decline*, 112–52. For these examples, see "Kinloch" clipping (n.d.), and "Kinloch: Yesterday, Today, and Tomorrow," 1983, both in box 2:23, SLCMC, WHMC; Jones, *Fragmented by Design*, 30–33; Dennis Judd, "The Role of Governmental Policies in Promoting Residential Segregation in the St. Louis Metropolitan Area," *Journal of Negro Education* 66, no. 3 (Summer 1997): 235–36; Transcript of the Record, *City of Moline Acres v. Heidbreder* (1963), RG 600, Supreme Court Judicial Case Files, Missouri State Archives, Jefferson City; Metropolitan St. Louis Survey, *Path of Progress for Metropolitan St. Louis* (University City: St. Louis Survey, 1957), 85–87; and Gordon, *Mapping Decline*, 145–52.

21. On this early era, see John McKerley, "Citizens and Strangers: The Politics of Race in Missouri from Slavery to the Era of Jim Crow" (PhD diss., University of Iowa [History], 2008); and Eric Sandweiss, *St. Louis: The Evolution of an American Urban Landscape* (Philadelphia: Temple University Press, 2001).

22. See John A. Wright, *St. Louis: Disappearing Black Communities* (Chicago: Arcadia, 2004). On the general pattern of such developments, see Leonard Blumberg and Michael Lalli, "Little Ghettoes: A Study of Negroes in the Suburbs," *Phylon* 27, no. 2 (Summer 1966): 125; Leonard Blumberg, "Segregated Housing, Marginal Location, and the Crisis of Confidence," *Phylon* 25, no. 4 (Winter 1964): 325–26; and Jack Pyburn, "Confronting Suburban Deterioration" (master's thesis, Architecture and Urban Design, Washington University, 1973), 10–11, 14, 21.

23. Lonnie Speer, *Meacham Park: A History* (self-pub., 1998), 1–9; Ida Scott, *The History of Elmwood Park* (self-pub., 2004), 8.

24. Gladys Gray Jones, "Elmwood Park Development Has Interesting History," *Pittsburgh Courier* (1911–1950), November 22, 1947, city edition, accessed December 1, 2009, http://www.proquest.com/.

25. Barbara Kodner, *Olivette: Chronicle of a Country Village* (Gerald, MO: Patrice Press, 1979), 28; Scott, *History of Elmwood Park*, 9–10; "Meacham Park: A History of American Change," *Webster-Kirkwood Times*, November 14–20, 1986, reprinted March 21, 2008.

26. All demographics calculated from manuscript census, 1910–1940, for Elmwood Park enumeration districts, accessed from ancestry.com/search/categories/usfedcen/.

27. St. Louis County Department of Planning, *Meacham '76: A Community Plan* (Clayton: St. Louis County, 1976), 6, folder 36, Kay Drey Papers, WHMC.

28. Ida Scott Oral History (transcript of interview by Doris Wesley, November 1996), box 4, folder 76, Lift Every Voice and Sing Oral History Project (SO609), WHMC; Kodner, *Olivette*, 71–72.

29. Marc Weiss, *The Rise of the Community Builders: The American Real Estate Industry and Urban Land Planning* (New York: Columbia University Press, 1987).

30. "Regulations Governing the Subdivision of Land in the Unincorporated Portions of St. Louis County," June 1940, Correspondence Files, reel 12; St. Louis Planning Commission, "A Preliminary Report on Zoning Problems: St. Louis County," February 1940, Black Binders, 50:3; St. Louis County Planning Commission to Bartholomew, August 10, 1940, Correspondence Files, reel 12; "A Report Upon the Proposed Zoning Regulations for the Unincorporated Areas of St. Louis County," October 1944, Black Binders, 50:3; and "Zoning Order for the Unincorporated Portions of St. Louis County," June 1946, Black Binders, 50:3, all in the Harland Bartholomew Papers, Washington University Archives.

31. *Globe-Democrat* clipping, June 21, 1961, reprinted in Scott, *History of Elmwood Park*, 57.

32. Gordon, *Mapping Decline*, 112–52; Steven Goldberg, "Annexations in Urban Counties: Missouri's Scheme and a Plan for Reform," *Washington University Journal of Urban and Contemporary Law* 29 (1995), 187–226; Illene Dubrow, "Municipal Antagonism or Benign Neglect: Racial Motivations in Municipal Annexations in St. Louis County, Missouri," *Journal of Urban Law* 53, no. 245 (1975–76): 250–52.

33. "Overland," n.d., box 20, folder 226; and "Overland: Trials and Trails," 1956, box 20, folder 234, St. Louis Counties Municipalities Collection, 1930–1976 (SL 74), WHMC. The details of incorporation and annexation in Overland, Olivette, Kirkwood, Crestwood, and Sunset Hills rely on a review of local ordinances by Carolyn Nolan of the St. Louis County Department of Planning. I am indebted to Carolyn for sharing these documents with me.

34. "Olivette: A Brief History of Its Development," 2005, box 19, folder 206, St. Louis Counties Municipalities Collection, 1930–1976 (SL 74), WHMC; "A Preliminary

Report on the Proposed Zoning Ordinance, Olivette, Missouri," August 1939, Black Binders, 46:2, Bartholomew Papers.

35. In 1953, Olivette attempted to annex three hundred acres to the west, a gambit that both neighboring Creve Coeur and St. Louis County viewed as an effort to capture the area's substantial commercial-tax base (which included Monsanto). This dragged through the courts, a case (*Olivette v. Graeler*) that Olivette ultimately lost in 1963 (in 1966, the land was annexed to Creve Coeur). See Gordon, *Mapping Decline*, 143–44.

36. "In the Matter of Additions and Properties within the Corporate Limits of the Town of Olivette," St. Louis County Court, September 11, 1950, in documents collected by Carolyn Nolan for Olivette Annexation History, St. Louis County Department of Planning, September 2010.

37. Olivette Annexation History, St. Louis County Department of Planning, September 2010; Ida Scott Oral History, WHMC; "In the Matter of the Incorporation of Additions and Properties within the Corporate Limits of the Town of Olivette," Certified Copy of Order, County Council of the County of St. Louis, June 22, 1955; "An Ordinance Certifying the Results of a Special Collection in the City of Overland, Missouri, Extending the Boundaries of the City of Overland," December 12, 1950; E. V. Lambrechts, "Highlight in the History of Olivette," 1963, box 19, folder 210, St. Louis Counties Municipalities Collection; *Hearings: St. Louis*, USCCR, 400–401 (January 1970) (testimony of Olivette officials); Dubrow, "Municipal Antagonism or Benign Neglect," 257–58; *Hearings: St. Louis*, USCCR, 384–85 (January 1970) (testimony of Herman Davis); Donald Hagman, "The Use of Boundary Lines to Discriminate in the Provision of Services by Race," *University of Detroit Journal of Urban Law* 54 (1976–77): 854.

38. "A Preliminary Report on the Proposed Zoning Ordinance, Olivette, Missouri," August 1939, Black Binders, 46:2, Bartholomew Papers; Dubrow, "Municipal Antagonism or Benign Neglect," 263–64; "Urban Renewal Plan: Elmwood Park," Project MO R-10, October 1962, *Brooks v. LCRA* case file, RG 600, Missouri State Archives; "A Report Upon the Proposed Zoning Ordinance: Olivette, Missouri," 1970, Brown Binders, 50:3, Bartholomew Papers.

39. Kirkwood Annexation History, St. Louis County Department of Planning, October 2010; Sunset Hills Annexation History, St. Louis County Department of Planning, September 2010; Crestwood Annexation History, St. Louis County Department of Planning, September 2010. Annexation histories and documents were compiled by Carolyn Nolan of the St. Louis County Department of Planning and provided to the author.

40. Dubrow, "Municipal Antagonism or Benign Neglect," 266–67; Speer, *Meacham Park*, 43; Kirkwood League to Mrs. Lloyd Thomas, March 1968, folder 190, Metropolitan League of Women Voters Records, WHMC; "Black Power Movement Affected Meacham Park," *Webster-Kirkwood Times*, November 14–20, 1986, reprinted March 21, 2008; "Rundown Meacham Park Finds Friend: Kirkwood," Nov. 1960 clipping, folder 190, League of Women Voters Records.

41. "Minutes of a Regular Meeting of the Land Clearance for Redevelopment Authority of St. Louis County," September 26, 1956, Records of the St. Louis County LCRA (hereafter cited as County LCRA Records), St. Louis County Economic Council, Clayton, MO; Speer, *Meacham Park*, 43.

42. Quoted in Dubrow, "Municipal Antagonism or Benign Neglect," 271.

43. "Tragic Fire Spurred Kirkwood Interest in Meacham Park," *Webster-Kirkwood Times*, November 14–20, 1986, reprinted March 21, 2008.

44. Dubrow, "Municipal Antagonism or Benign Neglect," 269; St. Louis County Department of Planning, *Meacham '76*, 1, 6–7; "Meacham Park: Annexation Ideas Failed in the 1970s," *Webster-Kirkwood Times*, November 14–20, 1986, reprinted March 21, 2008.

45. "Kirkwood Begins Bid to Annex Meacham Park," *SLPD*, May 2, 1991; "Council OKs Meacham Park Plan," *SLPD*, May 6, 1991; "Mayor Cites Reasons to Back Annexation of Meacham Park," *SLPD*, May 16, 1991; "Boundary Panel to Meet with Officials," *SLPD*, July 29, 1991; "Council Votes to Adopt Plan of Meacham Park Residents," *SLPD*, August 19, 1991.

46. "Council OKs Meacham Park Plan," *SLPD*; "Meacham Park Joins Municipality," *SLPD*, November 11, 1991.

47. See William H. Freivogel, "Kirkwood's Journey: Separating Myths and Realities about Meacham Park, Thornton, Part 2," *St. Louis Beacon*, February 7, 2010; Tim O'Neil, "Meacham Park Meeting Discusses Race," *SLPD*, February 8, 2008; Jeremy Kohler, "As City Recovers, Racial Tension Remains," *SLPD*, February 15, 2008; and "Racial Tensions Might Have Sparked Kirkwood Shooting," *Columbia Missourian*, February 11, 2008.

CHAPTER TWO

1. Jessica Trounstine, "Segregation and Inequality in Public Goods," *American Journal of Political Science* 60, no. 3 (July 2016): 709–10; Robert L. Lineberry, "Mandating Urban Equality: The Distribution of Municipal Public Services," *Texas Law Review* 53 (1974): 26, 5.

2. See Gerald Frug, "City Services," *New York University Law Review* 73, no. 1 (April 1998).

3. See L. Owen Kirkpatrick, "Graduated Sovereignty and the Fragmented City: Mapping the Political Geography of Citizenship in Detroit," in *Citizenship and Place*, ed. C. Lyon and A. Goebel (Latham, MD: Rowan and Littlefield, forthcoming).

4. Michelle Wilde Anderson, "Mapped out of Local Democracy," *Stanford. Law Review* 62, no. 4 (2009): 940–41; Ralph S. Abascal, "Municipal Services and Equal Protection: Variations on a Theme By Griffin v. Illinois," *Hastings Law Journal* 20, no. 4 (1969): 1391–92.

5. Missouri Advisory Committee to the USCCR, *School Desegregation in the St. Louis and Kansas City Areas* (Washington, DC: USCCR, January 1981), 2.

6. *Hearing in St. Louis, 1970*, USCCR, 384–85 (1970) (testimony of Herman Davis); *Hearing in St. Louis, 1970*, USCCR, 304–5 (testimony of Adel Allen).

7. "Tragic Fire Spurred Kirkwood Interest in Meacham Park," *Webster-Kirkwood Times*, November 14–20, 1986, reprinted March 21, 2008; *Globe-Democrat* clipping, June 21, 1961, reprinted in Ida Scott, *The History of Elmwood Park* (self-pub., 2004), 57.

8. Illene Dubrow, "Municipal Antagonism or Benign Neglect: Racial Motivations in Municipal Annexations in St. Louis County Missouri," *Journal of Urban Law* 53, no. 245 (1975–76): 272–73.

9. Ben A. Rich, "Equal Protection as a Means of Securing Adequate Municipal Services," *Urban Law Annual* (January 1973): 277–78; Michael P. Schumaecker, "Equal Protection: The Right to Equal Municipal Services," *Brookings Law Review* 37 (1971): 568, 587.

10. "The Right to Adequate Municipal Services: Thoughts and Proposals," *New York University Law Review* 44 (1969): 757–74; John Yinger, "State Aid and the Pursuit of Educational Equity," in *Helping Children Left Behind: State Aid and the Pursuit of Educational Equity*, ed. John Yinger (Cambridge, MA: MIT Press, 2014), 3–58.

11. Abascal, "Municipal Services and Equal Protection," 1388; Mary Bowen Little, "Potholes, Lampposts and Policemen: Equal Protection and the Financing of Basic Municipal Services in the Wake of Hawkins and Serrano," *Villanova Law Review* 17 (1972): 655, 687.

12. Andrew Hawkins et al., Plaintiffs-appellants, v. Town of Shaw, Mississippi, et al., Defendants-appellees, 437 F.2d 1286 (5th Cir. 1971).

13. Frug, "City Services," 42.

14. See *Hawkins v. Town of Shaw*, 437 F.2d 1286 (5th Cir. 1971); Kenneth W. Barton, "Equal Municipal Services for the Other Side of the Tracks," *Mississippi Law Journal* 43 (1972): 89; Little, "Potholes, Lampposts and Policemen," 687; and Michelle Wilde Anderson, "Cities Inside Out: Poverty and Exclusion at the Urban Fringe," *UCLA Law Review* 55 (2007–2008): 1111–12.

15. "Why We Should Have a Public Housing Project in North Webster Heights," 1956, box 12a, folder 1, St. Louis Urban League Papers, Washington University Special Collections.

16. Amy Gutmann, *Democratic Education* (Princeton, NJ: Princeton University Press, 1987), 136; see also Sarah Bruch and Joe Soss, "Schooling as a Formative Political Experience: Authority Relations and the Education of Citizens," *Perspectives on Politics* 16, no. 1 (January 2018): 36–57.

17. Gary Orfield, "The Housing Issues in the St. Louis Case," report to Judge William Hungate, US District Court (St. Louis, MO), *Liddell v. Board of Education* (April 1981); Carla Shedd, *Unequal City: Race, Schools, and Perceptions of Injustice* (New York: Russell Sage, 2015); Ansley Erickson, *Making the Unequal Metropolis: School Desegregation and Its Limits* (Chicago: University of Chicago Press, 2016).

18. For a concise summary, see Sean Reardon, "School Segregation and Racial Academic Achievement Gaps," *RSJ: Russell Sage Foundation Journal of the Social Sciences* 2, no. 5 (September 2016): 14–57.

19. See Gary Orfield, Jongyeon Ee, Erica Frankenberg, and Genevieve Siegel-Hawley, *Brown at 62: School Segregation by Race, Poverty, and State*, UCLA Civil Rights Project /Proyecto Derechos Civiles, May 16, 2016, https://www.civilrightsproject.ucla.edu /research/k-12-education/integration-and-diversity/brown-at-62-school-segregation -by-race-poverty-and-state; Sean F. Reardon, Elena Grewal, Demetra Kalogrides, and Erica Greenberg, "Brown Fades: The End of Court-Ordered School Desegregation and the Resegregation of American Public Schools," *Journal of Policy Analysis and Management* 31, no. 4 (Fall 2012): 876–904; and USCCR, *Public Education Funding Inequity in an Era of Increasing Concentration of Poverty and Resegregation* (Washington, DC: USCCR, January 2018).

20. Melanie Adams, "Advocating for Educational Equity: African-American Citizen's Councils in St. Louis, Missouri, from 1864 to 1927" (PhD diss., Education, University of Missouri–St. Louis, 2014); Claude Weathersby, "School Conversions in the Segregated St. Louis Public Schools District Prior to the Historic *Brown v. Board of Education* Ruling: An Urban School System's Response to the Migration of African Americans from the Rural South," *Journal of Urban History* 43, no. 2 (2017), 294–311.

21. Aaron Taylor, "Segregation, Education, and Blurring of Lines of Division in St. Louis," *St. Louis University Public Law Review* 33, no. 1 (2013–2014): 185; Gerald Heaney and Susan Uchitelle, *Unending Struggle: The Long Road to an Equal Education in St. Louis* (St. Louis: Reedy Press, 2004), 57.

22. Campbell Scribner, *The Fight for Local Control: Schools, Suburbs, and American Democracy* (Ithaca, NY: Cornell University Press, 2016), 9; Erica Frankenberg, "Splintering

School Districts: Understanding the Link between Segregation and Fragmentation," *Law & Social Inquiry* 34, no. 4 (Fall 2009): 869–909; David R. James, "City Limits on Racial Equality: The Effects of City-Suburb Boundaries on Public-School Desegregation, 1968–1976," *American Sociological Review* 54, no. 6 (December 1989): 963–85.

23. R. L'Heureux Lewis-McCoy, "Suburban Black Lives Matter," *Urban Education* 53, no. 2 (2018): 145–61; Heaney and Uchitelle, *Unending Struggle*, 60.

24. Heaney and Uchitelle, *Unending Struggle*, 63.

25. St. Louis Board of Education, "Desegregation Program," June 17, 1954, box 9, folder 2, St. Louis Urban League Papers; William Freivogel, "St. Louis: Desegregation and School Choice in the Land of Dred Scott," in *Divided We Fail: Coming Together through Public School Choice* (New York: Century Foundation, 2002), 209–35; Heaney and Uchitelle, *Unending Struggle*, 71–76; Missouri Advisory Committee to the USCCR, *School Desegregation in the St. Louis and Kansas City Areas*; Justin Smith, "Hostile Takeover: The State of Missouri, the St. Louis School District, and the Struggle for Quality Education in the Inner-City," *Missouri. Law Review* 74 (2009): 1149; USCCR, *Racial Isolation in the Public Schools* (Washington, DC: USCCR, 1967), 4, 60.

26. Leo Bohanon, "Negro Housing Problem vs. Discriminatory Public Housing Policy (the St. Louis Situation)," December 1951, box 12a, folder 1, St. Louis Urban League Papers; "Notes for School integration" (n.d), box 9, folder 2, St. Louis Urban League Papers; Orfield, 102–4, 110–11, 124.

27. "Notes for School Integration," n.d., box 9, folder 2, St. Louis Urban League Papers; Smith, "Hostile Takeover," 1149–51; Leo Bohanon, "Complaints Against the St. Louis School System," November 1959, box 8, folder 25, St. Louis Urban League Papers; Press Release, Alderman William Clay, March 1963, box 8a, folder 5, St. Louis Urban League Papers.

28. Colin Gordon, *Mapping Decline: St. Louis and the Fate of the American City* (Philadelphia: University of Pennsylvania Press, 2008), 112–52.

29. Orfield, "Housing Issues in the St. Louis Case," 10–11, 105–8, 114–17, Missouri Housing Development Commission member quoted at 119.

30. These eighteen districts were Affton, Bayless, Brentwood, Ferguson, Florissant, Hancock Place, Hazelwood, Jennings, Ladue, Lindbergh, Maplewood-Richmond Heights, Mehlville, Normandy, Parkway-Riverview Gardens, Rockwood, Valley Park, Webster Groves, and Wellston.

31. USCCR, *School Desegregation in the St. Louis and Kansas City Areas*; Orfield, "Housing Issues in the St. Louis Case," 1–4, 9–10; *Liddell v. Board of Education*, 491 F.Supp. 351 (E.D.MO. 1980); Missouri Advisory Committee to the USCCR, *School Desegregation in the St. Louis and Kansas City Areas*, 3; Heaney and Uchitelle, *Unending Struggle*, 112–13, 118–19.

32. Heaney and Uchitelle, *Unending Struggle*, 87–88, 122–23; Freivogel, "St. Louis: Desegregation and School Choice"; Amy Stuart Wells, "St. Louis Evaluates Its Pioneer Integration Plan," *New York Times*, June 8, 1988; Department of Justice, "Settlement Reached in St. Louis School Desegregation Case," 1999, http://www.justice.gov/opa/pr/1999/January/003cr.htm.

33. See Lewis-McCoy, "Suburban Black Lives Matter," 146–49; Jack Dougherty, "Shopping for Schools: How Public Education and Private Housing Shaped Suburban Connecticut," *Journal of Urban History* 38, no. 2 (2012): 205–24.

34. "A Preliminary Report Upon the Location of Elementary School Buildings: Olivette School District," September 1945, Black Binders, 46:2, Harland Bartholomew Papers, Washington University Archives; Patricia Lewis Williamson, *Ritenour: Our First*

132 Years (Overland, MO: Ritenour School District, 1978), 9–10, 16–18, 20–24, 30; Barbara Kodner, *Olivette: Chronicle of a Country Village* (Gerald, MO: Patrice Press, 1979), 2.

35. Lonnie Speer, *Meacham Park: A History* (self-pub., 1998), 15–20; "Meacham Park: A History of American Change," *Webster-Kirkwood Times*, November 14–20, 1986, reprinted March 21, 2008; USCCR, *School Desegregation in Kirkwood, Missouri* (Washington, DC: USCCR, July 1977), 2.

36. Scott, *History of Elmwood Park*, 17–18; Williamson, *Ritenour: Our First 132 Years*, 37.

37. *Hearing in St. Louis, 1970*, USCCR, 307 (testimony of Adel Allen).

38. Minutes of Kirkwood R-7 School District, July 12, 1954, reel 42506, St. Louis County Records, Missouri State Archives; Jeannette Cooperman, "The Kirkwood Shootings," *St. Louis Magazine*, May 2008; USCCR, *School Desegregation in Kirkwood, Missouri*, 2, 6 (Table 2), 7–8, 9–11.

39. Brenda Biles and James Ward, "A Guide to Missouri School Finance," 1981, American Federation of Teachers, https://files.eric.ed.gov/fulltext/ED208546.pdf; Missouri Budget Project, "A Shaky Foundation: Missouri Underfunding the School Formula," 2014, https://www.mobudget.org/files/A_Shaky_Foundation.pdf; Peter West, "Judge in Missouri Strikes the State's Finance Formula," *Education Week*, January 1993.

40. *United States v. State of Missouri*, 363 F. Supp. 739 (1973).

41. *United States v. State of Missouri*, 363 F. Supp. 739 (1973).

42. Education Field Services, Graduate School of Education, University of Chicago, *School District Organization in St. Louis County Missouri* (Chicago: Education Field Services, 1962), 17.

43. *United States v. State of Missouri*, 363 F. Supp. 739 (1973), quoting Dr. Clifford Hooker, the plaintiff's expert witness.

44. Education Field Services, *School District Organization in St. Louis County Missouri*, 48.

45. *United States v. State of Missouri et al.*, 515 F.2d 1365 (1975).

46. HOLC 1940 description for area C25, Records of the Home Owners' Loan Corporation (HOLC), 195.3, Records of the Federal Home Loan Bank Board, RG 195, National Archives, College Park, MD.

47. Nikole Hannah-Jones, "School Segregation, the Continuing Tragedy of Ferguson," *ProPublica*, December 19, 2014.

48. Nadav Shoked, "An American Oddity: The Law, History, and Toll of the School District," *Northwestern University Law Review* 111, no. 4 (2017): 997–1000.

49. Plaintiffs Trial Brief, *Missouri State Conference of the National Association for the Advancement of Colored People, Redditt Hudson, F. Willis Johnson, and Doris Bailey v Ferguson-Florissant School District and St. Louis County Board of Election Commissioners*, United States District Court for the Eastern District of Missouri, Civ. No. 14–2077 (2015); Colin Gordon, "Segregation and Uneven Development in Greater St. Louis, St. Louis County, and the Ferguson-Florissant School District," Expert Report submitted on behalf of plaintiffs in *Missouri NAACP et al. v. Ferguson-Florissant School District* (May 2015).

50. United States, District Court, Eastern District of Missouri, Eastern Division, Remedial Order, *Missouri NAACP et al. v. Ferguson-Florissant School District*, Case No. 4:14 CV 2077 RWS (November 2016), available at https://www.aclu-mo.org/sites/default/files/field_documents/ferguson_florissant_remedy_nov._2016_0.pdf.

51. Lindsey McLure Hartman, "Not in My Backyard: *Turner v. Clayton* and the Battle over Mandatory Open Enrollment," *Saint Louis University Public Law Review* 32, no. 1 (2012), 199–229; D. J. Wilson, "Five Years into the Turner Case the Fate of St. Louis

Schools Remains in Question," *St. Louis Magazine*, August 2012; Taylor, "Segregation, Education, and Blurring of Lines of Division," 183; Elisa Crouch, "Student Transfer Ruling Is Reversed by Missouri Supreme Court," *SLPD*, June 2013; Hannah-Jones, "School Segregation, the Continuing Tragedy of Ferguson."

52. Hannah-Jones, "School Segregation, the Continuing Tragedy of Ferguson." See also Chris McDaniel, "Francis Howell Parents Express Outrage Over Incoming Normandy Students," St. Louis Public Radio, July 2013, http://news.stlpublicradio.org /post/francis-howell-parents-express-outrage-over-incoming-normandy-students #stream/0; Nikole Hannah-Jones, "The Problem We All Live With," *This American Life*, July 2015, https://www.thisamericanlife.org/radio-archives/episode/562/the -problem-we-all-live-with.

53. Hannah-Jones, "School Segregation, the Continuing Tragedy of Ferguson"; Order and Judgment, *Janine Massey et al. v. Normandy School Collaborative*, Circuit Court of St. Louis County, Case 14SL-CCO2359.

54. Joe Soss and Vesla Weaver, "Police Are Our Government: Politics, Political Science, and the Policing of Race-Class Subjugated Communities," *Annual Review of Political Science* 20 (2017): 567–69, 574.

55. See Andrea S. Boyles, *Race, Place, and Suburban Policing* (Berkeley: University of California Press, 2015); Soss and Weaver, "Police Are Our Government," 573; Bennett Capers, "Policing, Race, and Place," *Harvard Civil Rights–Civil Liberties Law Review* 44 (2009): 65–66; Jeffrey Fagan and Garth Davies, "Street Stops and Broken Windows: *Terry*, Race, and Disorder in New York City," *Fordham Urban Law Review* 28, no. 2 (2000): 457–503; Albert J. Meehan and Michael C. Ponder, "Race and Place: The Ecology of Racial Profiling of African American Motorists," *Justice Quarterly* 19, no. 3 (2002): 399–430.

56. *Hearing in St. Louis, 1970*, USCCR, 304 (testimony of Adel Allen).

57. Frug, "City Services," 74; Brendan Beck and Adam Goldstein, "Governing through Police? Housing Market Reliance, Welfare Retrenchment, and Police Budgeting in an Era of Declining Crime," *Social Forces* 96, no. 3 (March 2018): 1183–210.

58. Khalil Gibran Muhammad, *The Condemnation of Blackness: Race, Crime, and the Making of Modern Urban America* (Cambridge, MA: Harvard University Press, 2011).

59. See Elizabeth Hinton, *From the War on Poverty to the War on Crime: The Making of Mass Incarceration in America* (Cambridge, MA: Harvard University Press, 2016); and Julilly Kohler-Hausmann, *Getting Tough: Welfare and Imprisonment in 1970s America* (Princeton, NJ: Princeton University Press, 2017).

60. See Bruce Western, *Punishment and Inequality in America* (New York: Russell Sage Foundation, 2006); Soss and Weaver, "Police Are Our Government," 569–73; and Rod Brunson and Jody Miller, "Young Black Men and Urban Policing in the United States," *British Journal of Criminology* 46 (2006): 622.

61. Tracey Meares and Benjamin Justice, "How the Criminal Justice System Educates Citizens," *Annals of the American Academy of Political and Social Science* 651 (January 2014): 162.

62. See Bryan Sykes and Michelle Maroto, "A Wealth of Inequalities: Mass Incarceration, Employment, and Racial Disparities in U.S. Household Wealth, 1996 to 2011," *Russell Sage Journal of the Social Sciences* 2, no. 6 (2016): 129–52; Daniel Schneider and Kristin Turney, "Incarceration and Black-White Inequality in Homeownership: A State-Level Analysis," *Social Science Research* 53 (2015): 403–14; Christopher Uggen and Jeff Manza, *Locked Out: Felon Disenfranchisement and American Democracy* (New York: Oxford University Press, 2008); Vesla Weaver and Amy Lerman, "Political

Consequences of the Carceral State," *American Political Science Review* 104, no. 4 (2010): 817–33; Devah Pager, "The Mark of a Criminal Record," *American Journal of Sociology* 108, no. 5 (March 2003): 937–75; and Becky Pettit and Bruce Western, "Mass Imprisonment and the Life Course: Race and Class Inequality in U.S. Incarceration," *American Sociological Review* 69 (April 2004): 151–69.

63. Tom Tyler, *Why People Obey the Law* (Princeton, NJ: Princeton University Press, 2007); Brunson and Miller, "Young Black Men and Urban Policing."

64. Weaver and Lerman, "Political Consequences of the Carceral State," 817–33; see also Joe Feagin, "The Continuing Significance of Race: Anti-black Discrimination in Public Places," *American Sociological Review* 56 (February 1991): 101–16.

65. "Why We Should Have a Public Housing Project in North Webster Heights," 1956, box 12a, folder 1, St. Louis Urban League Papers.

66. Kirkwood's 1966 *Proposed Plan of Action* quoted in Dubrow, "Municipal Antagonism or Benign Neglect," 271; "Tragic Fire Spurred Kirkwood Interest," *Webster-Kirkwood Times*.

67. Boyles, *Race, Place, and Suburban Policing*, 63.

68. Dubrow, "Municipal Antagonism or Benign Neglect," 272–73; "Tragic Fire Spurred Kirkwood Interest," *Webster-Kirkwood Times*; St. Louis County Department of Planning, *Meacham '76: A Community Plan* (Clayton: St. Louis County, 1976), 6, folder 36, Kay Drey Papers, WHMC; "A Local Crisis," *St. Louis Argus*, September 17, 1966, 3-B; "Citizen's Protest Mounting Wave of Police Shootings," *St. Louis Argus*, September 17, 1966, 1; Meacham Park/Kirkwood clipping, folder 192, Metropolitan League of Women Voters Records, WHMC.

69. Boyles, *Race, Place, and Suburban Policing*, 12 (quote), 93–132, 197; Jeremy Kohler, "Conviction Splits Kirkwood Neighbors," *SLPD*, November 11, 2007; Cooperman, "The Kirkwood Shootings."

70. Doug Moore, Stephen Deere, and Steve Giegerich, "A Smile That Gave in to Anger," *SLPD*, February 9, 2008; William H. Freivogel, "Kirkwood Debates Role of Race in Shootings," *St. Louis Beacon*, March 20, 2008; Stephen Deere, "Friends, Family Remember Thornton," *SLPD*, February 15, 2008; Stephen Deere and Doug Moore, "Charles Lee 'Cookie' Thornton: Behind the Smile," *SLPD*, May 4, 2008; Jeremy Kohler, "As City Recovers, Racial Tension Remains," *SLPD*, February 15, 2008; Cooperman, "The Kirkwood Shootings."

71. "Rising Crime and Police Problems in St. Louis," 1957, box 20, folder 8, St. Louis Urban League Papers.

72. Arch City Defenders, *Municipal Courts White Paper* (St. Louis: Arch City Defenders, 2014), 13, available at http://03a5010.netsolhost.com/WordPress/wp-content/uploads/2014/11/ArchCity-Defenders-Municipal-Courts-Whitepaper.pdf; Radley Balko, "How Municipalities in St. Louis County Profit from Poverty," *Washington Post*, September 3, 2014; Thomas Harvey and Brendan Roediger, "St. Louis County Municipal Courts, For-Profit Policing, and the Road to Reform," in *Ferguson Fault Lines: The Race Quake that Rocked a Nation*, ed. Kimberly Jade Norwood (American Bar Association, 2016).

73. Ryan Reilly and Rebecca Rivas, "In St. Louis, the Politics of Police Reform Are Tougher than Ever," *St. Louis American*, September 12, 2017.

74. See testimony of Larman Williams in *Equal Opportunity in Suburbia*, USCCR (Washington, DC: USCCR, 1974), 2.

75. US Department of Justice, Civil Rights Division, *Investigation of the Ferguson Police Department* (Washington, DC: Department of Justice, March 2015), 2, 63.

76. *Hearing Held in St. Louis, January 1970*, USCCR, 304–5 (testimony of Adel Allen).

77. US Department of Justice, *Investigation of the Ferguson Police Department*, 62–78.
78. Calculated from the Attorney General of Missouri's Vehicle Stops Reports (annual, 2000–2017), at https://www.ago.mo.gov/home/vehicle-stops-report.
79. Arch City Defenders, *Municipal Courts White Paper*. For the broader patterns, see Meehan and Ponder, "Race and Place," 399–430.
80. US Department of Justice, *Investigation of the Ferguson Police Department*, 79–80.
81. Max Ehrenfreund, "The Risks of Walking While Black in Ferguson," *Washington Post*, March 4, 2015; code available at https://library.municode.com/mo/ferguson/codes /code_of_ordinances/239430?nodeId=PTIICOOR_CH44TRMOVE_ARTVIIPE_S44 –344MAWAALRO, accessed September 2017.
82. US Department of Justice, *Investigation of the Ferguson Police Department*, 18–20, 25, 62.
83. US Department of Justice, *Investigation of the Ferguson Police Department*, 2.
84. Thomas Harvey and Brendan Roediger, "St. Louis County Municipal Courts, For-Profit Policing, and the Road to Reform," in *Ferguson Fault Lines*, ed. Norwood, 57.
85. Christopher Green, "Reverse Broken Windows," *Journal of Legal Education* 65, no. 1 (2015): 265–77.
86. Capers, "Policing, Race, and Place," 68–69; see also Bennett Capers, "Rethinking the Fourth Amendment: Race, Citizenship, and the Equality Principle," *Harvard Civil Rights–Civil Liberties Law Review*, 46 (2011): 1–49.
87. Statement of William Blanding, July 1978, box 6, Freedom of Residence, Greater St. Louis Committee (1961–) Addenda, 1957–1988, SO509, WHMC; *Hearing Held in St. Louis, January 1970*, USCCR, 304–5 (testimony of Adel Allen); US Department of Justice, *Investigation of the Ferguson Police Department*, 2; Arch City Defenders, *Municipal Courts White Paper*, 15.
88. W. E. Burghardt Du Bois, "My Evolving Program for Negro Freedom," in *What the Negro Really Wants*, ed. Rayford Logan (Chapel Hill: University of North Carolina Press, 1944), 37.
89. See Capers, "Policing, Race, and Place," 65–68; Vesla Weaver, "Why White People Keep Calling the Cops on Black Americans," Vox, May 17, 2018, https://www.vox .com/first-person/2018/5/17/17362100/starbucks-racial-profiling-yale-airbnb-911.
90. Abascal, "Municipal Services and Equal Protection," 1389–90.
91. *Hawkins v. Town of Shaw*, 437 F.2d 1286; Daniel Wm. Fessler and Charles M. Haar, "Beyond the Wrong Side of the Tracks: Municipal Services in the Interstices of Procedure," *Harvard Civil Rights–Civil Liberties Law Review* 6, no. 3 (May 1971): 442–43; Lawrence Simon, "Equal Protection in the Urban Environment: The Right to Equal Municipal Services," *Tulane Law Review* 46 (1971–72): 497–98.
92. Fessler and Haar, "Beyond the Wrong Side of the Tracks," 460; C. Ronald Ellington and Lawrence F. Jones, "*Hawkins v. Town of Shaw*: The Court as City Manager," *Georgia Law Review* 5 (1971): 739–40; Little, "Potholes, Lampposts and Policemen," 687.
93. Robert Lineberry and Robert E. Welch, "Who Gets What: Measuring the Distribution of Urban Public Services," *Social Science Quarterly* 54, no. 4 (1974): 700; Gershon M. Ratner, "Inter-Neighborhood Denials of Equal Protection in the Provision of Municipal Services," *Harvard Civil Rights–Civil Liberties Law Review* 4 (1968): 64.
94. *Report of the National Advisory Commission on Civil Disorders* (Washington, DC: Government Publishing Office, 1968), 148.
95. Speer, *Meacham Park*, 28; Charles B. Kaiser, "Organization of a Metropolitan Sewer District," *Journal of the Water Pollution Control Federation*, 38, no. 4 (1966), 555–61; Peter Mattei and Charles B. Kaiser, "Administrative and Financial Aspects of Operating a Municipal Sewer System," *Journal of the Water Pollution Control Federation*, 39, no. 4

(1967): 502; Charles B. Kaiser, "Creation and Operation of the Metropolitan St. Louis Sewer District," *Journal of the Water Pollution Control Federation* 54, no. 9 (1982): 1247.

96. L. L. Lumsden and William L. Jellison, "St. Louis Encephalitis in 1933: Observations on Epidemiological Features," *Public Health Reports* 73, no. 4 (April 1958): 340–53; Kaiser, "Creation and Operation of the Metropolitan St. Louis Sewer District," 1247; J. P. Leake, E. K. Musson, and H. D. Chope, "Epidemiology of Epidemic Encephalitis, St. Louis Type," *JAMA* 103, no. 10 (1934): 731–33.

97. Werner Troesken, "The Limits of Jim Crow: Race and the Provision of Water and Sewerage Services in American Cities, 1880–1925," *Journal of Economic History*, 62, no. 3 (September 2002): 734–72.

98. "Meacham Park," folder 193, Metropolitan League of Women Voters Records.

99. Kaiser, "Creation and Operation of the Metropolitan St. Louis Sewer District," 1247–49; Mattei and Kaiser, "Administrative and Financial Aspects of Operating a Municipal Sewer System," 501, 505–12.

100. "Minutes of a Regular Meeting of the Land Clearance for Redevelopment Authority of St. Louis County," October 29, 1956, County LCRA Records, St. Louis County Economic Council, Clayton MO; Ida Scott Oral History (transcript of interview by Doris Wesley, November 1996), box 4, folder 76, Lift Every Voice and Sing Oral History Project (SO609),WHMC, UMSL; Scott, *History of Elmwood Park*, 8; Matte and Kaiser, "Administrative and Financial Aspects of Operating a Municipal Sewer System," 513; HHFA, Urban Renewal Administration, Summary of Project Data, Elmwood Park MO R-10 (October 1962), Supreme Court file 52147, *Brooks v. LCRA*, Missouri State Archives, Jefferson City; Project Improvements, "Explanatory Memorandum . . . for Change in Plan," Elmwood Park MO R-10 (October 1962), Supreme Court file 52147, *Brooks v. LCRA*, Missouri State Archives.

101. "Meacham '76: A Community Plan" (typescript), folder 36, Kay Drey Papers (SL 241), WHMC, UMSL; St. Louis County Department of Planning, *Evaluation of Substandard Conditions, Selected Unincorporated Communities* (Clayton, MO: St. Louis County, 1973), 13; St. Louis County Department of Planning, *Meacham '76*, 15–17.

102. "Kinloch Passes Sewer Bond," *St. Louis Argus*, February 11, 1966, 1; *In Our Opinion* (Meacham Park newsletter), December 1970, folder 156, Metropolitan League of Women Voters Records, WHMC-UMSL; "Former Mayor Swoboda's Death Casts Pall on Kirkwood Healing Meeting," *St. Louis Beacon*, April 2008; "Meacham '76: A Community Plan," WHMC, UMSL.

103. Dubrow, "Municipal Antagonism or Benign Neglect," 273; *In Our Opinion* (Meacham Park newsletter), May 1970, folder 156, Metropolitan League of Women Voters Records, WHMC-UMSL; St. Louis County Department of Planning, *Meacham '76*, 17; Speer, *Meacham Park*, 56; *In Our Opinion* (Meacham Park newsletter), February 1969, folder 156, Metropolitan League of Women Voters Records, WHMC-UMSL; "Meacham '76: A Community Plan," WHMC, UMSL; "Tragic Fire Spurred Kirkwood Interest," *Webster-Kirkwood Times*.

104. *Report of the National Advisory Commission on Civil Disorders*, 81–83.

105. USCCR, *School Desegregation in Kirkwood, Missouri*, 2.

CHAPTER THREE

1. "Eminent Domain Plaintiff Will Keep Her House," *Los Angeles Times*, July 1, 2006; Kenneth R. Harney, "Eminent Domain Ruling Has Strong Repercussions," *Washington Post*, July 23, 2005; Ilya Somin, "The Limits of Anti-*Kelo* Legislation," *Reason*, August/September 2007; Richard Epstein, "*Kelo*: An American Original: Of Grubby

Particulars and Grand Principles," *Green Bag: An Entertaining Journal of Law* 8, no. 2 (Summer 2005): 355; "An American's Home Is Still Her Castle," *Economist* 381, no. 8505 (November 25, 2006).

2. See Wendell Pritchett, "Beyond *Kelo*: Thinking About Urban Development in the 21st Century," *University of Georgia Law Review* 22 (2005–2006): 909; David A. Dana, "The Law and Expressive Meaning of Condemning the Poor after *Kelo*," *Northwestern University Law Review* 101, no. 1 (2007): 366; and Amanda Goodin, "Rejecting the Return to Blight in Post-*Kelo* State Legislation," *New York University Law Review* 82 (2007): 178.

3. See Alexander von Hoffman, "A Study in Contradictions: The Origins and Legacy of the Housing Act of 1949," *Housing Policy Debate* 11, no. 2 (2000): 299; and Gail Radford, *Modern Housing for America: Policy Struggles in the New Deal Era* (Chicago: University of Chicago Press, 1996).

4. William G. Grigsby, "Housing and Slum Clearance: Elusive Goals," *Annals of the American Academy of Political and Social Science* 352, Urban Revival: Goals and Standards (March 1964): 107–18; Ashley Foard and Hilbert Fefferman, "Federal Urban Renewal Legislation," *Law and Contemporary Problems* 25, no. 4 (1960): 635–84; Urban Renewal Administration, Housing and Home Finance Agency, *Urban Renewal Manual: Policies and Requirements for Local Governments* (Washington, DC: Government Publishing Office, 1959), 1:2; von Hoffman, "A Study in Contradictions"; Martin Millspaugh, "Objectives and Criteria of Urban Renewal," *Proceedings of the Academy of Political Science* 27, no. 1, The Urban Problems (May 1960): 49.

5. Richard H. Leach, "The Federal Urban Renewal Program: A Ten-Year Critique," *Law and Contemporary Problems* 25, no. 4, Urban Renewal: Part 1 (Autumn 1960): 779.

6. Jon C. Teaford, "Urban Renewal and Its Aftermath," *Housing Policy Debate* 11, no. 2 (January 2000): 6.

7. *Schneider v. District of Columbia et al. Morris v. District of Columbia Redevelopment Land Agency et al.* Civ. Nos. 5791–52, 476–53; United States District Court for the District of Columbia 117 F. Supp 705; 1953 U.S. Dist LEXIS 4309, November 1953.

8. *Berman et al. Executors v. Parker et al.*, no. 22, Supreme Court of the United States, 348 U.S. 26; 75 S. Ct. 98; 99 L. Ed. 27; 1954 U.S. LEXIS 1463.

9. Millspaugh, "Objectives and Criteria of Urban Renewal," 49–50; Susan Fainstein, "Redevelopment Planning and Distributive Justice in the American Metropolis," in *Justice and the American Metropolis*, ed. Clarissa Rile Hayward and Todd Swanstrom (Minneapolis: University of Minnesota Press, 2011), 150.

10. Wendell Pritchett, "The 'Public Menace' of Blight: Urban Renewal and the Private Uses of Eminent Domain," *Yale Law and Policy Review* 21, no. 1 (2003): 12–13, 39–40; Goodin, "Rejecting the Return to Blight," 181; *Susette Kelo et al., Petitioners v. City of New London et al.*, Supreme Court of the United States, no. 04–108, On Writ of Certiorari to the Supreme Court of Connecticut (June 23, 2005); Dana, "The Law and Expressive Meaning of Condemning the Poor after *Kelo*," 368; Richard Epstein, *Takings: Private Property and the Power of Eminent Domain* (Cambridge, MA: Harvard University Press, 1985), 166–67, 178–79.

11. Pritchett, "The 'Public Menace' of Blight," 17–18; Colin Gordon, "Blighting the Way: Urban Renewal, Economic Development, and the Elusive Definition of Blight," *Fordham Urban Law Journal* 31, no. 2 (2004), 305–37; "Despotism by Stealth: Eminent Domain," *Economist*, February 19, 2005; Urban Renewal Administration, Housing and Home Finance Agency, *Urban Renewal Manual*, 3:1–2.

12. Millspaugh, "Objectives and Criteria of Urban Renewal," 52; Teaford, "Urban Renewal and Its Aftermath," 444–45; Herbert Gans, "The Failure of Urban Renewal,"

Commentary, April 1965, 29; Arnold Hirsch, "Searching for a 'Sound Negro Policy': A Racial Agenda for the Housing Acts of 1949 and 1954," *Housing Policy Debate* 112 (2000): 400–401; von Hoffman, "A Study in Contradictions," 299.

13. Hirsch, "Searching for a 'Sound Negro Policy,'" 396, 398, 421–26; Frank Horne, "Interracial Housing in the United States," *Phylon Quarterly* 19, no. 1 (Spring 1958): 16; Pritchett, "The 'Public Menace' of Blight," 44–46.

14. Hirsch, "Searching for a 'Sound Negro Policy,'" 410–11.

15. "Summaries of Local Redevelopment Programs," 1950, Papers of the NAACP, Part 5, The Campaign against Residential Segregation, 1914–1955, microform, reel 18:904.

16. Russell, Mullgardt, Schwarz, & Van Hoefen, "Study for a Comprehensive Plan for Redevelopment of the Central City Area," 1953, box 8, ser. 1, Raymond Tucker Papers, Washington University Archives; City Plan Commission, "Rebuilding Industry and Commerce in St. Louis" [1960?], box 8, ser. 1, Tucker Papers.

17. Alexander von Hoffman, "Why They Built Pruitt-Igoe," in *From Tenements to the Taylor Homes: In Search of an Urban Housing Policy in Twentieth-Century America*, ed. John Bauman, Roger Biles, and Kristin Szylvain (University Park: Pennsylvania State University Press, 2000), 186–93; Lee Rainwater, *Behind Ghetto Walls: Black Families in a Federal Slum* (Chicago: University of Chicago Press, 1970), 1–9.

18. See Joseph Heathcott and Maire Murphy, "Corridors of Flight, Zones of Renewal: Industry, Planning, and Policy in the Making of Metropolitan St. Louis, 1940–1980," *Journal of Urban History* 31, no. 2 (2005): 154, passim.

19. East-West Gateway Coordinating Council, *An Inventory of Housing Conditions, Programs, and Codes in St. Louis County*, HUD Mo. P-160, (St. Louis: East-West Gateway, 1970), 9.

20. USCCR Staff Report, "Housing in St. Louis," 1970, box 3:127, Freedom of Residence, Greater St. Louis Committee Records, WHMC, UMSL; Gary Orfield, "The Housing Issues in the St. Louis Case," report to Judge William Hungate, US District Court (St. Louis, MO), *Liddell v. Board of Education* (April 1981), 72; *Hearings: St. Louis*, USCCR, 299, 577–78 (January 1970).

21. "Judicial Review of Displacee Relocation in Urban Renewal," *Yale Law Journal* 77, no. 5 (1968): 968.

22. Henry W. McGee Jr., "Urban Renewal in the Crucible of Judicial Review," *Virginia Law Review* 56, no. 5 (1970): 826–94.

23. Advisory Commission on Intergovernmental Relations, *Relocation: Unequal Treatment of People and Businesses Displaced by Governments* (Washington, DC: Government Publishing Office, 1965), 17–19; Lawrence Christy and Peter Coogan, "Family Relocation in Urban Renewal," *Harvard Law Review* 82, no. 4 (1969): 870; Chester Hartman, "Relocation: Illusory Promises and No Relief," *Virginia Law Review* 57, no. 5 (1971): 747–52.

24. Wolf Von Eckhardt, *Bulldozers and Bureaucrats: Cities and Urban Renewal* (Washington, DC: New Republic Pamphlet, 1963), 6; House Committee on Banking and Currency, Subcommittee on Housing, *Slum Clearance and Urban Renewal* (Washington, DC: Government Publishing Office, 1956), 19–20; Hartman, "Relocation," 747–52; Martin Millspaugh, "Problems and Opportunities of Relocation," *Law and Contemporary Problems*, 26, no. 1, Urban Renewal: Part 2 (1961): 8–9; Advisory Commission on Intergovernmental Relations, *Relocation*, 17–19.

25. Hartman, "Relocation," 747–52; Christy and Coogan, "Family Relocation in Urban Renewal," 870; Millspaugh, "Problems and Opportunities of Relocation," 8–9; Advisory Commission on Intergovernmental Relations, *Relocation*, 17–19; Urban Renewal

Administration, Housing and Home Finance Agency, *Urban Renewal Manual*, 16:1–3; Von Eckhardt, *Bulldozers and Bureaucrats*, 6; Edgar Cahn, Timothy Eichenberg, and Roberta Romberg, *The Legal Lawbreakers: A Study of the Nonadministration of Federal Relocation Requirements* (Washington, DC: Citizens Advocate Center, October 1970), 21–22.

26. "Judicial Review of Displacee Relocation," 982; Terry J. Tondro, "Urban Renewal Relocation: Problems in Enforcement of Conditions on Federal Grants to Local Agencies," *University of Pennsylvania Law Review* 117, no. 2 (1968): 191–93; Millspaugh, "Problems and Opportunities of Relocation," 11–24; Charles Abrams, *The City Is the Frontier* (New York: Harper & Row, 1965), 81–33, 133; Teaford, "Urban Renewal and Its Aftermath," 448; Hirsch, "Searching for a 'Sound Negro Policy,'" 395.

27. "Judicial Review of Displacee Relocation," 966–87; *Norwalk CORE v. Norwalk Redevelopment Agency*, No. 227, Docket No. 31761, U.S. Court of Appeals (Second Circuit), 395 F.2d 920; 1968 U.S. App. LEXIS 6615; 12 Fed. R. Serv. 2d (Callaghan) 368; 8 A.L.R. Fed. 388.

28. *Norwalk CORE v. Norwalk Redevelopment Agency*, 42 F.R.D. 617 (D. Conn. 1967), rev'd, 395 F.2d 920 (2d Cir. 1968); Hartman, "Relocation," 767–69; Cahn, Eichenberg, and Romberg, *Legal Lawbreakers*, 53–54; McGee, "Urban Renewal in the Crucible of Judicial Review," 826–94.

29. House Committee on Public Works, Subcommittee on Roads, *Proposed Amendments to the Uniform Relocation Assistance and Real Property Acquisitions Policies Act of 1970* (Washington, DC: Government Publishing Office, 1972), 10–14, 92–94; Advisory Commission on Intergovernmental Relations, *Relocation*; Hartman, "Relocation," 769–81; New Jersey Department of Community Affairs, "A Staff Review and Assessment of the Relocation Program in New Jersey, 1967–1978," Bureau of Housing and Renewal Services (July 1979), v–vi.

30. Note, "In the Path of Progress: Federal Highway Relocation Assurances," *Yale Law Journal* 82, no. 2 (1972): 382–86; Daniel Thursz, *Where Are They Now? A Study of the Impact of Relocation on Former Residents of Southwest Washington* (Washington, DC: Health and Welfare Council, 1966), 2–3; Cahn, Eichenberg, and Romberg, *Legal Lawbreakers*, 2; Chester Hartman, "The Housing of Relocated Families," *Journal of the American Institute of Planners* 30, no. 3 (1964): 280; Abrams, *The City Is the Frontier*, 135 (quote). For examples from various cities, see Eric Hill and Associates, "Relocation Study: Technical Supplement, Atlanta Community Improvement Program" (Atlanta: Eric Hill, March 1967); Tondro, "Urban Renewal Relocation," 199; and Harry W. Reynolds, "Population Displacement in Urban Renewal," *American Journal of Economics and Sociology* 22, no. 1 (1963): 113–28.

31. Grigsby, "Housing and Slum Clearance," 109–10; Hartman, "Relocation," 804–5; Comptroller General, *Opportunity to Improve Allocation of Program Funds to Better Meet National Housing Goals*, HUD Report B-118754 (Washington, DC: Government Publishing Office, October 1970), 1–2, 13–19; Housing and Home Finance Agency, Urban Renewal Administration, *Local Plans for Residential Redevelopment and Family Relocation* (Washington, DC: Government Publishing Office, 1954), 7–8; Raymond Foley, "Statement on the Relationship of the Slum-Clearance and Low-Rent Housing Programs," June 1950, Papers of the NAACP, Part 5, The Campaign against Residential Segregation, 1914–1955, microform, reel 18:904; Cahn, Eichenberg, and Romberg, *Legal Lawbreakers*, 13–14; Christy and Coogan, "Family Relocation in Urban Renewal," 864.

32. Martin Anderson, *The Federal Bulldozer: A Critical Analysis of Urban Renewal, 1949–1962* (Cambridge, MA: MIT Press, 1964), 52–55; Ernest Norton Tooby, "The Interest

in Rootedness: Family Relocation and an Approach to Full Indemnity," *Stanford Law Review* 21, no. 4 (1969): 802.

33. The federal Urban Renewal Administration counts families and individuals. In this estimate, the number of families is multiplied by 3.67 (the average family size in 1960).

34. See Tooby, "Interest in Rootedness," 802; Millspaugh, "Problems and Opportunities of Relocation," 7; House Committee on Public Works, *Uniform Relocation Assistance and Land Acquisition Policies—1970 (Washington, DC: Government Publishing Office)*; Advisory Commission on Intergovernmental Relations, *Relocation*, 12–13; and Note, "In the Path of Progress," 377.

35. Christy and Coogan, "Family Relocation in Urban Renewal," 864; Chicago Plan Commission, *Report on Relocation*, Population and Housing Report #2 (Chicago: Chicago Plan Commission, December 1956), 8–9; Nick S. Fisfis and Harold Greenberg, "Note: Suburban Renewal in Pennsylvania," *University of Pennsylvania Law Review* 111, no. 1 (1962): 88, 91–93.

36. Teaford, "Urban Renewal and Its Aftermath," 448–49; Grigsby, "Housing and Slum Clearance," 110; Von Eckhardt, *Bulldozers and Bureaucrats*, 6–7; Reynolds, "Population Displacement in Urban Renewal," 117; Christy and Coogan, "Family Relocation in Urban Renewal," 874–78; Peter Marris is quoted in Thursz, *Where Are They Now?*, 25.

37. *Uniform Relocation Assistance and Land Acquisition Policies—1970*, House Committee on Public Works, 458–59 (1970) (statement by Kevin Philips, National Housing and Development Law Project); Advisory Commission on Intergovernmental Relations, *Relocation*, 25; Housing and Home Finance Agency, *Local Plans for Residential Redevelopment and Family Relocation*, 8; Note, "In the Path of Progress," 373. For the full sweep of projects, and their racial impact, see Digital Scholarship Lab, *Renewing Inequality*, American Panorama, ed. Robert K. Nelson and Edward L. Ayers, accessed January 4, 2019, https://dsl.richmond.edu/panorama/renewal/.

38. Chicago Plan Commission, *Report on Relocation*, 8–9; Atlanta Urban Renewal Department, *Relocation Housing Plan of the City of Atlanta* (Atlanta: Urban Renewal Department, November 1958), 17; Baltimore Urban Renewal and Housing Agency, *Ten Years of Relocation Experience in Baltimore, Maryland* (Baltimore: Urban Renewal and Housing Agency, June 1961), 3; Cahn, Eichenberg, and Romberg, *Legal Lawbreakers*, 12–13; Yale Rabin, *Discrimination in the Public Use, Control, and Development of Land in Selma, Alabama* (New York: NAACP Legal Defense Fund, March 1970).

39. Chicago Handbill, n.d., Papers of the NAACP, Part 5, The Campaign against Residential Segregation, 1914–1955, microform, reel 15:819.

40. "Memorandum Concerning the Present Discriminatory Policies of the Federal Housing Administration," October 1944, Papers of the NAACP, Part 5, The Campaign against Residential Segregation, 1914–1955, microform, reel 12:750.

41. Atlanta Urban Renewal Department, "Relocation Housing Plan," 32.

42. Hartman, "Relocation," 788–89; Thursz, *Where Are They Now?*, 19; Von Eckhardt, *Bulldozers and Bureaucrats*, 10.

43. See Hartman, "Relocation," 746–47; Chicago Plan Commission, *Report on Relocation*, 16–18; Hartman, "Housing of Relocated Families," 276–77; Herbert Gans, "The Human Implications of Current Redevelopment and Relocation Planning," *Journal of the American Institute of Planners* 25, no. 1 (1959): 18–19, also available at http://herbertgans.org/wp-content/uploads/2013/11/3-Human-Implications.pdf; Reynolds, "Population Displacement in Urban Renewal," 118; and "Judicial Review of Displacee Relocation," 966.

44. Anthony Downs, "Losses Imposed on Urban Households by Uncompensated Highway and Renewal Costs," in *Urban Problems and Prospects* (Chicago: Markham, 1970), 219–20; see also Tooby, "Interest in Rootedness," 805.

45. Thursz, *Where Are They Now?*, 57 (quote); Hartman, "Relocation," 746–47; Marc Fried, "Grieving for a Lost Home: Psychological Costs of Relocation," in *Urban Renewal: The Record and the Controversy*, ed. James Q. Wilson (Cambridge, MA: MIT Press, 1966), 359–60; Marc Fried and Peggy Gleicher, "Some Sources of Residential Satisfaction in an Urban Slum," *Journal of the American Planning Association* 27, no. 4 (1961): 309; Abrams, *The City Is the Frontier*, 142; Gans, "Human Implications of Current Redevelopment and Relocation Planning," 15–17; Tooby, "Interest in Rootedness," 808–18. See also Mindy Fullilove, *Root Shock: How Tearing Up City Neighborhoods Hurts America, and What We Can Do About It* (New York: Ballantine, 2004).

46. Fainstein, "Redevelopment Planning and Distributive Justice," 152; Gans, "Human Implications of Current Redevelopment and Relocation Planning," 9.

47. St. Louis City Plan Commission, *Technical Report on a Relocation Analysis for St. Louis, Missouri* (St. Louis: City Plan Commission, February 1972), 2.

48. "Land Clearance for Redevelopment Authority Projects," January 1961, box 2:17, Tucker Papers; Comptroller General of the United States, *Inadequate Relocation Assistance to Families Displaced from Certain Urban Renewal Districts in Kansas and Missouri* (Washington, DC: Government Publishing Office, 1964), 8–9; "Mill Creek Valley Urban Renewal Report," n.d., box 12:542, Freedom of Residence Records; *Urban Renewal in Selected Cities*, Senate Subcommittee on Banking and Currency, 142 (1957) (testimony of Charles Farris, St. Louis Housing Authority); St. Louis City Plan Commission, *Technical Report on a Relocation Analysis*, 2, 15, 20.

49. Comptroller General, *Inadequate Relocation Assistance*, quoted at 5; St. Louis City Plan Commission, *Technical Report on a Relocation Analysis*. See also Mark Gelfand, *A Nation of Cities: The Federal Government and Urban America, 1933–1965* (New York: Oxford University Press, 1975), 211–14; Tondro, "Urban Renewal Relocation," 194; (quote) "Mill Creek Valley Urban Renewal Report," n.d., box 12:542, Freedom of Residence Records.

50. St. Louis Economic Development Program, "Technical Program: History of Renewal" (St. Louis: St. Louis Economic Development Program, 1971), 14.

51. "Minutes of a Regular Meeting of the Land Clearance for Redevelopment Authority [LCRA] of St. Louis County," March 11, 1964, County LCRA Records, St. Louis County Economic Council, Clayton, MO.

52. *Hearings: St. Louis*, USCCR, 260, 299 (January 1970); *Hearings: St. Louis*, USCCR, 577 (January 1970) (USCCR staff report, Exhibit 21); Jack Wood (NAACP) to Margaret Rush Wilson (SL NAACP), January 25, 1962, Papers of the NAACP, Part 5 (supp.), The Campaign against Residential Segregation, 1914–1955, microform, reel 8:212; Gary Orfield, "School Segregation and Housing Policy: The Role of Local and Federal Governments in Neighborhood Segregation," *Equity & Excellence in Education* 17, no. 3 (1979): 51–52.

53. "Minutes of a Regular Meeting of the LCRA of St. Louis County," September 26, 1956, County LCRA Records; Ida Scott Oral History (transcript of interview by Doris Wesley, November 1996), box 4, folder 76, Lift Every Voice and Sing Oral History Project (SO609), WHMC, UMSL; "Minutes of the Organization Meeting of the LCRA of St. Louis County," September 10, 1956, County LCRA Records; Olivette official quoted in "Minutes of a Regular Meeting of the LCRA of St. Louis County," October 29, 1956, County LCRA Records; "Minutes of a Regular Meeting of the LCRA of St. Louis County," March 2, 1957, County LCRA Records.

54. Henry Deeken (Olivette mayor) to Olivette Planning and Zoning Commission, October 11, 1960; G. Bassett to Mr. Riley (Harland Bartholomew and Associates intra-office memo), October 16, 1960; Bartholomew to City of Olivette, February 23, 1959, all in Correspondence Files, reel 31, Harland Bartholomew Papers, Washington University Archives.

55. "Minutes of a Regular Meeting of the LCRA of St. Louis County," January 11, 1958, County LCRA Records.

56. "Minutes of a Regular Meeting of the LCRA of St. Louis County," March 8, 1958, County LCRA Records.

57. G. Bassett to Mr. Riley (Harland Bartholomew and Associates intra-office memo), October 16, 1960, Correspondence Files, reel 31, Bartholomew Papers.

58. "Minutes of a Regular Meeting of the LCRA of St. Louis County," April 19, 1958, County LCRA Records.

59. "Minutes of a Regular Meeting of the LCRA of St. Louis County," March 15, 1958, County LCRA Records; "Minutes of a Regular Meeting of the LCRA of St. Louis County," April 12, 1958, County LCRA Records; commissioner quoted in "Minutes of a Regular Meeting of the LCRA of St. Louis County," January 19, 1959, County LCRA Records.

60. "Minutes of a Regular Meeting of the LCRA of St. Louis County," December 13, 1958, County LCRA Records.

61. "Minutes of a Special Meeting of the LCRA of St. Louis County," November 19, 1958, County LCRA Records; "Minutes of a Regular Meeting of the LCRA of St. Louis County," February 8, 1958, County LCRA Records; "Minutes of a Regular Meeting of the LCRA of St. Louis County," January 10, 1959, County LCRA Records; "Minutes of a Regular Meeting of the LCRA of St. Louis County," February 14, 1959, County LCRA Records.

62. "Urban Renewal Plan: Elmwood Park," Project MO R-10, October 1962, *Brooks v. LCRA* case file, RG 600, Missouri State Archives, Jefferson City.

63. "Urban Renewal Plan: Elmwood Park," Project MO R-10, October 1962, *Brooks v. LCRA* case file, RG 600, Missouri State Archives.

64. "Minutes of a Regular Meeting of the LCRA of St. Louis County," May 9, 1961, County LCRA Records; "Minutes of a Regular Meeting of the LCRA of St. Louis County," January 16, 1962, County LCRA Records.

65. "Minutes of a Regular Meeting of the LCRA of St. Louis County," September 25, 1962, County LCRA Records; "Minutes of a Regular Meeting of the LCRA of St. Louis County," August 14, 1962, County LCRA Records.

66. "Minutes of a Special Meeting of the LCRA of St. Louis County," July 25, 1963, County LCRA Records; "Contract for Disposition of Land for Private Redevelopment," September 1963, Recorder Book 5196, p. 399, St. Louis County Recorder, Clayton, MO; "Minutes of a Special Meeting of the LCRA of St. Louis County," November 20, 1962, County LCRA Records; East-West Gateway Coordinating Council, *Inventory of Housing Conditions*, 156.

67. H. Black (St. Louis County NAACP) to Jack Woods, November 19, 1960, Papers of the NAACP, Part 5 (supp.), The Campaign against Residential Segregation, 1914–1955, microform, reel 1:561; *Hearings: St. Louis*, USCCR, 689–93, 699 (January 1970) (statement of the Olivette LCRA, Exhibit 46).

68. *Hearings: St. Louis*, USCCR, 408 (January 1970).

69. "Olivette Public Hearing," June 29, 1965, box 19, folder 214, SLCMC, 1930–1976 (SL 74), WHMC; "Quarterly Report: City of Olivette," Spring 1963, box 19, folder 212, SLCMC; Illene Dubrow, "Municipal Antagonism or Benign Neglect: Racial Motivations

in Municipal Annexations in St. Louis County Missouri," *Journal of Urban Law* 53, no. 245 (1975–76): 258–59, 260; "Minutes of the Citizens Committee in Support of the LCRA," October 1960, Papers of the NAACP, Part 5 (supp.), The Campaign against Residential Segregation, 1914–1955, microform, reel 1:563; H. Black (St. Louis County NAACP) to Jack Woods, November 19, 1960, Papers of the NAACP, microform, reel 1:561.

70. "Olivette Public Hearing," June 29, 1965, box 19, folder 214, SLCMC; Quarterly Report: City of Olivette (October, November, December 1969), box 19, folder 212, SLCMC; Quarterly Report: City of Olivette (October, November, December 1971), box 19, folder 213, SLCMC; East-West Gateway Coordinating Council, *Inventory of Housing Conditions*, 158; Quarterly Report: City of Olivette, Spring 1963, box 19, folder 212, SLCMC.

71. East-West Gateway Coordinating Council, *Inventory of Housing Conditions*, 89.

72. "Market Analysis and Reuse Appraisal of Meacham Park Urban Renewal Area," 1959, folder 74, box 3, Roy Wenzlick Papers, WHMC.

73. Dubrow, "Municipal Antagonism or Benign Neglect," 270.

74. "Minutes of a Regular Meeting of the LCRA of St. Louis County," March 30, 1960, County LCRA Records; "Minutes of a Regular Meeting of the LCRA of St. Louis County," February 20, 1962, County LCRA Records; "Minutes of a Regular Meeting of the LCRA of St. Louis County," May 15, 1962, County LCRA Records; "Minutes of a Regular Meeting of the LCRA," August 14, 1962; "Minutes of a Special Meeting of the LCRA of St. Louis County," June 10, 1964, County LCRA Records.

75. Testimony of Alma Grigsby, Transcript on Appeal, vol. 2, p. 675, *Brooks v. LCRA*, Supreme Court of Missouri (September 1966), Supreme Court file 52147, *Brooks v. LCRA*, Missouri State Archives, Jefferson City; Appellant's Brief, *Brooks v. LCRA*, Supreme Court of Missouri (January 1967), SC file 52147, *Brooks v. LCRA*.

76. Testimony of Daniel Witt, Transcript on Appeal, vol. 1, p. 164, *Brooks v. LCRA*, Supreme Court of Missouri (September 1966), SC File 52147, *Brooks v. LCRA*; Orfield, "Housing Issues in the St. Louis Case," 72.

77. Testimony of Daniel Witt, Transcript on Appeal, vol. 1, pp. 160–61, *Brooks v. LCRA*, Supreme Court of Missouri (September 1966), SC File 52147, *Brooks v. LCRA*.

78. *Hearings: St. Louis*, USCCR, 390, 414–15, 564–565 (January 1970); "Olivette Public Hearing," June 29, 1965, box 19, folder 214, SLCMC; "Olivette Seeks Solution to Elmwood Park Dilemma," *Globe-Democrat*, July 23, 1970, clipping in folder 64, Kay Drey Papers, WHMC.

79. "Minutes of a Regular Meeting of the LCRA of St. Louis County," September 25, 1962, County LCRA Records.

80. Testimony of Daniel Witt, Transcript on Appeal, vol. 1, pp. 204–5, *Brooks v. LCRA*, Supreme Court of Missouri (September 1966), SC File 52147, *Brooks v. LCRA*; Appellant's Brief, *Brooks v. LCRA*, Supreme Court of Missouri (January 1967), SC File 52147, *Brooks v. LCRA*.

81. "Relocation Plan," Elmwood Park MO R-10 (October 1962), SC File 52147, *Brooks v. LCRA*; "Urban Renewal Plan: Elmwood Park," Project MO R-10, October 1962, *Brooks v. LCRA* case file, RG 600, Missouri State Archives; Testimony of Daniel Witt, Transcript on Appeal, vol. 1, pp. 201–4, *Brooks v. LCRA*, Supreme Court of Missouri (September 1966), SC File 52147, *Brooks v. LCRA*; "Explanatory Memorandum . . . for Change in Plan," Elmwood Park MO R-10 (October 1962), SC File 52147, *Brooks v. LCRA*.

82. Appellant's Brief, *Brooks v. LCRA*, Supreme Court of Missouri (January 1967), SC File 52147, *Brooks v. LCRA*; Testimony of Ida Scott, Transcript on Appeal, vol. 2,

pp. 582–84, *Brooks v. LCRA*, Supreme Court of Missouri (September 1966), SC File 52147, *Brooks v. LCRA*.

83. Testimony of Daniel Witt, Transcript on Appeal, vol. 1, p. 208, *Brooks v. LCRA*, Supreme Court of Missouri (September 1966), SC File 52147, *Brooks v. LCRA*; "Contract for Disposition of Land for Private Redevelopment," September 1963, Recorder Book 5196, p. 399, St. Louis County Recorder, Clayton, MO; "Minutes of a Regular Meeting of the LCRA of St. Louis County," May 12, 1965, County LCRA Records.

84. *Hearings: St. Louis*, USCCR, 540–42 (January 1970) (USCCR staff report, Exhibit 21); "Market Analysis and Reuse Appraisal of Meacham Park Urban Renewal Area," 1959, folder 74, box 3, Wenzlick Papers; HUD memo cited in USCCR Staff Report, "Housing in St. Louis," 1970, box 3:127, Freedom of Residence Records.

85. Quarterly Report: City of Olivette, Spring 1963, box 19, folder 212, SLCMC; "Proposal for Redevelopment of Elmwood Park, MO R-10, First Phase," April 1963, SC File 52147, *Brooks v. LCRA*; "Minutes of a Special Meeting of the LCRA of St. Louis County," November 23, 1959, County LCRA Records.

86. "AFSC Experience and Recommendations re: Executive Order 11063 on Equal Opportunity in Housing," May 1967, folder 2, Kay Drey Papers.

87. *Hearings: St. Louis*, USCCR, 396–97 (January 1970) (testimony of Olivette officials); *Hearings: St. Louis*, USCCR, 261, 564 (January 1970) (USCCR staff report, Exhibit 21); Dubrow, "Municipal Antagonism or Benign Neglect," 260–62; "Olivette Seeks Solution to Elmwood Park Dilemma," *Globe-Democrat*; East-West Gateway Coordinating Council, *Inventory of Housing Conditions*, 152–54; "Minutes of a Regular Meeting of the LCRA," January 11, 1958.

88. "Minutes of a Special Meeting of the LCRA of St. Louis County," August 20, 1963, County LCRA Records; Transcript on Appeal, vol. 2, p. 641, *Brooks v. LCRA*, Supreme Court of Missouri (September 1966), SC File 52147, *Brooks v. LCRA*; "Urban Renewal Plan: Elmwood Park," Project MO R-10, Relocation Plan (n.d.), *Brooks v. LCRA* case file, RG 600, Missouri State Archives; East-West Gateway Coordinating Council, *Inventory of Housing Conditions*, 11; "Minutes of a Special Meeting of the LCRA of St. Louis County," October 9, 1963, County LCRA Records.

89. "Minutes of a Regular Meeting of the LCRA of St. Louis County," November 16, 1963, County LCRA Records; Testimony of Ida Scott, Transcript on Appeal, vol. 2, pp. 608–9, *Brooks v. LCRA*, Supreme Court of Missouri (September 1966), SC File 52147, *Brooks v. LCRA*; "Low-Cost Apartments" (*St. Louis Globe-Democrat* clipping), October 23, 1968, box 1, folder 17, SLCMC; East-West Gateway Coordinating Council, *Inventory of Housing Conditions*, 158, 165; Testimony of Ruby Koelling, Transcript on Appeal, vol. 2, pp. 691–92, *Brooks v. LCRA*, Supreme Court of Missouri (September 1966), SC File 52147, *Brooks v. LCRA*.

90. Handwritten notes on Olivette (n.d.), folder 64; "New Neighbors" newsletter, 1972, folder 10; "New Neighbors" Board Minutes, February 1973, folder 14, all in Kay Drey Papers.

91. Testimony of Ida Scott, Transcript on Appeal, vol. 2, pp. 445–643, *Brooks v. LCRA*, Supreme Court of Missouri (September 1966), SC File 52147, *Brooks v. LCRA*; Ida Scott, *The History of Elmwood Park* (self-pub., 2004), 12. See also Testimony of Ruby Koelling (LCRA), Transcript on Appeal, vol. 1, pp. 12–54, *Brooks v. LCRA*, Supreme Court of Missouri (September 1966), SC File 52147, *Brooks v. LCRA*.

92. Testimony of Clara Burden, Transcript on Appeal, vol. 1, pp. 309–10; Testimony of Mary Bryant, Transcript on Appeal, vol. 1, pp. 140–41; Testimony of Ida Scott,

Transcript on Appeal, vol. 2, p. 57, all in *Brooks v. LCRA*, Supreme Court of Missouri (September 1966), SC File 52147, *Brooks v. LCRA*.

93. Relocation Ledger (Plaintiff's Exhibit 1), *Brooks v. LCRA* (1966), RG 600, Supreme Court Judicial Case Files. Of the 102 relocatees reported in 1962, forty-six had purchased new homes. The relocation ledger records the purchase price of forty of these, from which the average is calculated.

94. Testimony of Elizabeth Harris, Transcript on Appeal, vol. 1, pp. 340–44, *Brooks v. LCRA*, Supreme Court of Missouri (September 1966), SC File 52147, *Brooks v. LCRA*.

95. "Minutes of a Regular Meeting of the LCRA of St. Louis County," June 19, 1963, County LCRA Records; "Minutes of a Special Meeting of the LCRA of St. Louis County," December 19, 1961, County LCRA Records; "Minutes of a Regular Meeting of the LCRA," August 14, 1962.

96. Final Report of the Grand Jury of St. Louis County, January Term, 1965, in *Brooks v. LCRA*, Supreme Court of Missouri (September 1966), Exhibits, SC File 52147, *Brooks v. LCRA*.

97. Testimony of Willis Corbett, Transcript on Appeal, vol. 1, pp. 86–87; Testimony of Lillie Lemmons, Transcript on Appeal, vol. 1, pp. 254–55; Testimony of Maria Fannie White, Transcript on Appeal, vol. 1, pp. 271–72, all in *Brooks v. LCRA*, Supreme Court of Missouri (September 1966), SC File 52147, *Brooks v. LCRA*.

98. "AFSC Experience and Recommendations re: Executive Order 11063 on Equal Opportunity in Housing," May 1967, folder 2, Kay Drey Papers.

99. Handwritten notes on Olivette (n.d.), folder 64, Kay Drey Papers; "Minutes of a Regular Meeting of the LCRA of St. Louis County," July 16, 1963, County LCRA Records; Testimony of Willis Corbett, Transcript on Appeal, vol. 1, pp. 63–64, 84–86, *Brooks v. LCRA*, Supreme Court of Missouri (September 1966), SC File 52147, *Brooks v. LCRA*; "Minutes of a Special Meeting of the LCRA," October 9, 1963.

100. "Urban Renewal Plan: Elmwood Park," Project MO R-10, October 1962, *Brooks v. LCRA* case file, RG 600, Missouri State Archives; "Minutes of a Special Meeting of the LCRA of St. Louis County," September 20, 1961, County LCRA Records; Scott, *History of Elmwood Park*, 8–9; "Minutes of a Special Meeting of the LCRA," August 20, 1963; Plaintiff's Exhibit 30, and Testimony of L.C. Chase (Reasor), Transcript on Appeal, vol. 1, pp. 172–75 , *Brooks v. LCRA*, Supreme Court of Missouri (September 1966), SC File 52147, *Brooks v. LCRA*; Dubrow, "Municipal Antagonism or Benign Neglect," 262.

101. *Hearings: St. Louis*, USCCR, 406–8, 41 (January 1970); Olivette LCRA to Residents of Olivette Elmwood Park Mo. R-35, folder 64, Kay Drey Papers (SL 241), WHMC, UMSL; Dubrow, "Municipal Antagonism or Benign Neglect," 263.

102. Quarterly Report: City of Olivette (October, November, December 1969), box 19, folder 212, SLCMC; Quarterly Report: City of Olivette (October, November, December 1971), box 19, folder 213, SLCMC; Quarterly Report: City of Olivette (January, February, March 1973), box 19, folder 213, SLCMC.

103. Relocation Ledger (Plaintiff's Exhibit 1), *Brooks v. LCRA* (1966), RG 600, Supreme Court Judicial Case Files.

104. Census Bureau, *Income of Family and Persons in the United States: 1963*, P-60, No. 43 (Washington, DC: Government Publishing Office, 1964); Appellant's Brief, *Brooks v. LCRA*, Supreme Court of Missouri (January 1967), SC File 52147, *Brooks v. LCRA*.

105. Appellant's Brief, *Brooks v. LCRA*, Supreme Court of Missouri (January 1967), SC File 52147, *Brooks v. LCRA*.

106. "Minutes of a Regular Meeting of the LCRA of St. Louis County," April 9, 1963, County LCRA Records; "Minutes of a Regular Meeting of the LCRA of St. Louis

County," May 14, 1963, County LCRA Records; "Minutes of a Special Meeting of the LCRA," October 9, 1963; Appellant's Brief, *Brooks v. LCRA*, Supreme Court of Missouri (January 1967), SC File 52147, *Brooks v. LCRA*; Testimony of Daniel Witt, Transcript on Appeal, vol. 1, p. 235, *Brooks v. LCRA*, Supreme Court of Missouri (September 1966), SC File 52147, *Brooks v. LCRA*.

107. Testimony of Daniel Witt, Transcript on Appeal, vol. 1, p. 151, *Brooks v. LCRA*, Supreme Court of Missouri (September 1966), SC File 52147, *Brooks v. LCRA*; "Minutes of a Special Meeting of the LCRA of St. Louis County," January 23, 1964, County LCRA Records.

108. Final report of the Grand Jury of St. Louis County, January Term, 1965, in *Brooks v. LCRA*, Supreme Court of Missouri (September 1966), Exhibits, SC File 52147, *Brooks v. LCRA*.

109. *Esther Brooks et al., Plaintiffs-Appellants, v. LCRA of St. Louis County*, Defendant-Respondent, No. 52147, Supreme Court of Missouri, Division One, 414 S.W. 2d 545; 1967 Mo. LEXIS 978 (March 13, 1967).

110. Lead plaintiffs Esther Brooks and Carl Bell (10008 Roberts), joined by Sallie Bell, Carl Bell, and Annie May Bass (10004 Roberts); Elizabeth and Leo Wallace (1501 Lamson Place); Fred Johnson (9733 Roberts); Elizabeth Johnson (9726 Meeks); Grace Robinson (10161 Roberts); Lena Hendrick (9803 Meeks); Earnest Hannah (10033 Chicago); Roy and Julia Broyles (lots 28 to 34 of block 13); William Broyles and Vivian Broyles (lots 5 to 12 of block 15); Charles Bryant and Mary Bryant (lots 1, 2, 37, and 38 of block 15); Randall Howard and Clara Howard (lots 32–34 of block 5); Charles Phenix and Elizabeth Phenix (10000 Chicago Avenue, lots 16–19 of block 24); and Daisy Nickels (9731 Chicago, lot 37, block 17). See Transcript on Appeal, vol. 1, pp. 2–3, 10–11, *Brooks v. LCRA*, Supreme Court of Missouri (September 1966), SC File 52147, *Brooks v. LCRA*.

111. Appellant's Brief, *Brooks v. LCRA*, Supreme Court of Missouri (January 1967), SC File 52147, *Brooks v. LCRA*; *Hearings: St. Louis*, USCCR, 385–86 (January 1970) (testimony of Herman Davis); *Hearings: St. Louis*, USCCR, 699 (January 1970) (statement of the Olivette LCRA, Exhibit 46); *Hearings: St. Louis*, USCCR, 390–92 (January 1970) (testimony of Olivette officials).

112. Transcript on Appeal, vol. 2, p. 614, *Brooks v. LCRA*, Supreme Court of Missouri (September 1966), SC File 52147, *Brooks v. LCRA*.

113. Scott, *History of Elmwood Park*, 13.

114. Appellant's Brief, *Brooks v. LCRA*, Supreme Court of Missouri (January 1967), SC File 52147, *Brooks v. LCRA*.

115. H. Black (St. Louis County NAACP) to Jack Woods, November 19, 1960, Papers of the NAACP, microform, reel 1:561; *Hearings: St. Louis*, USCCR, 689–93, 699 (January 1970) (statement of the Olivette LCRA, Exhibit 46); East-West Gateway Coordinating Council, *Inventory of Housing Conditions*, 158, 165; Scott, *History of Elmwood Park*, 13; Orfield, "Housing Issues in the St. Louis Case," 72; *Hearings: St. Louis*, USCCR, 394 (January 1970).

116. Untitled statistical appendix [1970?], folder 12, Kay Drey Papers.

117. "Urban Renewal Plan: Elmwood Park," Project MO R-10, Relocation Plan (n.d.), *Brooks v. LCRA* case file, RG 600, Missouri State Archives; untitled statistical appendix [1970?], folder 12, Kay Drey Papers.

118. Relocation Ledger (Plaintiff's Exhibit 1); Transcript on Appeal, 86, 412, 641–43, Elmwood Park Project Area: Relocation Plan (1962), all in *Brooks v. Land Clearance for Redevelopment Authority* (1966), RG 600, Supreme Court Judicial Case Files.

119. Ida Scott Oral History, WHMC, UMSL.
120. *Hearings: St. Louis*, USCCR, 360 (January 1970).
121. Scott, *History of Elmwood Park*, 13; undated relocation chart, Supreme Court files 52147, *Brooks v. LCRA*, Missouri State Archives; Appellant's Brief, *Brooks v. LCRA*, Supreme Court of Missouri (January 1967), SC File 52147, *Brooks v. LCRA*. Post-redevelopment residency based on cross-check with St. Louis County Directory, volume 1 (telephone listings by name) and volume 2 (head-of-household by street address), Special Collections, St. Louis County Public Library.
122. "Minutes of a Regular Meeting of the LCRA of St. Louis County," June 28, 1958, County LCRA Records; "Minutes of a Regular Meeting of the LCRA of St. Louis County," August 12, 1964, County LCRA Records; "Minutes of a Regular Meeting of the LCRA," March 15, 1958; East-West Gateway Coordinating Council, *Inventory of Housing Conditions*, 156.
123. East-West Gateway Coordinating Council, *Inventory of Housing Conditions*, 11, 152–54, 156.
124. East-West Gateway Coordinating Council, *Inventory of Housing Conditions*, 9; "Meacham '76: A Community Plan" (n.d.), folder 36, Kay Drey Papers.
125. St. Louis County Department of Planning, *Evaluation of Substandard Conditions, Selected Unincorporated Communities* (Clayton, MO: 1973), 1, 12, 24, 62; St. Louis County Department of Planning, *Meacham '76: A Community Plan* (Clayton: St. Louis County, 1976), 15, folder 36, Kay Drey Papers; East-West Gateway Coordinating Council, *Inventory of Housing Conditions*, 112–13; untitled statistical appendix [1970?], folder 12, Kay Drey Papers; *In Our Opinion* (Meacham Park newsletter), December 1968, folder 156, Metropolitan League of Women Voters Records, WHMC.
126. "Council OKs Meacham Park Plan," *SLPD*, May 6, 1991; St. Louis County Department of Planning, *Evaluation of Substandard Conditions*, 63–64; "New Housing to Improve Meacham Park," 1971 clipping, folder 190, League of Women Voters Records; Lonnie Speer, *Meacham Park: A History* (self-pub., 1998), 56; *In Our Opinion* (Meacham Park newsletter), December 1970, folder 156, League of Women Voters Records; "Kirkwood City Council Hears Meacham Park Master Plan," September 1972 clipping, folder 178, League of Women Voters Records; St. Louis County Office of Community Development, "Review of Key Community Development Operations," 1974, folder 36, Kay Drey Papers.
127. Meacham Park/Kirkwood clipping, folder 192, Metropolitan League of Women Voters Records; "Meacham Park Cool to Annexation," 1977 clipping, folder 192, League of Women Voters Records; "Meacham '76: A Community Plan" (typescript), folder 36, Kay Drey Papers.
128. "Mayor Cites Reasons to Back Annexation," *SLPD*, May 16, 1991; "Council Votes to Adopt Plan of Meacham Park Residents," *SLPD*, August 19, 1991; Jeannette Cooperman, "The Kirkwood Shootings," *St. Louis Magazine*, May 2008.
129. William H. Freivogel, "Kirkwood's Journey: Separating Myths and Realities about Meacham Park, Thornton, Part 2," *St. Louis Beacon*, February 7, 2010; "Annexation Brings Zoning Shift, Concern," *SLPD*, July 2, 1992; "Council Votes to Adopt Plan," *SLPD*.
130. "Shopping Center Would Aid City Revenue," *SLPD*, September 5, 1994; "To Redevelop or Not Redevelop?," *SLPD*, August 26, 1994; "100 Houses Would Go to Make Way for Mall," *SLPD*, August 18, 1994.
131. "Council Oks Special Taxing District," *SLPD*, December 5, 1994.
132. "To Redevelop or Not Redevelop?," *SLPD*; "100 Houses Would Go to Make Way," *SLPD*.

133. "100 Houses Would Go to Make Way," *SLPD*.

134. "New Developments: Meacham Park Project Put on Hold," *SLPD*, April 4, 1995; "Muddle in Meacham Park," *SLPD*, April 26, 1995; Freivogel, "Kirkwood's Journey."

135. All quotes from "Muddle in Meacham Park," *SLPD*.

136. "Lone Group with Plan Follows TIF," *SLPD*, June 17, 1996; "Developer Offers to Help Fix, Build Homes," *SLPD*, November 25, 1996; "$50 Million 'Kirkwood Commons' Plan Advancing," *SLPD*, April 17, 1997; "Kirkwood Target Store Will Be Moving a Mile, To Kirkwood Commons," *SLPD*, September 13, 1999.

137. "Developer Offers to Help Fix, Build Homes," *SLPD*; "Lone Group with Plan Follows TIF," *SLPD*; "$50 Million 'Kirkwood Commons' Plan Advancing," *SLPD*; "Council Expected to Back 'Commons,'" *SLPD*, August 14, 1997; Anna Jones, "Meacham Park Undergoes $20 Million in Improvements," *St. Louis Business Journal*, January 27, 2006.

138. "Developer Offers to Help Fix, Build Homes," *SLPD*; "Council Expected to Back 'Commons,'" *SLPD*; "Lone Group with Plan Follows TIF," *SLPD*.

139. Jones, "Meacham Park Undergoes $20 Million in Improvements"; Freivogel, "Kirkwood's Journey"; Swoboda quoted in Eddie Silva, "A Mayor Runs through It," *Riverfront Times* 26, no. 7, February 13, 2002. On the Stonecrest Apartments, see "Kirkwood OKs Meacham Park Apartment Complex," *SLPD*, July 31, 2001; and "Kirkwood Has Tentatively OK'd Plan for Apartments," *SLPD*, July 13, 2001.

140. Freivogel, "Kirkwood's Journey."

141. "Council Expected to Back 'Commons,'" *SLPD*; "Kirkwood Commons Signs 2 Big Tenants; But $56 Million Is Held Up on Meacham Park Project," *SLPD*, March 18, 1998; Jones, "Meacham Park Undergoes $20 Million in Improvements"; Cooperman, "The Kirkwood Shootings"; "The Disappearance of Meacham Park," *SLPD*, March 7, 1999.

142. Cooperman, "The Kirkwood Shootings"; Freivogel, "Kirkwood's Journey"; Jeremy Kohler, "Conviction Splits Kirkwood Neighbors," *SLPD*, November 11, 2007.

143. "Disappearance of Meacham Park," *SLPD*.

144. "Disappearance of Meacham Park," *SLPD*; Freivogel, "Kirkwood's Journey"; Cooperman, "The Kirkwood Shootings."

145. These estimates are drawn from Emek Basker, "Job Creation or Destruction? Labor-Market Effects of Wal-Mart Expansion," *Review of Economics and Statistics* 87, no. 1 (2005), 174–83; David Neumark, Junfu Zhang, and Stephen Ciccarella, "The Effects of Wal-Mart on Local Labor Markets" (Forschungsinstitut zur Zukunft der Arbeit Institute for the Study of Labor, Discussion Paper 2545, January 2007); and Annette Bernhardt, Anmol Chaddha, and Siobhán McGrath, "What Do We Know About Wal-Mart?," (Economic Policy Brief #2, Brennan Center for Justice, August 2005).

146. Freivogel, "Kirkwood's Journey."

147. Cooperman, "The Kirkwood Shootings"; Freivogel, "Kirkwood's Journey."

148. Margaret Jane Radin, "Property and Personhood," *Stanford Law Review* 34, no. 5 (1982): 957–1015 (quote at p. 991); Michelle Wilde Anderson, "Cities Inside Out: Poverty and Exclusion at the Urban Fringe," *UCLA Law Review* 55 (2007–2008): 1145–50; Gerald Frug, "Voting and Justice," in *Justice and the American Metropolis*, ed. Hayward and Swanstrom, 201–22.

149. *Report of the National Advisory Commission on Civil Disorders* (Washington, DC: Government Publishing Office, 1968), 82.

150. "Conversation with Kenneth Clark," (1963) in *Conversations with James Baldwin*, ed. Fred Stanley and Louis Pratt (Jackson University Press, 1989), 42.

CHAPTER FOUR

1. Colin Gordon, *Mapping Decline: St. Louis and the Fate of the American City* (Philadelphia: University of Pennsylvania Press, 2008), 69–71; Gary Orfield, "The Housing Issues in the St. Louis Case," report to Judge William Hungate, US District Court (St. Louis, MO), *Liddell v. Board of Education* (1981).

2. John Logan, *Separate and Unequal: The Neighborhood Gap for Blacks, Hispanics and Asians in Metropolitan America* (Providence, RI: US2010 Project, 2011); John Logan, Diversities and Disparities, American Communities Project, http://www.s4.brown.edu/us2010/SegCitySorting/Default.aspx.

3. Gordon, *Mapping Decline*, 69–71.

4. Gordon, *Mapping Decline*, 69–83.

5. Gordon, *Mapping Decline*, 81–83.

6. Yana Kucheva and Richard Sanders, "The Misunderstood Consequences of *Shelley v. Kraemer*," *Social Science History* 48 (2014): 212–33.

7. Gordon, *Mapping Decline*, 89–91.

8. Gordon, *Mapping Decline*, 78.

9. Allison Shertzer, Tate Twinam, and Randall P. Walsh, "Race, Ethnicity, and Discriminatory Zoning" (NBER Working Paper 20108, Cambridge, MA, 2014).

10. Gordon, *Mapping Decline*, 112.

11. Gordon, *Mapping Decline*, 131.

12. Gordon, *Mapping Decline*, 153.

13. Gordon, *Mapping Decline*, 164–67.

14. Gordon, *Mapping Decline*, 98–99.

15. Sarah K. Bruch, Aaron J. Rosenthal, and Joe Soss, "Unequal Positions: A Relational Approach to Racial Inequality Trends in the US States, 1940–2010," *Social Science History* 43, no. 1 (published online December 2018), 1–26; Robert Fairlie and William Sundstrom, "The Emergence, Persistence, and Recent Widening of the Racial Employment Gap," *Industrial and Labor Relations Review* 52, no. 2 (1999): 252–70; Kevin Lang and Jee-Yeon K. Lehmann, "Racial Discrimination in the Labor Market: Theory and Empirics," *Journal of Economic Literature* 50, no. 4 (2012): 959–1006; Kenneth Couch and Robert Fairlie, "'Last Hired, First Fired': Black-White Unemployment and the Business Cycle," *Demography* 47, no. 1 (2010): 227–47.

16. Paul Taylor, Rakesh Kochhar, Richard Fry, Gabriel Velasco, and Seth Motel, *Wealth Gaps Rise to Record Highs between Whites, Blacks and Hispanics* (Washington, DC: Pew Research Center, 2011); Thomas Shapiro, Tatjana Meschede, and Sam Osoro, "The Roots of the Widening Racial Wealth Gap: Explaining the Black-White Economic Divide" (Waltham, MA: Brandeis University Institute of Assets and Social Policy, 2013).

17. William Collins and Robert Margo, "Race and the Value of Owner-Occupied Housing, 1940–1990" (Levy Institute Working Paper 310, 2000); William Collins and Robert Margo, "Race and Home Ownership: A Century-Long View," *Explorations in Economic History* 38, no. 1 (2001): 68–92; Daniel Fetter, "How Do Mortgage Subsidies Affect Home Ownership? Evidence from the Mid-Century GI Bills," *American Economic Journal: Economic Policy* 5, no. 2 (2013): 111–47; Ira Katznelson, *When Affirmative Action Was White* (New York: W.W. Norton, 2005), 115–41; Thomas A. Hirschl and Mark R. Rank, "Homeownership across the American Life Course: Estimating the Racial Divide" (Center for Social Development Working Paper 06–12, 2006), https://openscholarship.wustl.edu/csd_research/237/.

18. Shapiro, Meschede, and Osoro, "Roots of the Widening Racial Wealth Gap."

19. Fetter, "How Do Mortgage Subsidies Affect Home Ownership?"; William Collins and Robert Margo, "Race and Home Ownership from the Civil War to the Present" (NBER Working Paper 16665, Cambridge, MA, 2011).

20. See, on this point, Katznelson, *When Affirmative Action Was White*, 115–41; Melvin Oliver and Thomas Shapiro, *Black Wealth/White Wealth: A New Perspective on Racial Inequality* (New York: Routledge, 1996).

21. Patrick Sharkey, *Stuck in Place: Urban Neighborhoods and the End of Progress toward Racial Equality* (Chicago: University of Chicago Press, 2013); Paul Jargowsky, *Poverty and Place: Ghettoes, Barrios, and the American City* (New York: Russell Sage, 1997).

22. Sarah Bruch and Colin Gordon, "Home Inequity: Homeownership, Race, and Wealth in St. Louis after 1940" (paper presented at the Population Association of America, Denver, CO, April 2018).

23. St. Louis County Department of Planning, Office of Community Development, *St. Louis County Housing Study* (Clayton, MO: St. Louis County Department of Planning, 2012).

24. One St. Louis, *Fair Housing Equity Assessment* (St. Louis: Metropolitan St. Louis Equal Opportunity and Housing Council, 2013).

25. St. Louis County Department of Planning, *St. Louis County Housing Study*.

26. One St. Louis, *Fair Housing Equity Assessment*.

27. Gordon, *Mapping Decline*, 206–11.

28. Dennis Judd, "The Role of Governmental Policies in Promoting Residential Segregation in the St. Louis Metropolitan Area," *Journal of Negro Education* 66, no. 3 (Summer 1997), 214–40; Lawrence Vale, *Purging the Poorest: Public Housing and the Design Politics of Twice-Cleared Communities* (Chicago: University of Chicago Press, 2013).

29. For a recent assessment, see For the Sake of All, *Segregation in St. Louis: Dismantling the Divide* (University City, MO: Brown School of Social Work, Washington University, 2018), available at https://forthesakeofall.org/segregationinstlouis/.

30. St. Louis County Department of Planning, *St. Louis County Housing Study*; see also East-West Gateway Council of Governments, *Where We Stand*, 6th ed. (St. Louis: East-West Gateway, updated September 2014), at https://www.ewgateway.org/library-post/where-we-stand-6th-edition/.

31. Elizabeth Kneebone, "Ferguson, Mo. Emblematic of Growing Suburban Poverty," *The Avenue: Rethinking Metropolitan America*, Brookings Institute, August 2015, https://www.brookings.edu/blog/the-avenue/2014/08/15/ferguson-mo-emblematic-of-growing-suburban-poverty/.

32. William Julius Wilson, *More than Just Race: Being Black and Poor in the Inner City* (New York: W. W. Norton, 2009); William Julius Wilson, *When Work Disappears: The World of the New Urban Poor* (New York: Alfred A. Knopf, 1996); Douglas S. Massey and Nancy A. Denton, *American Apartheid: Segregation and the Making of the Underclass* (Cambridge, MA: Harvard University Press, 1993); Christopher Jencks and Paul Peterson, eds., *The Urban Underclass* (Washington, DC: Brookings Institute, 1991). The unemployment rate for Ferguson and St. Louis County is from US Census Bureau, American Fact Finder, Selected Economic Characteristics, 2013–2017 American Community Survey 5-Year Estimates, at https://factfinder.census.gov/faces/nav/jsf/pages/community_facts.xhtml.

33. John L. Lewis, "Michael Brown, Eric Garner, and the 'Other America'," *Atlantic*, December 2014, https://www.theatlantic.com/politics/archive/2014/12/michael-brown-eric-garner-other-america-john-lewis/383750/.

34. US Department of Justice, Civil Rights Division, *Investigation of the Ferguson Police Department* (March 2015), available at https://www.justice.gov/sites/default/files/opa/press-releases/attachments/2015/03/04/ferguson_police_department_report.pdf; Arch City Defenders, *Municipal Courts White Paper* (2014), available at http://03a5010.netsolhost.com/WordPress/wp-content/uploads/2014/11/ArchCity-Defenders-Municipal-Courts-Whitepaper.pdf; Better Together St. Louis, *Public Safety–Municipal Courts* (St. Louis: Missouri Council for a Better Economy, 2014), available at http://www.bettertogetherstl.com/wp-content/uploads/2014/10/BT-Municipal-Courts-Report-Full-Report1.pdf.

35. Colin Gordon, "Patchwork Metropolis: Fragmented Governance and Urban Decline in Greater St. Louis," *St. Louis University Public Law Review* 34, no. 1 (2014): 51–70.

36. Mary Delach Leonard, "Ferguson's Yesterdays Offer Clues to the Troubled City of Today," St. Louis Public Radio, August 2, 2015, http://news.stlpublicradio.org/post/fergusons-yesterdays-offer-clues-troubled-city-today#stream/0.

37. Charles Tilly, *Durable Inequality* (Berkeley: University of California Press, 1998), 147–69.

38. Jamie Peck, *Austerity Urbanism: The Neoliberal Crisis of American Cities* (New York: Rosa Luxemburg Stiftung, May 2015).

39. Peck, *Austerity Urbanism*; L. Owen Kirkpatrick, "The New Urban Fiscal Crisis: Finance, Democracy, and Municipal Debt," *Politics and Society* 44, no. 1 (2016): 45–80; Linda Lobao and Lazarus Adua, "State Rescaling and Local Governments' Austerity Policies across the USA, 2001–2008," *Cambridge Journal of Regions, Economy and Society* 4, no. 1 (2011): 419–35; Jamie Peck, "Pushing Austerity: State Failure, Municipal Bankruptcy, and the Crises of Fiscal Federalism in the USA," *Cambridge Journal of Regions, Economy and Society* 7, no. 1 (2014): 17–18.

40. Robin Einhorn, *American Taxation, American Slavery* (Chicago: University of Chicago, 2006), 200–250; Katherine Newman and Rourke O'Brien, *Taxing the Poor: Doing Damage to the Truly Disadvantaged* (Berkeley: University of California Press, 2011).

41. Calculated from "Table 3: State Tax Collections by State and Type of Tax 2013," Quarterly Summary of State & Local Tax Revenue Tables, US Census Bureau, State and Local Government Finance, at https://www.census.gov/data/tables/2013/econ/qtax/historical.html.

42. City of Ferguson, *Combined Annual Financial Report [CAFR] 1984* (Ferguson, MO: Ferguson Finance Department, 1984).

43. Missouri Constitution, art. X, §§ 16–24, available at http://www.moga.mo.gov/mostatutes/ConstArticleIndexes/T10.html; Rhonda Thomas, "The Hancock Amendment: The Limits Imposed on Local Governments," *University of Missouri–Kansas City Law Review* 52, no. 1 (1983–84): 22–44; Henry Ordower, J. S. Onesimo Sandoval, and Kenneth Warren, "Out of Ferguson: Misdemeanors, Municipal Courts, Tax Distribution and Constitutional Limitations" (Saint Louis University Legal Studies Research Paper 2016–14, St. Louis, MO, 2016).

44. Walter Johnson, "Ferguson's Fortune 500 Company," *Atlantic*, April 26, 2015, https://www.theatlantic.com/politics/archive/2015/04/fergusons-fortune-500-company/390492/.

45. See Greg LeRoy and Leigh McIlvaine, *Ending Job Piracy, Building Regional Prosperity* (Washington, DC: Good Jobs First, 2014), available at http://www.goodjobsfirst.org/sites/default/files/docs/pdf/endingjobpiracy.pdf; and Alan Peters and Peter Fisher, "The Failures of Economic Development Incentives," *Journal of the American Planning Association* 70, no. 1 (2004): 27–37.

46. City of Ferguson, *CAFR 1994*.
47. Missouri Department of Elementary and Secondary Education, School Finance Reports (Ferguson-Florissant 2017; Clayton 2017), available at https://apps.dese.mo.gov/MCDS/Reports/SSRS_Print.aspx.
48. Pew Research, *The Local Squeeze: Falling Revenues and Growing Demand for Services Challenge Cities, Counties, and School Districts* (Washington, DC: Pew Charitable Trust, June 2012).
49. See Elizabeth Hinton, *From the War on Poverty to the War on Crime: The Making of Mass Incarceration in America* (Cambridge, MA: Harvard University Press, 2016); and Julilly Kohler-Hausmann, *Getting Tough: Welfare and Imprisonment in 1970s America* (Princeton, NJ: Princeton University Press, 2017).
50. See Loïc Wacquant, *Punishing the Poor: The Neoliberal Government of Social Insecurity* (Durham, NC: Duke University Press, 2009).
51. Brendan Beck and Adam Goldstein, "Governing through Police? Housing Market Reliance, Welfare Retrenchment, and Police Budgeting in an Era of Declining Crime," *Social Forces* 96, no. 3 (March 2018): 1183–210.
52. On the idea of "fiscal fracking," I am indebted to Devin Fergus. See his "Financial Fracking in the Land of the Fee," in *The Assets Perspective: The Rise of Asset Building and Its Impact on Social Policy*, ed. Reid Cramer and Trina Williams Shanks (New York: Palgrave MacMillan, 2014), 67–91.
53. Whitney Benns and Blake Strode, "Debtors' Prison in 21st-Century America," *Atlantic*, February 23, 2016; see also Henry Ordower, J. S. Onesimo Sandoval, and Kenneth Warren, "Out of Ferguson: Misdemeanors, Municipal Courts, Tax Distribution, and Constitutional Limitations," *Howard Law Journal* 6, no. 1 (2017): 113–46.
54. Ferguson Commission, "Dawn: Escaping the Cycle," *Forward through Ferguson* (St. Louis: The Ferguson Commission, 2015), https://forwardthroughferguson.org/stories/escaping-the-cycle/.
55. City of Ferguson, *CAFR 2006*.
56. Benns and Strode, "Debtors' Prison in 21st-Century America."
57. US Department of Justice, *Investigation of the Ferguson Police Department*, 11.
58. Arch City Defenders, *Municipal Courts White Paper*.
59. US Department of Justice, *Investigation of the Ferguson Police Department*, 14.
60. Benns and Strode, "Debtors' Prison in 21st-Century America."
61. US Department of Justice, *Investigation of the Ferguson Police Department*, 4–5, 62–70.
62. Stephen Deere, "Ferguson Depending on Tax Measures to Close Budget Gaps," *SLPD*, March 31, 2016.
63. Stephen Deere and Christine Byers, "Ferguson Turns Down Initial Justice Department Plan, Asks for Time to Come Up with an Alternative," *SLPD*, August 15, 2015.
64. U.S. v. City of Ferguson, United States District Court, Eastern District of Missouri, Consent Decree (January 2016), available at https://www.fergusoncity.com/DocumentCenter/View/1920.
65. Jason Rosenbaum, "Ferguson Puts Conditions on Consent Decree, Gets Angry Reaction from Residents," St. Louis Public Radio, February 10, 2016, http://news.stlpublicradio.org/post/ferguson-puts-conditions-consent-decree-gets-angry-reaction-residents#stream/0.
66. U.S. v. Ferguson, Complaint (February 2016), available at https://assets.documentcloud.org/documents/2709387/Show-Multidocs.pdf.
67. Missouri Senate Bill 5, 98th General Assembly (2015), available at https://legiscan.com/MO/text/SB5/2015.

68. City of Normandy et al. v. Eric Greitens, Supreme Court of Missouri en banc no. SC95624 (May 16, 2016), available at https://www.courts.mo.gov/file.jsp?id=112954.

69. Monica Davey, "Lawsuit Accuses Missouri City of Fining Homeowners to Raise Revenue," *New York Times*, November 4, 2015; "Policing for Profit in St. Louis County," *New York Times*, November 14, 2015.

70. Benns and Strode, "Debtors' Prison in 21st-Century America."

CONCLUSION

1. Jelani Cobb, "The Matter of Black Lives," *New Yorker*, March 14, 2016. See also Gary Younge, *Another Day in the Death of America: A Chronicle of Ten Short Lives* (New York: Nation Books, 2018); Keeanga-Yamahtta Taylor, *From #BlackLivesMatter to Black Liberation* (Chicago: Haymarket Books, 2016); Wesley Lowery, *"They Can't Kill Us All": Ferguson, Baltimore, and a New Era in America's Racial Justice Movement* (New York: Little & Brown, 2016); Marc Lamont Hill, *Nobody: Casualties of America's War on the Vulnerable, from Ferguson to Flint and Beyond* (New York: Atria Books, 2016); Chris LeBron, *The Making of Black Lives Matter: A Brief History of an Idea* (New York: Oxford University Press, 2017); and Ta-Nehisi Coates, *Between the World and Me* (New York: Spiegel & Grau, 2015).

2. Ta-Nehisi Coates, "The Gangsters of Ferguson," *Atlantic*, March 5, 2015, https://www.theatlantic.com/politics/archive/2015/03/The-Gangsters-Of-Ferguson/386893/.

3. Bennett Capers, "Rethinking the Fourth Amendment: Race, Citizenship, and the Equality Principle," *Harvard Civil Rights–Civil Liberties Law Review* 46, no. 1 (2011): 11; Joe Soss and Vesla Weaver, "Police Are Our Government: Politics, Political Science, and the Policing of Race-Class Subjugated Communities," *Annual Review of Political Science* 20 (2017): 567–69, 574.

4. Khalil Gibran Muhammad, *The Condemnation of Blackness: Race, Crime, and the Making of Modern Urban America* (Cambridge, MA: Harvard University Press, 2011); Ira Katznelson, *Black Men, White Cities: Race, Politics, and Migration in the United States, 1900–30, and Britain, 1948–68* (London: Oxford University Press, 1976).

5. See Arnold Hirsch, "Choosing Segregation: Federal Housing Policy Between *Shelley* and *Brown*," in *From Tenements to the Taylor Homes: In Search of an Urban Housing Policy in Twentieth-Century America*, ed. John F. Bauman, Roger Biles, and Kristin Szylvian (University Park: Pennsylvania State University Press, 2000), 206–25; Richard Rothstein, *The Color of Law* (New York: Liveright, 2017); Colin Gordon, *Mapping Decline: St. Louis and the Fate of the American City* (Philadelphia: University of Pennsylvania Press, 2008); Kevin Fox Gotham, *Race, Real Estate, and Uneven Development: The Kansas City Experience, 1900–2000* (Albany, NY: SUNY Press, 2002); Joe Trotter, *Black Milwaukee: The Making of an Industrial Proletariat, 1915–1945* (Urbana: University of Illinois Press, 2006); and Robert Fogelson, *Bourgeois Nightmares: Suburbia, 1870–1930* (New Haven, CT: Yale University Press, 2005).

6. See Douglas S. Massey and Nancy A. Denton, *American Apartheid: Segregation and the Making of the Underclass* (Cambridge, MA: Harvard University Press, 1993); Camille Zubrinsky Charles, "The Dynamics of Racial Residential Segregation," *Annual Review of Sociology* 29 (2003): 167–207; William Julius Wilson, *The Truly Disadvantaged: The Inner City, the Underclass, and Public Policy* (Chicago: University of Chicago Press, 1990); Patrick Sharkey, *Stuck in Place: Urban Neighborhoods and the End of Progress toward Racial Equality* (Chicago: University of Chicago Press, 2013); Thomas Pettigrew, "Racial Change and Social Policy," *Annals of the American Academy of Political and Social Science* 441 (1979): 114–31; Chenoa Flippen, "The More Things Change

the More They Stay the Same: The Future of Residential Segregation in America," *City & Community* 15 (2016): 14–17; and Raj Chetty, Nathaniel Hendren, Maggie R. Jones, and Sonya R. Porter, "Race and Economic Opportunity in the United States: An Intergenerational Perspective" (National Bureau of Economic Research, Working Paper 24441, March 2018).

7. Kyle Crowder and Maria Krysan, *Cycle of Segregation: Social Processes and Residential Stratification* (New York: Russell Sage Foundation, 2017).

8. See Daria Roithmayr, "Locked in Segregation," *Virginia Journal of Social Policy and the Law* 12, no. 2 (2004): 197–259; Roithmayr, *Reproducing Racism: How Everyday Choices Lock in White Advantage* (New York: New York University Press, 2014); George Lipsitz, *The Possessive Investment in Whiteness: How White People Profit from Identity Politics* (Philadelphia: Temple University Press, 1998); Richard Thompson Ford, "The Boundaries of Race: Political Geography in Legal Analysis," *Harvard Law Review* 107, no. 8 (June 1994): 1841–921; and Clarissa Hayward, *How Americans Make Race: Stories, Institutions, Spaces* (New York: Cambridge University Press, 2013), 68–69, 192–94.

9. See Allison Shertzer, Tate Twinam, and Randall P. Walsh, "Race, Ethnicity, and Discriminatory Zoning" (NBER Working Paper 20108, Cambridge, MA, 2014); Jonathan Rothwell and Douglas S. Massey, "Density Zoning and Class Segregation in U.S. Metropolitan Areas," *Social Science Quarterly* 9, no. 5 (2010): 1123–43; William Apgar and Allegra Calder, "The Dual Mortgage Market: The Persistence of Discrimination in Mortgage Lending," in *The Geography of Opportunity: Race and Housing Choice in Metropolitan America*, ed. Xavier de Souza Briggs (Washington, DC: Brookings, 2005), 101–21; and John Yinger and Stephen Ross, *The Color of Credit: Mortgage Discrimination, Research Methodology, and Fair-Lending Enforcement* (Cambridge, MA: MIT Press, 2002).

10. Christine Percheski and Christina Gibson-Davis, "Racial Inequalities in Wealth: The Unequal Impact of the Great Recession on Families with Children" (paper presented at the Population Association of America, Denver, CO, April 2018).

11. Sean Reardon and Kendra Bischoff, "Income Inequality and Income Segregation," *American Journal of Sociology* 116, no. 4 (2011): 1092–153.

12. See Melvin Oliver and Thomas Shapiro, *Black Wealth/White Wealth: A New Perspective on Racial Equality in America* (New York: Routledge, 2006); Dalton Conley, *Being Black, Living in the Red: Race, Wealth, and Social Policy in America* (Berkeley: University of California Press, 1999); Thomas Shapiro, Tatjana Meschede, and Sam Osoro, "The Roots of the Widening Racial Wealth Gap: Explaining the Black-White Economic Divide" (Institute on Assets and Social Policy, Research and Policy Brief, 2013); and Seymour Spilerman, "Wealth and Stratification Processes," *Annual Review of Sociology* 26 (2000): 497–524.

13. Oliver and Shapiro, *Black Wealth/White Wealth*, 5–6.

14. Jacquelyn Dowd Hall, "The Long Civil Rights Movement and the Political Uses of the Past," *Journal of American History* 91, no. 4 (2005): 1233–63.

15. See Donna Murch, "Ferguson's Inheritance," *Jacobin*, August 2015, https://www
.jacobinmag.com/2015/08/ferguson-police-black-lives-matter/; Elizabeth Hinton, *From the War on Poverty to the War on Crime: The Making of Mass Incarceration in America* (Cambridge, MA: Harvard University Press, 2016); and Julilly Kohler-Hausmann, *Getting Tough: Welfare and Imprisonment in 1970s America* (Princeton, NJ: Princeton University Press, 2017).

16. Charles Clotfelter, *After Brown: The Rise and Retreat of School Desegregation* (Princeton, NJ: Princeton University Press, 2006); Gary Orfield and Erica Frankenberg, *Brown*

at 60: Great Progress, a Long Retreat and an Uncertain Future (The Civil Rights Project, Los Angeles: University of California at Los Angeles, 2014), available at https://www.civilrightsproject.ucla.edu/research/k-12-education/integration-and-diversity/brown-at-60-great-progress-a-long-retreat-and-an-uncertain-future.

17. Michael Waldman, *The Fight to Vote* (New York: Simon and Schuster, 2016), 173–252.
18. See Robert Lieberman, *Shifting the Color Line: Race and the American Welfare State* (Cambridge, MA: Harvard University Press, 2001); Jennifer Mittelstadt, "Reimagining the Welfare State," *Jacobin*, July 2015; Michael Brown, *Race, Money, and the American Welfare State* (Ithaca, NY: Cornell University Press, 1999); and Sanford Schram, "Putting a Black Face on Welfare: The Good and the Bad," in *Deserving and Entitled: Social Constructions and Public Policy*, ed. Anne Schneider and Helen Ingram (Albany: State University of New York Press, 2005), 261–90.
19. Karen E. Fields and Barbara J. Fields, *Racecraft: The Soul of Inequality in American Life (London: Verso, 2012)*, 261–90 (quote on 286). See also Arlie Russell Hochschild, *Strangers in Their Own Land: Anger and Mourning on the American Right* (New York: New Press, 2016); Katherine Cramer, *The Politics of Resentment: Rural Consciousness in Wisconsin and the Rise of Scott Walker* (Chicago: University of Chicago Press, 2016); and Robert C. Lieberman, Suzanne Mettler, Thomas B. Pepinsky, Kenneth M. Roberts, and Richard Valelly, "The Trump Presidency and American Democracy: A Historical and Comparative Analysis," *Perspectives on Politics* (published online October 29, 2018), 5–6.
20. See Pettigrew, "Racial Change and Social Policy," 114–31 (quote at 118); Paul M. Sniderman, Thomas Piazza, Philip E. Tetlock, and Ann Kendrick, "The New Racism," *American Journal of Political Science* 35, no. 2 (1991): 423–47; and Eduardo Bonilla-Silva, *Racism without Racists: Colorblind Racism and the Persistence of Inequality in America* (New York: Rowan and Littlefield, 2014), chapter 2.
21. See Michael A. Pagano, "Metropolitan Limits: Intrametropolitan Disparities and Governance in U.S. Laboratories of Democracy," in *Governance and Opportunity in Metropolitan America*, ed. Alan Altshuler, William Morrill, Harold Wolman, and Faith Mitchell (Washington, DC: National Academies Press, 1999), 253–94; Richard Hill, "Separate and Unequal: Government Inequality in the Metropolis," *American Political Science Review* 68 (1974): 1557–68; Gregory Weiher, *The Fractured Metropolis: Political Fragmentation and Metropolitan Segregation* (Albany: State University of New York Press, 1991); and Margaret Weir, "Urban Poverty and Defensive Localism," *Dissent*, Summer 1994.
22. See Genevieve Siegel-Hawley, "Mitigating *Milliken*? School District Boundary Lines and Desegregation Policy in Four Southern Metropolitan Areas, 1990–2010," *American Journal of Education* 120 (May 2014): 391–433; and Erica Frankenberg, "Splintering School Districts: Understanding the Link between Segregation and Fragmentation," *Law and Social Inquiry* 34, no. 4 (2009): 869–909.
23. See Richard Legates and Chester Hartman, "The Anatomy of Displacement in the United States," in *Gentrification of the City*, ed. Neil Smith and Peter Williams (New York: Routledge, 2007); and David Harvey, "The Right to the City," *New Left Review* 53 (2008), 23–40.
24. Jelani Cobb, "The Ordinary Outrage of the Baltimore Police Report," *New Yorker*, August 12, 2016.
25. *Report of the National Advisory Commission on Civil Disorders* (Washington, DC: Government Publishing Office, 1968), 1.

INDEX

Page numbers in italics refer to maps and figures.